Inspired by a personal moment of profound love
and generosity, Trent Dalton, bestselling author
and one of Australia's finest journalists, spent
two months in 2021 speaking to people from
all walks of life, asking them one simple and
direct question: 'Can you please tell me a
love story?' The result is an immensely warm,
poignant, funny and moving book about love
in all its guises, including observations,
reflections and stories of people falling into
love, falling out of love, and never letting go
of the loved ones in their hearts. A heartfelt,
deep, wise and tingly tribute to the greatest
thing we will never understand and the only
thing we will ever really need: **love**.

Praise for *Boy Swallows Universe*

'The best Australian novel I have read in more than a decade ... The last 100 pages of *Boy Swallows Universe* propel you like an express train to a conclusion that is profound and complex and unashamedly commercial ... A rollicking ride, rich in philosophy, wit, truth and pathos' *Sydney Morning Herald*

'*Boy Swallows Universe* is a wonderful surprise: sharp as a drawer full of knives in terms of subject matter; unrepentantly joyous in its child's-eye view of the world; the best literary debut in a month of Sundays' *The Australian*

'The book is plotted like a murder mystery, with the requisite twists and turns providing illuminating surprises right to the last page. Scenes are rendered in intimate detail, the characters are as real as your family and the writing is glorious' *The Advertiser*

'A towering achievement. It is the *Cloudstreet* of the Australian suburban criminal underworld' *Herald Sun*

'One of the best Australian novels I've ever read ... The characters are human and complex, the writing is fast-paced and heartfelt, and every sentence is surprising ... This book will stay with me for a long time' *The Guardian*

'*Boy Swallows Universe* hypnotizes you with wonder, and then hammers you with heartbreak' *Washington Post*

'Filled with beautifully lyric prose ... the characterization, too, is universally memorable, especially of Eli and August. At one point Eli wonders if he is good. The answer is "yes," every bit as good as this exceptional novel' *Booklist* (USA)

'Funny, tender and raw ... It is a remarkably compelling story, but what really makes *Boy Swallows Universe* shine is its use of language. Dalton has invented a kind of clipped, poetic vernacular that colours the entire book ... there's something distinctly picturesque about Dalton's language that makes it inherently Australian ... A wonderful, unexpectedly beautiful portrayal of boyhood and destiny' Better Reading

'It's fresh, original, it's dripping with promise. A voyage of wide-eyed wonder' Radio New Zealand

'A true Australian masterpiece' *Marie Claire*

Praise for *All Our Shimmering Skies*

'I think *All Our Shimmering Skies* is even better than *Boy Swallows Universe* ... There's a whiff of southern gothic here, with Molly reminding me of Scout Finch from *To Kill A Mockingbird*' Stephen Romei, *The Australian*

'A work of shimmering originality and energy, with extraordinary characters and a clever, thrilling plot ... unputdownable' Toni Jordan, *Sydney Morning Herald/The Age*

'His keen eye for detail and vivid sense of place take us on another tumultuous and ultimately beautiful Australian journey. It is a novel Molly Hook herself would hail poetic and full of grace' *Herald Sun*

'A spellbinding saga of survival and transformation in WWII Australia … This is a wonder' *Publishers Weekly* (starred review)

'Achingly beautiful and poetic in its melancholy, *All Our Shimmering Skies* is a majestic and riveting tale of curses and the true meaning of treasure' *Booklist* (starred review)

'The book is alight with joyous candour, extravagantly beautiful writing and a series of intriguing jungle-set pieces' *The Advertiser*

'A magical realist epic grounded by a vividly evoked sense of place and a cheeky sense of humour' *West Australian*

'As Australian as outback red dirt and as universal as the sky young Molly Hook's journey takes place beneath, *All Our Shimmering Skies* is an open-hearted wonder, by turns heartbreaking and full of hope, no less than an instant classic' Venero Armanno

'A glinting, big-hearted miracle of a book' Richard Glover

LOVE STORIES
TRENT DALTON

FOURTH ESTATE

Fourth Estate
An imprint of HarperCollins*Publishers*

HarperCollins*Publishers*
Australia • Brazil • Canada • France • Germany • Holland • Hungary
India • Italy • Japan • Mexico • New Zealand • Poland • Spain • Sweden
Switzerland • United Kingdom • United States of America

First published in Australia in 2021
by HarperCollins*Publishers* Australia Pty Limited
Level 13, 201 Elizabeth Street, Sydney NSW 2000
ABN 36 009 913 517
harpercollins.com.au

A catalogue record for this book is available from the National Library of Australia.

ISBN 978 1 4607 6093 2 (hardback)
ISBN 978 1 4607 1403 4 (ebook)
ISBN 978 1 4607 4013 2 (audio)

Cover design by Darren Holt, HarperCollins Design Studio
Author photo by Fiona Franzmann
Typeset in Bembo Std by Kirby Jones
Printed and bound in Australia by McPherson's Printing Group

MIX
Paper from
responsible sources
FSC
www.fsc.org   FSC® C001695

For Kathleen Kelly

CONTENTS

Author's Note   1

Two Believers   11
Love Is Blindness   21
It Follows   24
Sakura Tomii and the Good Things, Part 1   29
Prince Joseph   39
The Actress Breaking Up with Her Boyfriend in
    Her Underwear After a Two-Day Drive
    from Tasmania   42
The Crossing   48
Pictures of You   53
The Three-Second Rule   60
A Wide Expanse of Water   66
Pinky Promise   70
Good Evil   90
Henny and Denise   94
Buried Treasure   102
The In-Between   110
Yes   115
Ambiguous Gain   124
Magic Hour   129
The Big Cherry Taste   140
Sursum Corda   150
Lovebird Waltz   157

The Importance of Bear Hugs and Falling in Love
    with a Married Man Back When Telephones Were
    Still Stuck on Walls   162
The Story of Why I Reckon My Old Man Was Not
    Much of a Hugger   169
Found Under Tree   181
The Evangelist   186
We Lighten   199
Naomi   201
Waiting for the Icicle to Fall   204
Two Poets   208
Arlo   213
Gypsy Stuff   222
Cumulus People   229
Pay No Worship to the Garish Sun   242
The Last of the Rowing Whalers   248
Love and the Institute of Chartered Accountants, 1913   255
Later Ron   271
Square Two   276
The Find   290
Everywhere I Go   293
Sakura Tomii and the Good Things, Part 2   298
Blood Chemistry   304
The Cradle   309
Good to See You Again, Fe Brown   316

Acknowledgements   337

Author's Note

This book, from start to finish, is a joyous, heart-on-the-sleeve tribute to the wonder of love. But it also contains brief references to suicide, racism, homophobia and institutional abuse that some readers may find distressing. Some names have been changed for legal reasons. Deepest thanks to the storytellers herein who gently opened the window on their dark in order to blind me with their light.

Dear Kath,

I got your gift. Might be the most beautiful gift I
ever got.

I'm looking at your face in the funeral booklet
as I write this letter. Kathleen Kelly 15.01.1931 –
25.12.2020. You look like an angel, Kath, some
strange Irish cross between early Kate Hepburn and
every star in the Milky Way.

You bowed out on Christmas Day. We all thought
that was kinda perfect. The memorial was beautiful
and true. Lakeview Chapel, Albany Creek Memorial
Park. You were so loved, Kath. You must have done
it right. Life, I mean. You must have known the
point of it all: live a life so full and selfless
that latecomers struggle to find a spare seat at
your funeral.

The January heat outside the chapel broke the
airconditioner and the photo montage broke me
in two. All tears and no tissues. Funeral photo
montages get me every time. The journey of it all.
You as a kid. You as a mum. You as a grandmother to

all those grandkids who did you so proud in that chapel.

Judy and Greg, those beautiful children of yours, said the most beautiful things about you. True-love things. Maybe that's the trick to parenting: just love your kids so hard and so fully that when you go they won't be able to spit out a single word about you without trembling.

They told the love story of you and Jim. They told the love story of you and the sixty-seven years you spent in the Jack Street house, how much you loved the people in your neighbourhood, how you listened to all their stories for hours until the hours turned into years and the years turned into decades. You knew the secret to it all, how the greatest gift we can give to the world is to shut up and listen to it.

Greg spoke of you and your beloved Olivetti Studio 44 typewriter, the sky-blue one that you'd been tapping away on since the early 1970s, writing fiery letters about women's rights and human rights and doing life right to politicians and principals and popes. He spoke about the letter you wrote to the Catholic Leader in 1970, railing against Canon Law demanding the covering of women's heads in church. You were so furious and brilliant. 'I cannot see anything disrespectful about a woman's bare head,' you wrote. 'Surely it is what is in the heart, not the scrap of fabric on the head, that counts.' I turned to my daughter Beth beside me when Greg read that bit out. She's fourteen now, Kath, and she nodded at me because she heard every word you said.

After the memorial service, as per your instructions, we all went out to Greg's car in the parking lot and he pulled out an Esky filled with the thirty stubbies of XXXX Gold that were still chilling in your fridge the day you were rushed to hospital. We gladly sank those stubbies like you wanted, Kath, and we toasted your good name. I told Greg some things he didn't know about you, like how you wrote me those beautiful and tender emails when Dad was finally killed by the durries. 'He's not dead while his name is still spoken,' you reminded me.

Then Greg told me some things I didn't know about you, how you cut my journo stuff out of the paper and glued the clippings into those sacred scrapbooks that documented your life and all that you cared for. I was so touched that a mate's mum would take the time to do such a thing. 'Well, wait till you see this,' Greg said. And he leaned into the boot of his car and pulled out your sky-blue Olivetti Studio 44 typewriter. 'She wanted you to have it,' he said.

I told Greg that I'd write something special on
your typewriter. I said I would write something
filled with love and depth and truth and frankness
and heart because you were loving and deep and
true and frank and heartfelt. I said it wouldn't
be cynical and glib, Kath, because I can't do
cynical and glib anymore. The global market for
cynical and glib has been flooded. The cynics bob
up in your cornflakes, pop out of your toaster in
the morning like a burnt slice of mouldy Tip-Top.
Some four million people and counting are dead
from a virus and, hell no, I don't feel like being
sarcastic. I feel like being open and true and
right flippin' here, right flippin' now.

I told Greg I wanted to walk through the streets
of Brisbane's CBD for two months asking random
strangers to tell me love stories. I told him I
then wanted to sit for two straight weeks with
the Olivetti on the corner of Adelaide and Albert
streets, on the edge of King George Square, and
ask random strangers to stop and tell me more
love stories, and then I wanted to write about all
those love stories on your beautiful Olivetti. 'I
don't know, man, something inside me is telling
me I need to do this,' I said. And maybe it's this
awful arse-boil of a pandemic that refuses to be
lanced. And maybe it's just me and maybe it's just

something I need to do. 'I know Kath would say it sounds cheesy as hell,' I said to Greg. 'But do ya reckon she'd mind if I did something like that with her typewriter?'

He didn't hesitate, Kath. I can't remember when your son was ever hesitant. 'I think she'd love nothing more,' he said.

So here I am, Kath. I'm writing this letter to you on the Olivetti as I sit on the corner of Adelaide and Albert streets at a small fold-up table that I bought from BCF for $50 and will use as my writing desk. I've just spent two months walking through the streets of Brisbane, asking random strangers to tell me love stories. I've been shutting up and listening to the world. Back and forth through the city streets for sixty days, talking to people about love and what it means and what it is and where it comes from and what it feels like to find it, lose it, keep it and cherish it in the good years and the bad years and the arse-boil years like these ones we're living in now. Back and forth from the Orient Hotel at the end of Queen Street and down to the brown Brisbane River that rises every fifteen or thirty years to remind us we're only ever three steps away from the mop and the bucket.

And here I am now, spending two weeks sitting on this corner on a $15 fold-up blue chair I bought at Big W on Edward Street, with another $15 chair beside me that random strangers keep sitting in as they kindly, gently, wildly, courageously, beautifully tell me the love stories of their lives. Between the stories I'm tapping out letters to the people I love, inspired by the stories I've just heard. Just yesterday I wrote a letter to Joni Mitchell. This morning I wrote a letter to Whitney Houston.

The Olivetti is working like a dream, Kath. I took it to Garry Hill, the typewriter repairer in Everton Hills. He put a new ribbon in it and cleaned the letter hammers. Garry worked for Olivetti from 1974 to 1991 and he was so impressed by the way you'd looked after your typewriter, Kath. 'Beautiful machine,' Garry whispered. He dated the Olivetti to the mid-to-late 1960s. 'There's no parts available for this, but I don't think you're going to need any,' he said. 'What are you using it for?'

'I'm gonna sit with it on the corner of Adelaide and Albert streets for two weeks and listen to complete strangers tell me love stories. It's my gentle middle finger to eighteen months of global pandemic.'

Garry smiled. 'Good for you,' he said. Garry said my 'o' letter hammer on the typebar might get clogged with ink, but I can clean that ink out with a pin. I told Garry that was good to know: I needed that 'o' hammer in good working order because I was about to type the word 'love' maybe two thousand times.

It really is a beautiful machine, Kath. This machine kills fascists. This machine needs no power beyond stories and ideas. It carries no emails, no internet connection, no Spotify, but it carries my dreams.

There's a sign resting against my desk: 'Sentimental writer collecting love stories. Do you have one to share?' You would not believe the things people will tell you when you take the time to shut the hell up and listen. The wisdoms, the secrets and the stories so heartbreaking, triumphant, romantic, exhilarating, hilarious, tragic and wondrous, just like life. Sometimes people say things so perfect and true that it feels like they've been wanting to say those things all their life but the timing was never right. Maybe the timing is right now and maybe it's this awful pandemic that's been making us all think so damn hard about what we care about, about what we love.

I've already made some friends on my corner, Kath. Three metres to the left of my writing desk are the ladies from the anti-Chinese Communist Party petition group. They're tough as nails but caring, always giving me snacks and advice on being sunsmart when working on the street. Five metres to my right is Reuben Vui, a kind-hearted Kiwi who's signing people up to child sponsorship programs. Some days I'm joined at my desk by Tony Dee, a crooner living with spina bifida, who sings note-perfect Sinatra love songs from his wheelchair at the entry to King George Square. Sometimes I'm joined by my new Belgian busker mate, Jean-Benoit Lagarmitte, who plays drums on an upturned empty Osmocote fertiliser tub. Jean-Benoit was born during the Rwandan Civil War and left for dead under a tree as a baby, and he might be the happiest man I've ever met.

And now here's another friend, a woman named Helen Clark, standing in front of my writing desk. 'I've got a love story,' she says. And that means I've gotta go, Kath, because that's how it always begins and I'll never know how it ends if I don't shut the hell up and listen. I'll write again, soon. I know I said I just wanted to tell you I got your gift. But what I really wanted to tell you was thanks. Thanks for the stories, Kath. And thanks for the love.

Trent

TWO BELIEVERS

I believe we are not alone in the universe, teachers are underpaid, Harold Holt drowned, the Big Mac still has a role to play on earth, Connery was the best Bond, there is no best Beatle, Vegemite never goes out of date, preventions and cures are equally valid, injecting rooms work, Test cricket is not dead but Elvis is. I believe that somewhere in the world is a woman who has tattooed the true meaning of life on the upper inside of her left thigh. I believe I'll die before I see peace in the Middle East but my daughters won't because I believe in them. I believe in dancing badly, farting politely, kissing sloppily, hoping realistically, grieving openly, fishing silently, dreaming wildly, making up quickly, making love slowly, writing daily, whistling hourly, weeping freely, singing loudly, screaming internally, thanking everybody and failing at least once a week. I believe it is good to whisper to plants as long as nobody gets hurt. I believe in forty-plus sunscreen and sixty-plus bus drivers. I believe in standing up to bullies, sitting down with nuns, jogging in Dunlop KT26 runners, drinking in immoderation every once in a while and that lawn mowing cures a hangover. I believe redback spiders chill my bones, seeing Jodie Foster happy warms my heart and the onion belongs on top of the sausage. I believe the change you've been seeking all this time is sock-sock-shoe-shoe instead of sock-shoe-sock-shoe and the tomato goes on top of the beetroot. I believe Colonel Mustard did it, there is still good in Morrissey, quixotism is more than a useful Scrabble word, there are lessons to be learned from soldier crabs, Russell Crowe is Australian, revenge is a dish best served to people who double park, the truth will send you to prison, nurses are underpaid, living room rugs are good, living room drugs are bad, Murray was the most gifted Wiggle, pineapple belongs on only one kind of pizza, sky-diving will kill us, Kylie Minogue will save us, black lives matter, slow-motion replays will ruin rugby league, women's rights are human rights, normal people don't exist, *Die Hard* is not a Christmas movie, only the lawyers ever truly win, *Brokeback Mountain* should have won Best Picture and I still have time to fix all the things in my life that need fixing. I believe in duck-diving under waves at Burleigh Heads, laughing until your ribs hurt in the Birdsville Hotel, talking to the sky on the steps of the Sydney Opera House, leaving the poo rope in a Christmas prawn, tracing shapes in the stars and making a wish before you blow out the candles. I believe in the songs of Barry Gibb and text messages from family and friends. I believe there's not a train that ever passes that I don't want to jump on. I believe in standing your ground, running for your life, working, trying, attempting, struggling, losing, healing, winning, ending and always beginning.

'I believe in love,' I say to the woman sitting in the blue fold-up chair beside me on the corner of Adelaide and Albert streets.

'Oh, me too,' says Helen Clark.

And she tells me a love story about believing. She's always believed in love as affection, the smitten kind of love, the one that swells the heart and a couple of other body parts besides. She's always believed in the blood kind of love, the one that means we'd die for that person sleeping across the hallway. But the older she gets, the more she believes in the existence of a kind of love that's pulling the strings of our lives. The star-crossed kind of love, the one that's harder for us to believe in but the kind she must trust in if she's to believe the whole wild and improbable love story that was Norm and Helen Clark.

She's seventy-nine years old. Lives in Enmore, inner-west Sydney, but she's in Brisbane today visiting one of her two sons and her seven-year-old granddaughter, Dimity, the light of her twilight life.

'I'm not the former New Zealand prime minister Helen Clark,' she says, just in case I was wondering. She's the Helen Clark from Gunnedah, north-eastern New South Wales.

'That's Gunnedah, not Gundagai,' she says.

'I know Gunnedah,' I say. 'Once had to write a magazine profile of Miranda Kerr.' I share the brief and tragic history of Miranda Kerr's connection to Gunnedah, a love story I can recall in surprising detail. Kerr grew up there. Loved the place. Her sacred space as a girl was lying in the grass at her grandmother's house beneath a sprawling weeping willow. She fell in love with a local boy named Christopher, but then Christopher died in a car accident at the age of fifteen and Kerr's heart snapped in two. She always found it hard to go back to Gunnedah because it always reminded her of Christopher. But then time did what it does so gracefully – ticked forward – and the further Kerr was spirited away from thoughts of Christopher and Gunnedah by the pull of fashion and fame, through New York and Paris and London, the more she found comfort in thoughts of both. Today, her oldest child carries Christopher's name and she returns to Gunnedah precisely because it reminds her of her first true love.

'Hmmmm,' Helen says, with a puzzled look that suggests she thought Miranda Kerr was the woman who ran the Gunnedah hot bread shop.

Helen was raised by Greek parents who could never understand how two people with dark hair and brown eyes made a fair-haired girl with bright blue eyes.

'Greek girls back then in Gunnedah were supposed to be virgins when they married,' Helen says. 'So the Greek boys were always on the search for foreign women because they thought they might have a bit more luck. I had the blue eyes and the fair hair, so they thought I wasn't Greek and so they were always' – she thinks on the right word for it – '*persistent.*'

Gunnedah was where she started smoking and she tells me to listen carefully now because the durries play a major part in the love story of Norm and Helen Clark. She doesn't smoke anymore but she might consider it if you're offering after a roast dinner. She wishes she'd never smoked at all and that's more to do with true love than good health. 'When I was seventeen, I was old enough to smoke and I used to go to the Greek cafés and sit out back at the tables and I drank Greek coffee and sat for hours and smoked my cigarettes.'

Her parents wanted her to marry a good Greek boy in a good Greek Orthodox church, but that star-crossed kind of love wasn't having it. True love pulled her strings, she says, all the way to the University of New England, Armidale, where she studied education and met a girl named Carolyn Muir who, she realises now, as she sits on this bustling corner in the heart of Brisbane city, was the precise friend she had to meet in order to meet Norm Clark. After uni, Helen and Carolyn moved into an apartment in Bondi, Sydney, and it was there that Carolyn put to Helen what now seems to her a truly absurd question: 'Would you like to come to a fencing class with me?'

Fencing the sport, not the farm job. And she smiles and shakes her head at this memory because she can't grasp the laughably long odds of any human on earth ever being asked such a question. Who is ever asked such a thing? *Would you like to come to a fencing class with me?* A string-pull if ever there was one.

'It's incredible when I think about it now, the chances of it,' she says. 'Carolyn wanted to do fencing and I just went along to fencing class with her and that's how I met Norm. That's where it all began.'

No fencing class equals no Norm equals no sons equals no Dimity and that's a thought more terrifying to Helen than climate change. She sits back in the blue chair and she watches people pass. Hundreds of Brisbane lovers, coming and going. Eastern lovers. Western lovers. Lovers going north. Lovers headed south. A man in olive-green slacks and old brown leather boots like the ones my grandfather slipped over his wooden leg. There's a young man in a suit carrying three black takeaway bowls of Korean beef. Here's an older man who looks like Barry Humphries in a white silk slip dress. Lips covered in smudged red lipstick, his long black hair pulled roughly into a ponytail. He reads my sign and talks aloud. 'Sentimental writer collecting love stories,' he says. He runs a hand over Kath's typewriter and his interest causes Helen Clark to smile warmly at him.

'The politicians believe in an educated world, but I don't think they have a clue what that is,' he says, apropos of diddly-squat.

'I think you're right,' Helen says, nodding in her chair.

'You know the biggest problem we've got in the world?'

'What?' Helen asks.

'Lack of education.' The man in the white dress shakes his head furiously. 'Sorry,' he says, the way people say sorry when they really mean 'Don't get me fuckin' started.'

'Don't be sorry,' Helen says. She spent her life in education; she couldn't agree more. But the man in the white silk slip seems painfully sad now.

'No, I am sorry for interrupting,' he says, admonishing himself, and he waves at us both before he walks on down Adelaide Street towards Central railway station.

Helen scratches her chin, still studying the man as he walks. 'Fascinating,' she says. She turns to me, assesses my cheap writing desk, my cheap sign, my costly motivations. 'So, what, you just sit here all day talking to people about love?'

'Yeah, that's pretty much it,' I say. 'I also look at things.' Tiny leaves spinning as they fall from the sky and land on my writing hat. Junkie couples threatening to bash each other with tuna cans. A man staring at the sky through a telescope fashioned from an Australia Post mailing tube.

'I think it could turn out to be the most fulfilling work I've done in my life,' I say. 'Just sitting here.'

Helen sinks deep into her chair, arms resting on her thighs. She scans the street. 'I think you could be right,' she says.

'It's the pandemic,' I say. 'People seem to want to talk a bit more than usual. Go a bit deeper, maybe.'

'People have always wanted to talk,' Helen says. 'People haven't always wanted to listen.'

Norm Clark listened. Norm Clark was enthusiastic. When he fenced, he leaped across the floor, slashing his foil like Errol Flynn bouncing on the taffrails of a pirate ship. Norm was a listener and a talker, too. Norm was a thinker. He was a man of science who would one day devote his life to research into acoustics and vibrations at the CSIRO. He absorbed. He sensed. He felt. Helen says he was instrumental in creating materials for the lining of motorcycle helmets in Australia that protected the brain in moments of high impact. Norm was a member of an exclusive cheap living room club of rapier-witted conversationalists and coffee guzzlers who called themselves the Dawn-Busting Phantoms. 'The deal with being a member of the Dawn-Busting Phantoms was that you talked all night at someone's house and you weren't allowed to go home until the break of dawn.' Helen was welcomed into the thought-provoking sanctum of the Dawn-Busting Phantoms and for two years Norm kindly drove her home from club gatherings through the empty sunrise streets of Sydney and for two years Helen secretly hoped her kind friend, Norm, would end one such trip by switching the ignition off and slowly leaning across to the passenger seat and planting a kiss on the lips of a girl who would have planted a longer one right back.

'We were just friends, for so long I thought, Is this man even interested in me?' Helen says. 'Then, after two long years, he finally gives me a kiss.'

A perfect kiss, a soft lip-lock filled with anticipation and expectation, filled with the past and all the gloriousness of the future. A star-crossed kind of kiss.

'Why did it take so long for you to kiss me?' Helen whispered.

'I never got a chance,' Norm said. 'You always had a cigarette hangin' from your mouth.'

And Helen slaps her knees in the small blue Big W chair beside my desk. 'He was right, I bloody chain-smoked back then,' she says, shaking her head in disgust.

Marriage was complicated. Too many expectations from parents. Too much tradition and religion. Too much discussion about what they were supposed to do and not what their hearts were telling them to do.

'So, we eloped,' Helen says. 'We married in the registry office in Sydney. That must have been 1972.'

She wore a pink dress and a petticoat she'd sewn herself.

'I was a high school English teacher by then,' she says. 'I sewed that petticoat in class while the students were doing their reading. One day a student stood up. "Excuse me, Miss, but are you sewing that petticoat for anything special?" And I didn't tell them.'

'Pretty beautiful secret,' I say. 'Just for you and Norm.'

'Yep.'

'You knew exactly what it was for.'

'Yep,' she says. 'Took a day off on the Friday, we got ourselves married, and I came back into class on the Monday as Mrs Clark.'

Helen's parents took the elopement hard. She wonders if her mum and dad ever truly forgave Norm for it. 'It was very sad because my father expected to walk me down the aisle,' she says. 'He wanted to give me away at the Greek Orthodox church and have all that comes with that. That was tough. But I remember one day we all went to a function, and my father had died by then and my mother had no partner, so Norm took me by the arm on one side and my mother by the arm on his other side and he proudly walked us both into that function. After that, I think Mum realised what a good man he was.'

Helen pauses for a moment to think about her husband. And she looks painfully sad now, just like the man in the white slip who was standing at the typewriter only minutes ago. 'Norm died ten years ago,' she says, softly. She misses him every day but she's grateful for the forty-plus years she got to spend by his side.

'Were you able to tell Norm how much you loved him before he went?' I ask. 'Did you get it all out?'

'Yeah, he knew,' Helen says. 'He always knew.'

She has only one regret about all that time. She regrets the chain-smoking, she says, and that's more about true love than good health. If she could go back and do it all over again she'd spit all those dawn sunrise darts out of her mouth without a second thought. 'Two years with a cigarette in my mouth,' she says. 'Can you believe that?'

'I think it's all kinda sweet how it happened like that,' I say. 'I reckon Norm was just being chivalrous.'

'Yes, but what a waste of time!' Helen insists. She needs me to fully understand what got wasted. She clenches her fist. A fistful of the time she can't get back. 'Don't you understand? You must understand!' And she shudders with the ache of the thought in her head and she reaches out to grab my hand. 'I missed out on two whole years of being kissed by him,' she says.

And she rests back in her chair with the deflation of that sentence, and now I know what love is. Love is two years of not being kissed by Norm Clark.

`Love is a fistful of the time you can't get back.`

I believe in Helen Clark, the one from Waikato, New Zealand, and the one from Gunnedah, New South Wales. I believe supermodels have feelings, too. I believe in curried egg sandwiches for lunch, staring through telescopes at midnight, flipping through World War II diaries, bunny-hopping on a Mongoose BMX and the never-say-die attitudes of bathroom-tile cockroaches stuck on their backs. I believe in frying barramundi in butter and cracked pepper and I believe we should be comforted by the fact that whales have hip bones. I believe in the smell of 5 p.m. summer rain hitting bitumen and the sound my girls make when they laugh at Jennifer Aniston being funny on *Friends*. I believe in earnest Christening toasts, off-colour wedding speeches and sad eulogies. I believe in hailstorms, rainbows, forked lightning splitting the night sky, sleight-of-hand magic tricks, fever dreams, gravestone poems, cheap beer, expensive shiraz, birdsong, wishful thinking, and Neapolitan ice cream for the young. I believe in welfare, taxes, death, fate, chance, destiny, happenstance, dumb luck, talking, smelling, seeing, touching, hearing, listening, belonging, holding on, letting go and letting rip. I believe white silk slips look good on anyone and I believe in love.

LOVE IS BLINDNESS

Only two of us gathered on the street in this small circle of five are lucky enough to see each other clearly. Me with the typewriter and Cassie, the black Labrador guide dog with the sloppy kisses. Cassie's owner, Rene Crawley, leans down and wraps her arms around her neck. 'I dooooo love yooooouuuuu,' Rene coos.

Rene is sixty-one years old. When she was thirty-six she was diagnosed with retinitis pigmentosa, an inherited eye disease that causes her light-sensitive retina cells to degenerate slowly. Rene's been listing the great loves of her life and after Cassie she comes to her daughter and her grandson.

'I could see my daughter clearly until she was about twelve years old,' Rene says. 'By about the time she was fourteen, I'd started to have real problems.'

But she committed that face she loves so much to memory – every contour of her daughter's cheekbones, what her lips do when she smiles, the colours in her eyes – that it doesn't hurt so bad not being able to see her daughter's face at the age of sixty-one. 'But I would love to be able to see my grandson,' she says, sorrowfully. 'He was born on Mother's Day. He'll be eleven in two weeks.'

If, by some quirk of the universe, Rene was granted five bittersweet minutes of perfect sight, she would, without doubt, spend all of them staring at her grandson. No sunsets required. No starry night skies. No dazzling displays of light and colour. Just the perfect face of the boy she loves most in this world.

Two of her best friends and coffee mates, who are standing beside her in our small circle, nod their heads in understanding. Graeme Ferguson is fully blind and his wife, Dianne, is legally blind. They met thirty years ago, when Graeme was forty-six, and he and Dianne, then a single mother of three kids from a previous marriage, were starting up the Queensland branch of what would become Retina Australia, a sight-loss support network and research charity.

Graeme had been raised in a house in Yeronga, south Brisbane, with a family that had no fewer than seven members living with retinitis pigmentosa. He and his siblings leaned on each other through early life and their teen years in a way that most clear-sighted people could never comprehend. To get even a small measure of the kind of love he has for his siblings, you'd have to sit in a room in darkness for five unbroken years. When it came time for Graeme to help others through his support work with Retina Australia, he simply decided to treat every person with the same love and care he'd given his siblings.

'He tries to get them to see not what they can't do but what they still can do,' Dianne says. 'He's been there for so many people and I know for a fact he's talked people out of ending their lives.'

Graeme nods slowly, mournfully. 'And unfortunately there's been a couple we haven't been able to save,' he says.

I ask Graeme if he's ever entertained those useless thoughts about what he'd do with five miracle minutes of clear sight, apologising at the same time for all the clumsy, clear-sighted privilege inherent in my question.

'Oh, I've thought about that a lot,' he says. He switches his walking stick to his left hand so his right hand's free to wrap around Dianne's shoulders. 'What I'd like to see is my wife,' he says. 'I've never seen her.'

Water wells in his eyes and Dianne rests her head on his shoulder. And he pushes another sentence out of his mouth while he fights back tears. Same sentence as the last. 'I've never seen her,' he says.

And I wipe a tear away from my own eye, relieved that he can't see me doing that, and then I can't help myself from saying something that feels sentimental and dumb and awkward and maybe more than a little insensitive, but I have to say it because I just saw the amount of love in Dianne's eyes that she has for her husband. 'She's beautiful, Graeme,' I say.

'I know,' he says, warmly and softly, gently nodding his head, more tears welling in his broken eyes. 'I don't have to see her to know that.'

IT FOLLOWS

Cold morning wind pushing through the city and a large McDonald's soft drink lid sliding along Adelaide Street. The clear plastic disc seems to roll for a magic-trick moment on its side like a wagon wheel. These are the John Lennon mornings of our lives. Just watching the wheels go round and round. We all love to watch them roll, but where do we find the sacred time? I guess that's what writing the White Album buys you. The time.

Robert McCulley can take his time because he bought it with a lifetime of work. He sips a takeaway coffee at a bench seat in Albert Street, waiting for his 10.30 a.m. appointment at the skin cancer clinic. 'I've got a little thing here,' he says, pointing to the top of his nose, where some skin's peeling away. 'It'll be all right. They'll burn it off.'

Monday. First day of Robert's retirement. He spent the previous eight years of his sixty-six years on earth delivering letters across Brisbane on a remarkably reliable motorcycle serviced regularly by his employer, Australia Post. He loved being the messenger. He loved nothing more than handing a letter marked 'To Grandma' to a lonely old woman waiting by her letterbox. The letters of love were the best. All those ones marked 'To Dad', 'To Mum', 'To Pop'.

'One of the sad things I started noticing towards the end was that nobody seemed to be sending meaningful letters anymore,' Robert says. 'You would occasionally see a letter addressed to "Dear Dad" and you would think about the whole journey of that relationship between sender and receiver, the lives they've shared.'

Robert shrugs his shoulders inside his grey T-shirt. His hair is white and his eyebrows are black and bushy. 'But all you see now are bills and corporate letters,' he says. 'The romance is gone.'

Yet the messenger still knows a thing or two about love.

It's essential to Robert that his skin cancer clinic appointment goes smoothly today because it's essential to Robert that he spends every day of his retired life in good health beside his wife of thirty-one years, Julia McCulley. He says I would understand how essential this is to him were I ever fortunate enough to meet Julia McCulley.

'She's special,' he says.

'How so?' I ask.

'Love follows her around,' he says.

I smile at this unusual line and Robert the retired postman knows from the way I squint my eyes and bite my top lip and nod my head that I don't fully understand what he means.

'If you have a lot of love in your life, if you put a lot of love out into the world, then love follows you around,' he says, with a knowing smile. 'It follows.'

I like this notion. What if love was less an idea than a physical thing, as real as air and just as visible? And then I see in my head Robert's version of love as something that floats above us all like the cartoon scent cloud following Pepé Le Pew through the woods. We all walk in our invisible clouds and some clouds are bigger than others; our clouds expand when they brush against or chemically blend with other clouds.

That's how Robert and Julia ended up together. He saw her face. She walked ahead. He followed her cloud.

'Caring people have this sphere around them,' Robert says. 'People feel it and they want to be a part of that sphere. That's how it works. That's how caring people move through the world. That's how Julia moves through the world.'

*

Robert was born in Wrexham, North Wales. His mother and father had met on a Wrexham dance floor. His father was a leather trader. Robert was in school when he met a classmate who was part of an amateur dramatics society. Robert thought he wanted to be a physical education teacher, but he soon realised he wanted to act. He later landed a place at London's prestigious Guildhall School of Music and Drama.

'You know Julia Ormond?' Robert asks.

'I frickin' love Julia Ormond.'

'She's a friend,' he says.

'You know Alfred Molina?'

'I frickin' love Alfred Molina.'

'I met them through drama school,' Robert says. 'You know Art Malik?'

'You kidding me?' I say. 'Brilliant. The villain in *True Lies*. Gets strapped to that missile when Arnie shoots it through the sky.' And now my best Arnold accent: '"You're fired!"'

'Art's one of my best friends,' Robert says with a smile.

He landed some great acting roles over the years. He once trod the boards with the late Alan Rickman. He starred in the first episode of the BBC science fiction show *Red Dwarf.* But the best gig he ever landed through acting was a lifetime loving Julia McCulley.

It was the late 1980s and Robert was performing in a production of *Much Ado About Nothing* in Williamson Park, Lancaster, north-west England. Julia was singing in the theatre company's choir. At post-performance drinks in a nearby pub called The Gregson, Robert stood transfixed as he watched Julia enter through the bar door and breeze like a crimson-brown autumn leaf up the pub stairwell to the second-storey dance hall. Her hair flamed red with an ancient Irish fire and Robert had to summon every sweaty hour of his Guildhall School acting study just to play it cool.

'She went up the stairs and I followed,' he says.

They had two kids together. Boy and girl. They came to Australia via New Zealand, where Robert spent five years juggling part-time acting jobs with full-time postman work.

Nowadays, Julia's one of more than three hundred Teachers of the Deaf working in Australia. Dedicated and tireless, she brings every ounce of her love to her job and her students. Robert remembers the love she gave to their son during an early battle he eventually won against childhood cancer.

Damn, now he wishes he hadn't mentioned the C-word. Pancreatic cancer took his father's life at the age of fifty-six. Robert's mum died in the UK last year and it was hell for him because he couldn't be there to oversee the burial and funeral arrangements; he couldn't be there for her. All her possessions were sent to Australia and currently reside in boxes inside a Kennards storage shed in Coorparoo, south Brisbane, that he can't bring himself to open.

'I'll open all those boxes up and I'll see my mum's whole life,' he says. 'The mixture of all those feelings. The past, the present and the possible futures.'

But all possible futures are bright enough for Robert and Julia. They just sold their home in East Brisbane. They're making a new start on a hectare of land at Boonah, in Queensland's rural Scenic Rim. And true love will be the central theme of their coming months. Their son is about to marry. It was the darndest thing, Robert says. His son fell in love with a woman he literally bumped into while walking down the street. 'Imagine the chances,' Robert says. The terrifyingly long odds of true love. His son stumbling into love like that. The miracle of timing. It's almost as if love was there just waiting to be found, or had been following him around like a cloud the whole time.

Robert nods his head. 'It follows,' he says.

SAKURA TOMII AND THE GOOD THINGS
Part 1

Sakura Tomii wears a love-heart pendant on a necklace she found in Portugal. She likes eating almond croissants for breakfast and trimming her rosemary bush. She often stares for ten minutes at the caterpillars crawling along her lemon tree.

She carries a diary in her shoulder bag, in which she dutifully documents at least three good things she has observed in any given day. It was the advice of a friend named Robyn: 'Sakura, you must find three good things about each day of your life.' A blue butterfly flying through a crowded restaurant. An elderly couple kissing for forty seconds beneath the Story Bridge. A man whistling a Beatles song while he waits for a Boost Juice. The good things.

Rescued a stray dog. Harvested two pumpkins, one got rotten. Made risotto.

Cool but sunny winter day. Sewing. New laundry detergent smells good.

White chocolate. Eggplant for dinner. Lift from Pilates, thank you Hazel.

British murder doco, scary, lots of blood. Caterpillars survived. An email from Dad in Japan.

There is so much she wants to say about love and the human heart. She sees love as a thing that is expanding like the universe and if love is a universe then she's travelled to the very edge of it. She has stood on the edge of love and looked over the side and stared into the abyss of it, and she has seen death down there, then rebirth and death again.

But first, coffee. Her favourite coffee shop is a short walk from my writing desk on Adelaide Street. She likes the café, Coffee Iconic, for its coffee menu and because it has a laneway that customers can walk down off George Street that expands into a lush secret garden of ferns and potted plants that makes her feel like she's stepping out of one world – the one with car horns and concrete and deadlines – into another world – one of conversation and dreams and bottomless cups of black Brazilian coffee. She's a freelance English-to-Japanese translator with qualifications in IT and cybersecurity. She writes blogs about the cafés she visits across Brisbane. She's been coming to Coffee Iconic for seven years and she knows the manager, David, well enough to let him choose her coffee based on her tastes and what's new on the menu. She takes her coffee sugarless and black. I order a flat white.

'Ninety per cent of Australians drink flat whites,' she says.

'Does that make me boring?' I ask.

'No!' she insists. 'And there's nothing wrong with boring.'

Boring is safe. Boring is manageable. People who have led extraordinarily eventful lives such as Sakura Tomii always have a soft spot for boring.

She takes two sips of what she recognises as Market Lane coffee from Melbourne and she determines it to be some of the best coffee she's tasted in Australia.

Love is an imported Brazilian coffee bean that tastes like toasted almonds with notes of red apple and brown sugar. But, a word to the wise, love can also be an eight-dollar tin of International Roast that should have stayed in the back of the pantry.

One more sip and she's ready to tell me the long and eventful story of how her mother, Masumi, and father, Keisuke, followed their hearts and fell in love.

*

They were raised in a town that was slowly dying. 'A very rough mining town,' Sakura says. It's called Yubari, in the Sorachi Subprefecture of Hokkaido, the northernmost island of Japan. Yubari is Japan's 'greyest' city. One in every two citizens is older than sixty-five. The city was founded in 1943 as the country's coal-mining capital, but then the collieries closed and the town population plummeted from 120,000 in 1960 to roughly 9000 today. The town declared bankruptcy in 2007. It's ice-cold and snowbound most of the year, and large areas of Yubari have been 'rewilded', with local deer roaming freely through shopping strips and wild bush reclaiming concreted land where schools and coal mines once stood.

'Masumi is a male name in Japan,' Sakura says. 'My mum was really kind of' – she searches for the right word in English –

'weak. She tended to get very sick as a girl. That's why her parents gave her a male name, to make her stronger, to give her courage.'

Masumi's parents ran a successful restaurant. The family was rich enough to have a maid. 'But my mother's parents kept all their savings in cash inside a safe,' Sakura says, and I wince because I know where this is going. 'Then one day someone took all the money from the safe and the family went bankrupt. My mother was sixteen years old at the time. She had seven sisters and one brother and two of her sisters were younger than her. All of the older sisters and her brother got married. Her parents took care of the youngest girl, but insisted Masumi look after her other little sister.'

Life soon proved that Masumi had an inner strength, stemming from a source far deeper than her strong male birth name. 'She raised that younger sister by herself from the age of sixteen, in a very rough mining town,' Sakura says. 'She never talked about how she and her sister survived those years and I think that's because it was too traumatic for her to talk about.'

Lime marmalade. Sealed the shower cubicle after seeing ants coming through the gap. Watched The Great Escape.

*

Masumi met Keisuke in school. They went to primary and high school together, then Masumi moved seventy kilometres from Yubari to the city of Sapporo, the largest city in Hokkaido, to begin her training as a nurse. She chose nursing because the job came with free food and free clothing.

While Masumi was making plans to become a nurse, Keisuke was by his mother's bedside, nursing her through the cancer battle that eventually killed her. When he was twenty years old, Keisuke entered medical school in Sapporo, fulfilling a promise he had made to himself in the long months he'd spent watching his mother slowly dying – gradually being swallowed up by cancer as sure as the town around her was being swallowed up by wild green overgrowth – with not the faintest clue of how he might heal her or simply ease her pain.

For her first three years of nursing Masumi wore outfits that were hand-sewn or bought second-hand or found in a damaged-goods bin. Quite possibly the first truly happy day of her adult life was the day she had enough money to purchase her first brand-new fashion item from a Sapporo boutique: a sky-blue overcoat to wear to the city's famous annual Snow Festival, running for seven days every ice-cold February since 1950. And quite possibly the first truly happy day of Keisuke's adult life was the day he visited the Sapporo Snow Festival and saw a genuine earth angel standing in a sky-blue overcoat in an avenue of majestic ice sculptures. Snowflakes were falling over towering representations of famous historical figures and animals and creatures of myth and legend, but for all the sculptures' miracle artistry not one of them could steal Keisuke's gaze from the sweet and not-so-weak girl he knew from high school, who had transformed into the beautiful and seemingly invincible woman standing in all that white snow.

'And he summoned all of his courage,' Sakura says, 'and he walked up to her and he said, "Excuse me, are you Masumi?"'

Masumi loved him for his kindness. Masumi loved him for his tenderness. Masumi loved him for the fact he had no money and no car and for the way he showed his love for her every single day by walking one torturous hour across the city of Sapporo through freezing blankets of snow just to warm his eyes again by the fire of her perfect face. And from that time on, all Masumi and Keisuki ever had to do was follow their hearts.

Homemade lemon curd. Ordered audiobook from library. Found a packet of salty caramel biscuits in the pantry.

*

David, the coffee shop manager, brings new coffees to our table. 'This one's Rwandan,' he says. 'Tastes like lychees, with a red apple finish on it. Have you ever had a jazz apple?'

We nod.

'Just like that,' David says. 'Lychee is most noticeable, then it goes into a honey thing and then comes that ending, like biting into an apple.'

Nice ending. Everybody loves a happy ending.

Sakura remembers when she was a girl in primary school on parents' day, when all the local mums and dads visited the school and all the students compared and contrasted the many flaws of their guardians. 'Your mum is so beautiful,' the kids exclaimed when Masumi walked through the classroom door. Sakura swelled with pride, but she later learned about the many complexities that were masked and manifested by Masumi's beauty.

'I think my mother had anorexia,' she says. 'She was always underweight. I remember she didn't eat much. She was very good-looking but I think she hated being a woman.' Sakura thinks harder on this, her fingers pushing her coffee cup in semicircular rotations. 'I think she had trouble with men in that mining town.

She had lots of issues, all stemming from that childhood. Fear of abandonment. Fear of being poor again. She had a bad habit of spending money. I think she was genuinely terrified of living in poverty again. Then, when she was sixty years old, she was diagnosed with dementia.'

Sakura was in her late twenties and working as a computer programmer. She has a gift for info tech. To her, navigating complex software systems is as straightforward as running a pencil over a dot-to-dot image of the Sapporo Snow Festival. Her job paid well but it was a difficult workplace. Deeply stressful. The job became so taxing that one afternoon she found herself standing at a traffic-light crossing outside a Sapporo elementary school, thinking about jumping in front of the next car that passed. 'I thought that would make me feel better,' she says. 'But then I thought, I shouldn't do this, because it's just across the road from an elementary school. I don't want the schoolkids to see.'

She was terrified by the thoughts in her head and wondered where thoughts like that came from and how much the thoughts in our heads are related to the generational blood that runs through our veins. So she sat with Masumi, told her about her thoughts. She wanted Masumi to tell her to stop working immediately. She wanted Masumi to tell her to follow her heart, to run away and be free and never hold tight to something that causes pain.

But her mother told her she needed to hold tight to her job. Keep working. Never stop pushing, her mother said. Push through the pain of it, Sakura Tomii, because there's no pain like the pain of poverty.

'But then I thought, Wow, it's just a job, surely no job's worth dying for? So I quit. I decided to follow my heart, start doing what I wanted to do in life.'

She needed to leave Sapporo. She moved to Brisbane in 2001 to study international business and marketing and to improve her English. In January 2005, she was thirty-seven years old when she met and fell in love with an Australian man. They met online. She was first struck by his writing. He could spell. 'You'd be surprised how many English-speaking Australian men can't write proper English in the online dating world,' Sakura tells me. Sickening collections of misspelled sweet nothings; declarations of love that land with a thud because of numbskull prep-school spellings: *Maybe we should try that new reschaurant on Edward Street? We defenately belong together, I'm curtain of it! You compleet me, Sakura Tomii.*

'I wanted someone to spend time with, and also to practise my English with,' she says. 'We organised to meet in the city. He was polite. He studied agricultural science. He was really interesting, and I'd always wanted to meet someone intelligent like him.'

They shared the same birth date, 21 October. It felt so right. He was outgoing and Sakura was shy back then. She lacked confidence because of her tenuous grip on the English language, but that was fine because he was a good talker and she was a good listener who wanted to hear more English speakers talk. 'And Australian English is very different from normal English,' she says. 'He had a very strong Queensland accent, too. But he was really nice.'

They spoke for three straight hours in that first meeting, sipping coffee at the Milano café at the top of Queen Street Mall. 'He told me later he was so nervous, which was why he didn't stop talking the whole time,' Sakura says.

They dated for a whirlwind four months. Then Sakura said she needed to return to Sapporo to see Masumi, who was battling the creeping intensity of her dementia. She was going for walks and getting lost and having to be brought home by police. Sakura said she would stay in contact, assured her new boyfriend this was not an end to their relationship. Then he spoke of his fears that Sakura would meet someone else in Japan and never return to Australia. So he swung for the fence and followed his heart. He laid all of his chips down on life's roulette table. 'Will you marry me?' he asked. The proposal was as unsettling to Sakura as it was exhilarating. She was confused. She phoned a regular confidante in Japan, Aunty Ritsuko.

'I met someone,' Sakura said. 'He's really nice and he wants to get married. What should I do? I'm okay with getting married, but we've only known each other for four months.'

Aunty Ritsuko thought for a long moment. 'Well, if he's okay, maybe you just need to get married,' she said. 'Follow your heart, Sakura! If you don't like him, just get divorced!'

'Okay,' Sakura said. 'All right. I will.'

It seemed so romantic to Sakura. The rush of it all. The heart-on-the-sleeve all-or-nothing roulette-wheel spin of it all. It felt like the universe was whispering to her, *Just follow your heart, Sakura Tomii. What could possibly go wrong if you just follow your heart?*

'But here's something I learned through my time with him,' she says. 'We all put too much weight on romance. You go right back, maybe all the way to the early nineteenth century. People didn't put so much weight on romance. Marriages were arranged. People married people they knew. People who were connected to families. You knew who you were marrying. You knew their values. You knew what sort of person they were. Then the notion of romance came in. "Ohhhh, you have to follow your heart!"'

Sakura shakes her head and dwells on a thought for a moment at the coffee table. There's a bitter taste in her mouth and it's not the jazz–apple finish in the coffee. It's the taste of memory. 'How much can you really know about someone you meet online?' she wonders.

Now she forms a cross with her arms, rests her hands on her biceps. It's like she's hugging herself, warming a chill that seems to be pulsing through her body.

'Follow your heart,' she whispers. 'Ha! Follow it right into hell.'

PRINCE JOSEPH

Joseph Mpofu was eleven years old when he said goodbye to his mum in Zimbabwe. He'd known about physical pain well enough back then, sprinting and chasing and tripping his way through city streets and village laneways, tumbling down dirt hills, falling off cheap rickety bicycles, bruising arms and legs. But there was another kind of pain he learned about on the day he said goodbye to his mum. That was the heart pain, the worst kind of pain, the kind that stays with you and the one an eleven-year-old boy feels when he stares out an aeroplane window and watches the vast blue African sky fill the space between him, the boy up there with the clouds and the future and the promise, and the mum back down there with the land and the hunger and the fight.

He remembered feeling something like that before, when he was about nine years old and was told his dog, a scrappy and loyal neighbourhood mongrel named Scooby, had been run over by a car. He's embarrassed to say it now at the age of twenty – sitting here dressed in sharp clothes, in the bustling heart of a fortunate city – but when he was a boy he would find a spare corner of his spartan home and he would share a lollipop with Scooby. One lick for Joseph, one lick for Scooby. He loved that dog. Scooby was all he had. He needs me to understand that there's a big difference between being poor in Australia and being poor in Zimbabwe. Poor in Australia is a kid missing out on soccer for the winter season; poor in Zimbabwe is a kid kicking a soccer ball made from rags, yarn and a handful of condoms. Poor in Australia means no roast chicken for Sunday dinner; poor in Zimbabwe means an eight-year-old boy working a street stall on Sunday night, selling roasted chicken heads wrapped in newspaper.

But Joseph's mum had the magic about her. Joseph's mum cast a spell over her son that made him believe he was rich, convinced him he was living through his early childhood like a young prince. *Even princes eat like this, Joseph. Even princes dress like this, Joseph. Even princes cry like this, Joseph.*

He was bright. He was insightful. He knew the truth like everybody else. He knew they had nothing, but his mum made him feel like they had everything, so when it came time to leave Zimbabwe – to fly away to Australia with his father in search of work and education – he couldn't help but think he was leaving everything behind.

But now he's twenty and he's a man and he's working on getting everything back. He's studying veterinary science here in Brisbane. One day soon he'll be a paid veterinarian. One day soon he'll fly his mum over to his new home in Australia and one day soon he will have everything. He will show his mum all the sad, funny, wondrous differences between here and there, and he will show her the one thing that always stays the same no matter where on earth we are: the love. The buildings change. The dinners change. The clothes change. The love stays the same.

The best kind of love, the kind that stays with you, the kind an eleven-year-old boy can carry in his heart for a decade. So maybe, he thinks, love is something that exists just to remind us what it means to have everything. Or maybe it's just something to ease the pain.

THE ACTRESS BREAKING UP WITH HER BOYFRIEND IN HER UNDERWEAR AFTER A TWO-DAY DRIVE FROM TASMANIA

They'd spent the afternoon building IKEA furniture. Ashlee Cairns had just moved into her new apartment in Brisbane, having driven from Hobart via Melbourne and Dubbo. It was baking hot inside the bedroom, so she slipped her pants off to take a shower.

'Oh, before you go,' her boyfriend said. 'Can we talk?'

Ashlee stood in her T-shirt and underpants. She made a joke. 'Wait, are you about to break up with me in my underwear?'

Her boyfriend did not laugh. 'Well, I tried to catch you before you took your pants off.'

It's been three months and Ashlee still recalls every detail of the break-up moment. She studies acting at the Australian Performing Arts Conservatory, a short walk from my writing desk. Her class has been learning about staying inside a single moment in time, noting every detail of a single moment: every smell, every sound, every picture on the wall of a room, the carpet beneath your toes, the sweat-stick of a T-shirt, the size of the pupils in the eyes of the actor sitting across from you. Sitting on the corner of Adelaide and Albert streets, she stays inside the single moment her heart broke.

*

They fell in love three years ago in Hobart, just two months before he was due to leave for army basic training. He'd signed up well before they met. She wrote him love letters through the three-month training period, full-hearted confessions and sugar-sweet declarations. She wrote those letters like she was some 1940s lover sending urgent messages to her beloved, who would be warmed by her words when he read them tucked deep in the muddy shelter of a bomb-struck battlefield trench in France. His letters in return lacked a certain romantic flair – updates on weather, nutrition, mess-hall dining options – but his love was true and boundless and greater than the sum of his adjectives.

'But then, with the army stuff, it was three years of seeing each other every three or four months for a weekend,' she says. 'He was posted to Darwin. Then, during Covid, we couldn't see each other for ten months. The plan was he was going to come home at the end of four years, and we didn't really know how it was all going to work with my acting.'

Acting is Ashlee's dream. Always was, always will be. Not a lot of acting work in Tasmania, which is why landing a place at the Australian Performing Arts Conservatory on Adelaide Street, Brisbane, felt like her dream was starting to come true.

Now here's the problem with true love and dreams. Her boyfriend's dream was to go home to Hobart and join the police force like his father and brother before him. He wanted to buy a house in Hobart and raise a family and care for a loyal dog and then maybe open a café somewhere nice where he and Ashlee and the kids could spend their days making flat whites and macchiatos for grateful customers as loyal as their dog.

'But I wanted to come to Brisbane and do this,' Ashlee says. 'I wanted to act. I don't want children. I don't want to be a mum. I just turned thirty two weeks ago. I'm at a time in my life when I need to make a decision. And for a long time I think he thought I might change my mind about kids. But if I was ever going to change my mind then it would have only been for him and that wouldn't have been fair on either of us.'

So Ashlee sat down in her underwear three months ago with her boyfriend of three years and, perched on the end of the new bed they had just assembled together, she patiently waited for her heart to break.

'Eventually one of us is going to have to sacrifice what we want,' her boyfriend said, gently. He wept when he said those words and Ashlee recalled how he never wept over much at all. The great stonewall. The soldier. Unflappable. Invincible. He cried on the end of that bed and he said he worried that Ashlee would sacrifice her acting dream if he asked her to but he knew that wasn't fair or right or smart. And that was all he had to say.

Ashlee figures it might have been that very moment that her heart broke because she realised the relationship had probably had an expiration date on it from the start.

'You know the difference between you and me,' her boyfriend had once said. 'You always assume that a relationship is just going to work out.' And she knows he was right about that. She always trusted in true love. She trusted in the string-pull of fate, and maybe that was the Shakespearean stage actor inside her. The romantic in her. It hurt so much for Ashlee to sit on the end of that bed because it hurt to hear the bottom-line truth her boyfriend was telling her: *Your dreams are stronger than our love.*

She absorbed his words, soaked in the moment like a seasoned thespian. She didn't understand why he'd travelled with her all the way to Brisbane only to break up with her. She didn't understand why they had just enjoyed one of the best weeks of their three-year relationship – driving across Australia listening to music, shopping for furniture, duck-diving under waves at the beach – and now it was all coming to an end. She tried for a moment to hate him for doing it, for ending things like that, but hate wasn't possible. Only love was possible.

'I wouldn't be here if it wasn't for him,' Ashlee says, tears forming in her eyes. 'I wouldn't have believed in myself enough to come here and follow this dream. He drove me here and helped me find a home and then he helped me build all my bloody furniture.'

Ashlee sat on the end of the bed in silence for a long moment and then she wiped away her tears and she took her partner's hand. 'Well, thank you for not breaking up with me when I was in the shower,' she said. 'At least I wasn't naked when you did it.'

*

Ashlee laughs as she wipes away a tear, resting in the blue chair by my desk on Adelaide Street.

'It sounds like he was careful,' I say. 'Us blokes can be so clumsy in those moments. We get it so wrong so often.'

'He did it beautifully,' she says. 'It was very grown-up and it was very hard.'

'I feel like you might have said it if he hadn't said it first,' I say.

'No, I probably would have never said anything,' she says. 'I would have tried to make it work forever and ever.'

'You know that about yourself?'

'I know that because I loved him I would have kept going. We could have tried fighting for it and ended up hating each other and maybe I could have gone home and had kids and in fifteen years resented him. I thought about it all for a few weeks after we broke up. One of my very good friends gave birth and I had all these thoughts like maybe I was wrong, maybe I could do this, maybe this would be enough for me? And I was seeing the alternative life I could have had. Maybe I could have been a mother and a wife and continued working in a job in an office in Tassie and been happy with the kids and the dogs, living on a bit of land like he wanted. I think I could have done all that, but there would still have been a part of me that knew that wasn't enough.'

Ashlee hopped off the end of the bed that day. She had her shower. She and her boyfriend spent one last night together and in the morning he drove back to his army base in Darwin. Weeks later, Ashlee sent her ex-boyfriend a text. She doesn't know why she sent it, but she's glad she did:

That last week I was so, so happy. We did all these great things like going to the aquarium and the beach and the movies and just spending time together and getting to hug and touch each other. But when I look back on it, I'm scared it wasn't real or that it didn't mean anything because you were planning on leaving. So, was it real? Did it matter?

Then a return text landed in her phone:

Of course it was real. Of course I knew how the week was going to end. But I wanted to end on a high, not just fizzling out. That's why I wanted to do all those things.

I mention to Ashlee a nice little love story that a woman told me this morning on this corner. She was talking about how much she missed a very close friend who had passed away recently. She said this friend was the one person in the world who brought out a silly side in her. She adored it whenever the friend did this, because she adored her silly side. Her silly side made her feel good. But when her friend died she was worried that her silly side had died with her.

'We are all just amalgams of the people we love,' Ashlee says. 'And we take good parts from people and try to build ourselves from them.'

'Where will this guy remain in your life?' I ask.

'I have these really great parts of him,' she says. 'He was so confident and self-assured, and I wasn't, and I learned a lot of that stuff from him. I learned a lot about myself through him. How I want to be treated and how I don't want to be treated. I learned all that from him. And from us.'

Ashlee beams a wide smile, the kind you'd find on a Hollywood billboard. 'Always in my heart,' she says. 'I think everyone I've ever loved still lives inside my heart. He's always going to live there.'

THE CROSSING

See this restless city. See the way that dad in the business shirt and tie reaches his right arm out to grip the left hand of his daughter. Waiting for the little green man to flash and tell them when to walk across Adelaide Street and into Queen Street Mall. The girl's in her school uniform and looks about twelve, and if she's anything like my twelve-year-old daughter she probably doesn't hug her old man as much as she used to. But look at them at the traffic lights. He's reaching for her hand instinctively because there are fast-moving cars about and at least six grumbling council buses. He's probably been doing that protective reach for her hand ever since she could run. Nothing more terrifying than a wide-eyed toddler on the loose and approaching the ever-enticing push-button of a busy traffic-light crossing.

She'd probably refuse his hand if her friends were about, but there are only strangers here, so he knows he can hold her hand tight and she knows she can let him. And for the next ten seconds of that dad's life he knows for certain that she is safe and she is secure and he is so clearly and definitively doing the one thing he is certain now that he was put on this earth to do: to be a father for her. And I know for a fact he wishes he could stop time

48

here and now because he knows that she will grow. He wishes he could change the world and the way it spins, but he knows the only person with the power to change the world is her. She will grow because she must. She will soon discover the music of The Smiths and she will teensplain Johnny Marr's guitar playing to her father like she was the first person in the world to ever truly appreciate it. She will take two or three puffs on a joint at her friend Kayla's seventeenth birthday party and realise she gets a better high from the words of Emily Brontë. Her first car will be a second-hand red Toyota Yaris and she will fall in love with a boy named Arizona who plays bass in a punk band called Forked Tongue, and that boy will break her heart. She will work hard for no money and then she will work hard for lots of money and she will meet someone true and then one perfect and quiet afternoon she will ask her father to walk her down the aisle of Our Ladies of Victories Church, Bowen Hills, and they will hold each other's hands as tightly as they hold them now at this crossing but there'll be no flashing green man to tell them when to walk down that aisle safely and securely; they'll have to make that decision for themselves – daughter and dad, together. He would do anything for her, but at the end of that church aisle he'll have to do the one thing he never really ever wanted to do for her: let go of her hand. But for now, for the next ten seconds of that father's life, she can stay right there in his grip. She can stay.

Then comes the inevitable push-button buzz of life. And she lets go of his hand. *She lets go of him.* And she's off, two paces ahead of Dad as she crosses the street, and the little green man rushes more than anyone because the little green man knows that life's too short and moves too fast for fathers and that particular one in the business shirt and tie crossing the street has about as much chance of keeping up with his daughter as he does of stopping time.

*

See the family walking their bikes across King George Square, on their way to Roma Street Parkland. See the mum fitting a bike helmet to her young son's head. Never seen love until you've seen a mum tighten the straps on a young child's bike helmet. Always too tight. Always too much love in the tightening. 'Nope, still not tight enough,' she says.

*

See the man in the kilt with the heavy bagpipes under his big right arm. His name's Piper Joe and he's here to help. Help us think. Help us feel. 'These things stir emotions,' Joe McGhee says. He was born and raised in Glasgow, moved to Australia in 1982 with the love of his life, Liz, and their two kids, Sharon and Neil. In 1995, Joe was forty-two years old and a drum major for the Ipswich Thistle Pipe Band when a dear friend named Sally asked him if he would play 'Amazing Grace' for her on the bagpipes as she walked down the aisle on her wedding day. 'I would love to,' Joe said, 'but I don't play the bagpipes.' He'd never picked up a set of pipes, but his son, Neil, could play 'Amazing Grace' with his eyes closed and, come the day of the wedding, Joe stood with Liz in the church pews and watched Sally slowly march down the aisle with her father to the sound of Neil's heartfelt piping. Unexpectedly, Joe felt a bell of regret chime in his heart and he leaned over and whispered to Liz, 'I should have been doing that.'

'Well, you better get your finger out then,' Liz said, smiling.

He blew the bagpipes almost every day from that moment on – a cacophonous explosion of bum notes and spent breath – until, twelve months later, he could play a note-perfect rendition of 'Amazing Grace' and make his beloved wife weep tears of pride and relief in the process.

'It takes people back to wherever they've come from,' Joe says. 'It stirs all that emotion. It gets you thinking about the ones you love.'

*

See the man with the baby boy in his arms. See the way he holds him, nurses him, nestles him, like a ball of thin blown glass.

'Excuse me,' I say. 'Would you mind if I ask you what it feels like to hold that boy in your arms?' The father's name is Harsh Gondaliya. The boy is twelve months old and his name is Ari. Harsh and his brother were raised by their mum and dad on a peanut farm in western India. He came to Australia to study and he was supposed to return to India to run the farm, but he enjoyed his life in Australia too much. He went home to break the hard news to his mum and dad that he wanted to live permanently in Australia, and his mum and dad told him to follow his heart because they loved him with all of theirs. Just one request, they said: please marry a girl in India. His marriage to Ari's mother was arranged, but he was allowed to speak to her before they were wed and Harsh knew immediately in those early conversations that he was going to marry the woman of his dreams. Their love, he says, grows stronger every day.

Harsh works as a nurse in a hospital emergency ward. He sees the fragility of life writ large on a daily basis. The whole world is a ball of thin blown glass. Young mums diagnosed with aggressive cancers. Young fathers left brain-damaged by car accidents. Young dads the same age as him walking through hospital wards with newborn baby boys nestled in their arms.

Harsh thinks about my question. What does it feel like to hold that boy in your arms? 'World-changing,' he says, smiling.

PICTURES OF YOU

She stared at the pictures again last night. The photographs of Chris she keeps on the refrigerator. Handsome Chris in various poses and periods of his life. He catches her eye almost every night. When she's taking a bag of frozen peas from the freezer. Reaching for a wine. Drying the dishes. There he is, stopping her in her tracks again. And there she stands, still in her work clothes, tea towel over her shoulder, maybe fixing a dinner for Fin. A working single mother in her mid-fifties, frozen and mesmerised at the refrigerator. Then she puts her hands to her face and cries. Silently, so her big warm rock of a son doesn't hear her again.

She's not depressed. She's not broken and she's not lost.

Kerry Shepherd is in love.

*

It was two days before Christmas, 2012. Chris Walton woke at dawn and slipped quietly out of the house in Currumbin Valley, south Gold Coast, that he shared with his wife, Kerry Shepherd, and their then thirteen-year-old son, Fin. A surfing tragic, off for a morning wave. Healthy, fit and fifty-four years of age.

Chris phoned home after his surf. A couple they knew who were expecting a child were coming over, and Kerry was preparing lunch for them. He said he was going to the shops at Burleigh Heads to buy a baby book for the couple.

He went to a bookshop he knew on West Burleigh Road, but it had closed down. He phoned Kerry again to tell her he was going to another bookstore among the boutique shops near the Burleigh Heads beachfront.

'Honey, it's Sunday,' she said. 'It won't be open.'

'It's Christmas, maybe it will be,' Chris replied. 'I'm just going to have a look.'

'All right,' Kerry said. 'But it's nearly lunchtime, can you hurry back?'

'Okay, no probs,' Chris said. 'See you, honey.'

Chris was walking down one side of the James Street shopping strip when he saw the parents and sister of a close friend and the sister's two young sons on the other side. He crossed over and greeted his friend's parents beneath the awning of a place called Equity House, which sheltered three small fashion boutiques. Chris introduced himself to the sister's two boys.

Chris was exactly the kind of outgoing man who kneeled when meeting children for the first time. He was exactly the kind of man who went out of his way to meet people on their level. He was kind. He was optimistic. He was enthusiastic. He was a dreamer. A property developer with a passion for ecological sustainability. Chris and Kerry had spent the past decade of their lives creating the Currumbin Ecovillage, which thrives to this day, a 110-hectare village of sustainable housing and architecture for 450 residents living self-sufficiently. In 2008, the development was given a 'Prix d'Excellence' award by the International Real

Estate Federation and described as 'the world's best environmental development'.

Chris loved community. Chris loved people. Chris loved children. That's why he was kneeling down when the heavy shopping strip awning above him collapsed suddenly. That's why the last act of Chris Walton's life was to push those two boys to safety before he was killed by the crushing impact of the falling awning.

*

Sometimes Kerry thinks about taking the pictures down from the refrigerator. Putting the pictures in a drawer somewhere safe. Protecting herself from the feeling of his love. The ache of it.

'I get a physical feeling,' she says. 'It feels like an unrequited love, but it's not because of someone not loving me. It's that they're not here anymore. It's unrequited, but it's not painful in the sense that I love someone and they don't love me back. I love someone, I just can't be with him because he's not here anymore.'

Kerry changes the refrigerator photographs every six months or so. 'There's one on the fridge at the moment where we both went to a ball and we really dressed up,' she says. 'Your mind can go straight back to that night. A photograph can do that. And when someone's not here, a photograph can do that even more.

'If the person is still here, if you're still married, if you're still living together, your mind doesn't need to recall all that deep stuff because you're still seeing that person on a daily and nightly basis. When the person's not here, your mind needs to recall that very moment so strongly, and it does. It works. It's lovely. It's a really beautiful feeling.'

Kerry Shepherd is silent for a moment.

'But it's tragic as well,' she says. 'How can a human being possibly hold two completely opposite feelings in one moment in time? Polar-extreme-opposite feelings of love in that one moment.'

Sometimes the photographs feature Chris and Fin when Fin was little. Chris holding Fin as a baby. Chris at the beach with Fin. Kerry asks me if I've ever heard of 'agape love'. 'It's a Greek term,' she says. 'It's the over-arching love, the love you feel for humans or for pets, for everything.' Then there's 'eros love', she continues, 'the love between a man and a woman. And there's the love that comes through experience. So when I see a photo of us at a ball I can feel the love of what it felt like to stand so close to him. And when I see him in a photograph holding Fin, I can feel the love of seeing him be a father.'

Some nights she'll stare at a fridge photograph of Chris surfing and she will laugh because that's a fun memory. The love of knowing he loved something so much. But then she will cry because the photograph means something else, too: all the years he missed out on doing what he loved.

'So there's a sadness as well with anything,' she says, and she cries when she says that. 'And it comes from the love I have for him, from wishing more for him than what he got.'

So that's the catch of love. The hardest things inside us, the saddest things, stem from the best things inside us, the sweetest things. The fridge pictures hurt sometimes. The fridge pictures make her cry sometimes. When she looks at the picture of Chris at the ball she can remember how he felt about dancing and she can remember the way he danced, but she can't remember what it felt like to hold him close and move across a dancefloor.

'I wish I could,' she says. 'That fades. It's really just a memory and there's no more than that. Nothing physical. I kept some articles of clothing, of course. For the smell. But those smells have now gone. I can't smell him anymore. So now I have a reconciled view of love. If that smell hasn't lasted, then maybe lots of other things won't last either. Maybe the memories will go, too.'

*

Fin's been the great revelation through it all. His strength. His growth. His heart. 'It was survival,' she says. 'It was just keeping the wheels on. Watch him. Help him. He kind of shut up shop for a while. But as long as the wheels were turning, as long as he had normality – and an incredible friendship group – he was handling it, even though he wasn't dealing with it. Where the love comes in is, while I had ideas that he should be grieving – why isn't he crying? – I realised that was none of my business. My love for him helped me pull back from any aspirations I had about how he should be dealing with it, and just let him be. Just be there and keep the wheels turning. And that is so hard to do as a parent.'

She says she became a duo with Fin. They were a domestic double act existing in the darkness of true love lost. She will never know another human being better than she knows Fin right now at the age of twenty-one. She will never love another human being more. She will never appreciate another human being more. His teen years flew by in a flash. There was the day she told her son about the awning. And then it seemed like only a rushed series of goodbyes after that. Goodbye as he went to that party. Goodbye for the last day of high school. Goodbye for the first day of uni. 'And suddenly I'm in my fifties and I'm alone and it wasn't meant to be like that,' she says.

*

When Kerry lost Chris, the normal everyday domestic questions of life seemed suddenly absurd. What's for dinner? Should we eat at the dining table tonight? Would you like parmesan cheese on that? She has a group of friends who have a welcome and healthy respect for speaking about what she calls 'the deep shit'. 'We so regularly and often talk about Chris,' she says. She loves them for their listening, their endlessly open ears and their full hearts. She's almost certain now she doesn't need to meet another man. 'So many of my friends my age, and some even younger, could not care less if they never have sex again,' she says. 'I can have a good chat with those friends and be just as fulfilled. Some of my married friends aren't actually sleeping with their husbands. But it's about love for each other. They still have a good life. But, sex? No, thanks.'

She doesn't want the baggage of a partner. But then she wonders if that's just something she tells herself because she hasn't let Chris go. But what the hell does that mean, anyway? Letting go. Who would ever do such a thing? Let go of the one you love? Let them go from your heart, from your memory, from the door of your fridge?

And don't you dare see that as a 'Kerry hasn't dealt with her deep shit' type of thing. That's actually a romance thing, she says. That's a true-love thing. She will never let him go. She will never stop staring at the pictures on the refrigerator. She will not protect herself from the feeling of his love. She will cry her eyes out when she needs to until the day she dies and she will feel every bit of the ache of true love. She will weep, she will hurt, she will feel and then she will breathe and then she will dry her eyes and then she will smile and then she will take the frozen peas out of the freezer.

THE THREE-SECOND RULE

Two middle-aged women meet beside my writing desk. One from the south end of the street, one from the north. A long embrace. The hug lasts thirty seconds, at least. So much emotion in it. So much story.

The average duration of a human hug is three seconds. A developmental psychologist named Emese Nagy from the University of Dundee, Scotland, wrote a paper on the wonders of the human hug. She conducted a frame-by-frame timed analysis of 188 filmed hugs given by athletes from 32 nations across 21 sports through the finals of the 2008 Beijing Olympics. Athletes hugged partners and coaches the longest (3.8 seconds), opponents the shortest (1.8 seconds), but, overall, each hug averaged 3.2 seconds. We humans like to operate in three-second bursts of emotion. A three-second greeting, a three-second wave goodbye. Infants rambling sentences and gesturing wildly: three seconds. More primally, we breathe deep in three-second bursts, we chew food in three-second bursts. Same in the animal kingdom. A giraffe chews a leaf, a panda has a scratch, a kangaroo takes a dump. Three seconds. A whole world turning in three-second life-units that build upon themselves to form a truly wondrous twenty-four-hour miracle that we so insufficiently call 'Wednesday'.

'Excuse me,' I say. 'I'm sorry to bother you, and I know this question sounds bizarre, but can you please tell me why you two just hugged for so long?'

Rhonda Wittmann howls with embarrassed laughter, her left hand still gripping her friend Rachele's right shoulder.

'We've been friends since kindergarten,' she says.

'There was so much love in that hug,' I say. 'It felt to me like you hadn't seen each other in a decade?'

Rachele howls now. 'We saw each other last Friday.'

They caught up for coffee. Rhonda lives on the south side of the Brisbane River, Rachele lives on the north side. They caught up in the middle, at South Bank. 'Rhonda had a few issues she wanted to talk about and we got straight into it, didn't we?' Rachele says. 'It was friendship stuff. There's some things you can't talk to anybody else about. She always talks to her husband, obviously, but, I don't know, sometimes husbands get sick of it all.'

Rhonda finds a text message on her phone that she sent Rachele after that catch-up. She reads it aloud:

Thought of real warmth, love and affection for you when we caught up this week. Thanks for always being there. I missed you so much when you were gone in your head for those few years.

Rhonda shoots a half-smile at her friend and Rachele laughs.

'Gone in the head?' Rachele replies.

'No, not gone in the head, gone in *your* head,' Rhonda clarifies.

Rachele gives a half-smile back.

'We all go into our heads sometimes,' I say.

'Nah, I was gone in the head,' Rachele says. She wants to tell me about all that because it was her best friend, Rhonda Wittmann, who pulled her out of her head, but talking about all that is tricky and treacherous and hard to do in the middle of the city. Rachele will send me an email weeks later. She will tell me the truth; she will tell me exactly why she hugged Rhonda for so long.

Dear Trent,

I hope that you are well and enjoying discovering stories for your new book.

So, Rhonda and I went to the same kindergarten together. I don't remember her there. Year 1 at school, we were definitely friends and continued to be, on and off all through primary school. Same through high school. We did nursing together and then Rhonda moved away to Wagga. I studied midwifery and I was working as a midwife and was really struggling mentally. I developed an eating disorder and lost a lot of weight. I used sleeping tablets to make me sleep so I wouldn't eat. Before long, I was overdosing on the tablets. One day, I was unconscious so long I damaged the nerve in my leg, and I wasn't able to walk. My leg swelled up, I developed foot drop, and I needed a splint to walk. Rhonda and I had drifted apart a bit by this stage, but I remember I hand-wrote her a six-page letter about all that had transpired. Rhonda was shocked and saddened.

This letter brought us close again. She moved to Saudi with her husband but we remained close. I was sick for a while but gradually got better and was well for about eighteen years. I had changed workplaces because of the problem with my leg. It was fine for a long time. I loved my job and did it well. However, the workplace was toxic because of management and I became very unwell again. I ended up quitting work in 2015 because I got a new job but I only lasted one day because I was too unwell to do it. I was very self-destructive, overdosing two to three times a week sometimes. My husband had to lock up my medication or I would take too many. I hated myself. I didn't want to be conscious because being awake was too hard. I didn't want to die either, so, after I had taken the tablets, often I knew I had to go to the hospital because if I didn't, I may not make it. That made me feel worse. Sometimes I got treated like a leper. I was so ashamed. The shame made me do it again, and so the cycle went on. Hundreds of times for the next few years. I think a part of me wished I would die. I certainly went close. I know people were angry at me. Family, friends. People didn't understand. I didn't understand.

But Rhonda was there. Rhonda tried to understand. She asked me questions. She knew me. She was sad. It was hard for her. So hard. I'll probably never understand just how hard. But that's how amazing she is. She doesn't give up easily. She's loyal.

Everyone loves Rhonda. At high school, she was school captain. She's not the kind of girl you would expect to be school captain. She was kind of quiet, well behaved, a good student. Everyone liked her, though. You couldn't dislike her. It's the same today. She goes and does nursing contracts in different states. People just like her because she's so lovely. And I just think to myself, 'How did I get to be Rhonda Wittmann's best friend?' I am blessed beyond belief. I can talk to her about anything. She is the same with me. There's safety in a friendship like ours.

Anyway, I just thought I'd throw a bit more in there, see if it's of any use.

Best wishes,
Rachele

*

'I did get angry at you sometimes,' Rhonda says, sitting beside my writing desk.

'Well, of course you would,' Rachele says.

'I didn't really understand everything you were going through,' Rhonda says.

'I couldn't understand it myself. I was so angry at myself.'

'But you're back,' Rhonda smiles.

And Rachele shrugs her shoulders, not willing just yet to confirm that. Sometimes Rachele slips back down into what she calls the 'wormhole' of her head. 'I had a wormhole weekend, actually,' Rachele says, softly. 'I actually took some pills and I hadn't done that for a while.'

This is news to Rhonda and she receives it on this busy street like a gut punch.

'I lost the last two days,' Rachele says. 'I can't even remember yesterday. Yeah, it's still a struggle sometimes.'

And Rhonda nods. Listening, empathising, understanding, best-friending.

'But why am I saying this to you?' Rachele asks, turning to me. 'You're a complete stranger.'

'I'm not now,' I say. 'We've been talking flat out for half an hour.' That's about as long as I've conversed with some touch-footy mates I've known for thirty years. 'I reckon you're generously saying this stuff because it all relates to love,' I say.

If Rachele's not all the way back permanently from being gone in her head, from being lost in the wormhole, then she figures she's at least a lot more than halfway back. 'So what is it that brings you back, Rachele?' I ask.

She dwells on this for a long moment. She turns to her best friend. 'I think it's realising that people do actually love me,' she says. And she smiles at Rhonda Wittmann for exactly three seconds.

A WIDE EXPANSE OF WATER

She says she will tell me a love story, but the story can only last as long as it takes to smoke her last Winfield Blue. It's 8 a.m. I'm on my way to my corner on Adelaide and Albert streets. Same journey every morning. Drive a Toyota into the city. Park in the Queensland Performing Arts Centre carpark, where the all-day $17 parking is about as cheap as I can find anywhere in the CBD. Pull the heavy Olivetti along South Bank in a small black portable suitcase, my sign and my collapsible table resting in a $4 Big W red, white and blue chequered jumbo zip bag slung over my right shoulder, two collapsible blue camping chairs hanging on my left shoulder.

I pass her most mornings having smoko by the caramel milkshake churning of the Brisbane River. Her favourite smoko spot is the rock edge of a garden bed between the sandstone-block Victoria Bridge Abutment and the bikeway that curls up from the shadowed underside of Victoria Bridge to the sunshine topside that takes pedestrians and cars and buses across the river and into the city. A Polynesian woman raised in New Zealand, quick with a smile and a morning nod of the head. She's fifty-eight years old. She wears a wide-brimmed straw hat and high-vis yellow and blue workwear. She's been holding a stop-go sign for a gang of roadworkers laying fresh bitumen and concrete outside the underground parking lot of the nearby Queensland Museum. This morning she lights her cigarette and takes a drag, looking deep into the brown Brisbane River.

'You don't always have to love a person,' she says. 'I'm in love with this city. I came to this city to run away from a lot of things and this city saved me. It saved me from a very sad story.'

I like the way she says that, like we're all just products of stories, all moving in and out of sad stories and happy stories and all the stories in between.

'That story was suicide,' she says. 'Depression. Brisbane lifted me out of all of that.'

She takes another drag. A quarter of her cigarette has already disappeared.

'You ever seen this river at night?' she asks.

I nod.

'How it lights up?'

I nod again. There's no brown in the dirty brown Brisbane River at night. You can look across the river from Victoria Bridge under a full moon and all you see are flashes of light bouncing off ripples and if you squint your eyes you can almost tell yourself it's the River Seine and this is the city of lights, the city of lovers.

'But look around here this morning,' she says. 'The trees. The flowers. The random people you meet, like you coming up and asking me about love.' She looks again into the river. 'I love this river,' she says. 'I mean, it doesn't seem much to anyone else. To me, it's everything.'

Ten years ago she flew in to Brisbane from New Zealand. 'I came here on the very day of the big flood,' she says. 'Eleventh of January 2011. This river was risin' so high.'

'That was your introduction to Brisbane?' I exclaim. 'The 2011 flood?' Surely Brisbane's most dramatic day of the twenty-first century, to date. Some twenty thousand homes across the city were destroyed. I reported on some of the things I saw that day. Like how this river broke its banks a little after lunchtime. I watched the river tear up a three-hundred-metre floating walkway that joggers used to run on at dawn while admiring the gentle flow of their sleepy brown river. I watched a riverside restaurant being torn from its footings and spat down the river like a piece of scrap paper. In the inner-western suburbs I joined a group of thirty strangers who formed a human furniture removal chain stretching from the flooded living room of a widowed grandmother to dry land some eighty metres along her street. Thirty perfect strangers up to their necks in toxic, sewage-filled floodwater passing antiques and photo albums and jewellery boxes and armchairs from one raised pair of hands to another. I didn't report on some other things: people having nervous breakdowns as their life's possessions washed away; my own wife and our two confused kids evacuating our house in the south-west; the thirty-three people who died and the three people who are still missing.

'I came here that day and I saw so much devastation for everyone here,' she says. 'But then I watched all these families coming together, all these strangers coming together. I decided to join the Mud Army myself.'

The flood had peaked by the night of Thursday, 13 January. Then a call was put out to anyone across the city with a bobcat, a front-end loader, a water tanker, a high-pressure hose, a garden hose, a mop, a bucket, a water pistol or just a toothbrush to register with the Brisbane City Council as a volunteer for a city-wide clean-up that coming weekend. Council expected maybe six thousand volunteers if they were lucky. Some twenty-five thousand volunteers rolled up their sleeves, got themselves covered in mud and grit and grime, and earned themselves a name that will be whispered and toasted and remembered in the corners of riverside Brisbane bars and restaurants for decades to come: the Mud Army.

She'd been a Brisbane resident for precisely three days, and she still decided to enlist. And she doesn't know how to explain it, but something changed inside her during that long, hard, beautiful weekend she spent in the hallowed ranks of the Mud Army. She had been feeling a little broken herself, a little bit broken like this city. 'Then I watched this place being rebuilt and it felt like I was being rebuilt with it,' she says. 'That's how it saved me. That's why I love this city.'

I ask her about the things she was running from. I ask her about the sad story this city saved her from. And she smiles and holds up her cigarette now burnt down to the butt between her fingertips. 'Sorry,' she says. 'Gotta get back to work.'

'Would you let me write something about how you love this city?'

'Yeah, all right,' she says.

'Can I use your name?'

'Yeah, but just my first name.'

'What's your first name?'

'Moana,' she says.

'That's a beautiful name, Moana.'

'It is,' she says. 'It means ocean, sea, or' – she turns her eyes again to the river – 'a wide expanse of water.'

PINKY PROMISE

'Early start, bro?'

'Early bird gets the love story, Reuben.'

It's 8.30 a.m. and Reuben Vui smiles so wide I can see the gold flecks on each of his cuspid teeth. He's twenty years old and built like one of those mighty All Blacks from his cloudy and perfect homeland. He shuffles over to my writing desk with an iPad under his left arm, filled with electronic ChildFund Australia sponsorship forms. Reuben looks at Kath's typewriter, locked and loaded with a piece of white A4 paper covered in random typed-up morning revelations.

```
The human heart pumps enough blood over a
lifetime to fill a football stadium.

Is there a better love story in the world
than the fact the female superb fairy-wren
teaches her chicks to sing while they're still
incubating in their eggs?
```

'You finding some stories?' Reuben asks.

I tell him about some of the people he's seen sitting in the chair by the desk. We talk about our weeks, the ups and downs of street work. He asks me if I've ever wanted to sponsor a child and I tell him that I always have, but then I give a pained and squirmy account of how I was thinking about signing up with him but I don't know much about the background of his group, ChildFund Australia, and, maybe more than all that, I'm not too keen on handing my credit card details over to random dudes in the street. 'Does that make any sense?'

'No worries,' he says.

'I'm really sorry I can't sign up right now.'

'No worries, bro,' he says, smiling again so those gold flecks stuck to his teeth glisten in the morning sun.

*

Now it's 11 a.m. and a couple from Perth push a pram through King George Square. The mother's name is Sarah Brown. The father is Ben Stafford. The handsome four-year-old boy holding Sarah's hand is named Finn. The baby boy sleeping in the pram is Will. Ben works at sea on large commercial vessels: oil-rig supply ships, cargo transports. Sarah runs a jewellery and clothing shop at the Fremantle Markets. Sarah and Ben met twelve years ago in Kalbarri, a small tourist town on the coast of Western Australia, 570 kilometres north of Perth. Ben was drunk and dancing in a pub when Sarah first set eyes on him. 'I'd never seen anyone dance like that,' she says. 'He has a special kind of dance. He's got some flamenco-type thing going on, definitely not a modern man's dance, which I liked.'

Sarah was almost twenty-one, Ben was twenty-three. They met at a party after the pub. They realised they lived near each other, so they walked home together that night. Along the way, they stopped at a pirate-themed children's amusement park enclosed by a high-security fence. Buoyed by drink and the glow of the Kalbarri moon, they decided, in a shared rush of blood, to scale the security fence and leap onto a trampoline. They bounced high into the air and they howled with laughter and they felt four years old again. They felt as old as Finn is now, and they were just as happy, bouncing and bouncing until it was time to breathe and steady their dream-night universe by steadying their feet. And they caught their breath and they smiled as they stared into each other's eyes and the amusement park was silent and the stars above were twinkling and the man in the moon was eating his popcorn with a smile and that big heart inside Sarah's chest felt like it was going to run off into the Indian Ocean.

'Then we kissed,' she says.

Sarah is a brave woman but she wasn't brave after that first kiss. Days later, Ben was helping build a house for his grandparents. Sarah asked her sister, Alex, to casually walk with her past the worksite. Sarah couldn't bring herself to talk to Ben, so she begged her sister to approach her future brother-in-law and pass on Sarah's phone number.

Sarah made Ben tacos at home on their first official date. She put the taco shells directly on the wire rack of the oven and was so caught up in conversation with Ben that the shells overheated and caught fire. Then they ordered pizza. Sarah lived next door to a man with a learning disability who insisted on bringing his guitar over to Sarah's house that night and providing a live musical accompaniment to their increasingly awkward first date.

Sarah's neighbour's guitar playing sounded something like a garbage truck reversing into a guitar shop, but Ben was so kind and patient with her neighbour and he never once asked him to stop playing during a relentless set that lasted two hours.

And that, she says, is Ben all over. Gentle but not weak. Patient but never wasting a single moment. Sarah places her hand atop Finn's head. 'And the rest is history,' she says.

'That's so beautiful that you said that as you put your hand on Finn's head,' I say.

And it seems as though Sarah is tracking back through that perfect history in her head, and now she's come to the most profound moment of her life. 'Well, you make these kids for nine months,' she says. 'Then they come out and they have these squishy little heads with red faces and these slimy, slippery bodies and it's pretty amazing.'

'Instant tears,' Ben says. 'And just so proud of what Sarah had done.'

I remember that feeling. 'Hell yeah, that whole new level of worship for your wife,' I say.

'It's so impressive,' Ben says. 'You just can't imagine yourself going through something as intense as that. There's nothing we can do that matches that.'

They've got the young parent weariness. The round-the-clock numbed joy of caring for babies and toddlers. Sarah says she looks forward to the time when she can read novels again. 'Or poo with the door closed,' she laughs.

I share my loose theory about how we're all just underground miners working away at the thick and never-ending coal seam of life and we all spend our shifts at the coalface. Early parenthood might be the most gruelling shift of them all, making you feel like you're hacking away with a blunt rock axe at a wall that won't change shape, never fully certain that the twisting wormhole tunnel of your existence isn't going to collapse around you. But then, sure enough, after a shift that lasts five years or ten years or twenty, some other family takes your place at the coalface and you wonder why you're so bloody envious of them.

Sarah has an ouroboros tattoo on her arm: a circle formed by a serpent eating its own tail. 'It's life, death, regeneration,' she says. 'It's all connected. Nothing really dies.'

Sometimes Ben and Sarah go deep on the big stuff. Sometimes they dwell on the big purpose of it all. Ben's decided it's a ride. It's a pirate-themed amusement park thrill ride and he's just gotta buckle in and hold on and hope it all doesn't get too dizzy for him. Just be a good dad. Just help Finn and Will grow into good men who are kind and patient and always willing to help others.

'We get so caught up in life,' Sarah says. 'We're just going about our days and we get so caught up in life that it's nice to reconnect with the story of how we all came to be here.'

Then Ben says something beautiful about Sarah. He hopes his boys get to grow up and know something of the kind of love he feels for Sarah. He knows that's been the greatest gift of his time on earth so far. Being allowed to love someone so fully like that. He tells a story about what it feels like to leave Sarah for long periods when he travels for work on the long-journey cargo ships. The toughest mornings are the ones when he finds himself watching the sun come up after an all-night shift. That's the exact moment when he starts to think how perfect it would be to have Sarah beside him. And he sees no land. Not a single suggestion of grass and dirt – of home – to the north, south, east or west. Nothing but the endless blue ocean. And that's when he gets a sense of what it would mean to be alone. But then the days pass and Ben witnesses enough sunrises on his own on the deck of a cargo ship that, one morning, without fail, he eventually sees a thin horizon of land again and he knows he's almost home. And every coastal bird he sees in the sky flies in the direction of Sarah. And all that grass and dirt on the horizon is Sarah. Because home is Sarah. And Sarah is home.

*

Now it's midday and I know that face. A man in a suit walking with a slight limp. It's John Coates. Mr Olympics. He made that whole wild Sydney 2000 Olympics national fever dream come true. Some thirty-one years as Australian Olympic Committee president. Quite likely the most influential Australian sports administrator who ever lived, and here he is passing my corner on Adelaide and Albert because he's in town with another impossible dream, bringing the Olympics to this city in my soul for the year 2032.

'Love?' John Coates says. And he ponders the word for a moment and he thinks of his second wife as well as his first. 'I'm on my second marriage and I still get massive support from my first wife as well as my second wife.' Then he thinks of Cathy Freeman and Cathy Freeman makes him think of the Olympic Games and he tells a love story about a boy who fell head over heels in love with sport but was never much chop at sports because he was born with a congenital dislocation of the hips. 'They didn't pick it up until I was five,' he says. 'I was not a good athlete myself. I had a disability, so I coxed for a rowing team. And then I coached in rowing and then they grabbed me and stuck me in administration. And then I got to mix with all these superstar heroes.'

He says he has another love story for me. Imagine being the poor blighter given the task – the nerve-racking, bone-rattling honour – of asking Cathy Freeman if she would mind lighting that Sydney Olympics cauldron before the eyes of 6.1 billion people across the world, and imagine knowing full well the pressure that would put on someone like Cathy Freeman, but also knowing full well what such a moment might mean to the Indigenous people of Australia, her people, and where it might fit inside a history stretching back more than sixty thousand years. Then imagine the love and gratitude you feel for someone like that when she turns to you and says that perfect three-letter word that always changes everything: 'Yes.'

'Woah,' I gasp, shaking my head. 'Not a bad story, John.'

'Not a bad story,' he says.

*

Now it's 1 p.m. and a woman passes and slaps a slab of roasted hazelnut chocolate on my writing desk. 'Just thought you might be getting hungry,' she says with a smile, then walks on down the street.

'Thank you!' I holler after her. She turns and gives a thumbs-up as she scurries back to work. No more thanks needed.

I turn back to a woman I've been talking to, Karen Seeto, who's sitting in the blue chair beside my desk. 'Humans are amazing.'

'They really are,' Karen says. She points at the chocolate slab. 'I get it now,' she says. 'This whole thing has been a ploy to get free chocolate from the people of Brisbane.'

'Ya got me,' I say. 'Want some?'

'I'm good,' Karen says.

And she is good. Now. She wasn't so good in 2020.

'Such a shit year,' she says. Covid-19. She quit her job. Her parents divorced. Her relationship severed without warning. She can't even talk about that break-up. Tears escape from the corner of her eyes just thinking about it. 'Really, don't ask,' she says, laughing. 'It's triggering.'

But she wants to say something about the good parts of that horrible year: 'Change.' There was a beauty to that awful year, she says. Every one of those downsides had an upside. She didn't like her full-time job, so she quit, which meant she was free to pursue her passions. She's now studying graphic design and chasing her dreams. She's unemployed but she's never been happier. Her mum and dad's separation meant that Karen could finally be the rock for her mum, a woman who was raised in China and was forced to work from the age of sixteen because her own mother had died and somebody needed to be the rock for her family in place of the beautiful rock that had been lost. Karen's mum had never leaned on anyone. She was always the one being leaned on.

'We didn't grow up with a lot of money, but we had so much of what really mattered,' she says. 'Love. And we got so much of it from her. I was blinded, never really noticing it while growing up, probably because I was always comparing myself to everyone else, always measuring myself against what everyone else had. Last year helped me realise that what we had was actually really, really good, and as bad as that year was, it was also a time for us to give all that love back to Mum and that was a beautiful thing.'

Love is appreciation.

Love is Karen Seeto being motivated by the times we live in, by a pandemic that made her see that life is nothing but a glorious lottery. Some days are rocks and some days are slabs of roasted hazelnut chocolate.

*

And now it's 3 p.m. and I'm packing up my chairs to go home.

'Long day, bro.'

Reuben Vui smiles, shuffling towards my desk, the iPad still tucked under his left arm. 'Hey, you got time for one more story?'

'Course I do.'

Reuben wants to tell me a story about the gold flecks on his teeth. 'See, my parents weren't really able to be there for me when I was young,' he says. 'My grandparents took me and my brothers in and they showed me what it was to be a parent and I loved them with all my heart.'

This was back in New Zealand in Reuben's primary school years. There were times before his grandparents took care of him when he had to sleep rough, or was dragged between inadequate homes, coming face to face with violence, pain, fear and a couple of other things he won't mention because he doesn't want to spoil a good day. 'I know what it's like to have no one,' he says. And that's why he works so hard here on Adelaide Street, hawking those child sponsorship packages to dozens, hundreds, thousands who pass him every day. I know how hard he works because I've watched him fist-bumping and high-fiving his way into the hearts of strangers for six straight hours spent on his feet. 'I'm saving up enough money to create my own real estate business,' he says. 'Once I finish that I want to build homes for the homeless and help them. That's why I wake up in the morning. That's my dream.'

Every weekend, Reuben says, he volunteers at a local homeless shelter. 'I see kids in that shelter and they don't know where they're getting their next meal from and it breaks my heart because I was there at one point and the only thing that saved me was my grandparents.'

He spells their names out for me. Nivea and Tagaloa. The kindest people he ever met. 'Where are they now?' I ask.

'My grandpa died of a heart attack,' he says. 'Then my grandma had dementia and she died of cancer. They were real hard times, seeing two of the most important people in my life disappear.'

He smiles wide again. 'Can you see the gold in my teeth?'

'Yeah, I can see it.' Leaf-shaped slivers of gold fixed to each large cuspid.

'That's gold from my grandparents' wedding rings,' he says.

'No shit.'

He laughs. 'Nah, man, my grandma always said to me her favourite part of me was my smile, and so whenever I get lost or whenever I get a little troubled I just look into the mirror and smile and I think of my grandma and I remember who I am and I remember where I've come from, *who* I've come from, and then I'm not so lost.'

I picture Reuben in my mind, smiling into his bathroom mirror on a lost and lonely night. 'Mate, I think I'm gonna cry,' I say.

'Noooooo, don't cry, bro. It's a huge blessing for me. My grandparents are with me, always, and they're with every person I smile at.' Then he smiles at me and now his grandparents are with me, too, because that's how it works.

'I know I'll face my trials again,' he says. 'I know I'll face my hardships, but I'll just go to that mirror and smile and I'll be strong again because I know they're with me.'

He stops talking and takes two steps back because he's crying. 'Sorry, man,' he says.

'Man,' I say, because I always start saying 'man' around young people when they start saying 'man' around me. 'Don't be sorry.'

'I still miss them, but I keep it all inside and then I'll walk around the corner and have a little tear.'

'Nothing wrong with that.'

He nods. 'Yeah, I reckon we should show our emotions more when there's shit happening.'

He's talking about us blokes. He says it's better for us blokes to walk forward weeping than to walk backwards with it all bottled up inside. 'Even though there might have been shit things in your life, you can never let it be your excuse for going backwards,' he says.

'Man, I wrote a whole novel about that.'

'Ya did?'

'I did.'

'We gotta try and be sharks, bro,' Reuben says.

'Sharks?'

'Sharks always go forward,' he says. 'A shark never swims backwards, because it will die. A shark never stops swimming, because it would sink and die. The shark never stops. Carries on. Keeps going. Always forward.'

'Reuben, I reckon you're gonna swim all the way to that real estate agency.'

'Ha!' He laughs, shrugging his shoulders.

'All right,' I say, pointing at his iPad, 'show me those forms.'

'Aww, really, bro? Ya don't have to.'

'Nah, ya got me,' I say. 'You had me at the smiling in the mirror stuff. I'll give you my credit card details. I really do want to sponsor one of those kids.'

'Aww, man, that's great.'

Reuben takes my name and address, date of birth. He taps in my credit card details and then he hands me a pack of papers and leaflets. 'This welcome package tells you who your sponsor child is and what he does, where he lives and what his livelihood consists of,' Reuben says. He hands me a photo. A young boy with a smile as warm and soothing as a Cat Stevens song. A message next to the photograph: 'Hi, I'm Eric, and I live in Uganda.'

The story of Eric's life has been typed out on the back of the photograph. He lives in a small two-room house with his parents, who are small-scale farm workers who earn the equivalent of $20 each month, which they spend on essentials such as soap and medical supplies. Eric's favourite colour is yellow and the best part of his day is when he gets to collect the yellow flowers he finds on his way to school and church.

'What a beautiful kid,' I say.

'Yeah, man,' Reuben says over my shoulder. 'You can talk to him anytime. Check on how's he going, tell him about yourself and your family and where you come from.' Reuben points at Kath's typewriter. 'Hey, maybe you can type him a letter!'

'I might just do that.'

We shake hands and Reuben shuffles away a few steps before he stops on the spot, thinking deeply about something. Then he shuffles back to my side. 'Listen,' he says. 'You're a good guy, man, so now I'm gonna tell you the story about the love of my life. You want to hear that one?'

'Course I do.'

Around the time when Reuben was starting high school, he reconnected with his parents and his family moved to working-class Ipswich, South East Queensland.

'I was born in Ipswich,' I say.

'You have my respect, man,' Reuben says with a clenched fist to his chest.

In Year 8 at Ipswich High School, Reuben met a girl. 'The loveliest girl, man,' he says. 'Her name was Isis. She was half-Chinese, half-Australian. We dated and we went all the way to Year 11 and that's when I found out she had cancer. She didn't tell me until she had to, after I saw her pass out once. I called an ambulance and they did all these tests. I was devastated. I knew I wanted to spend my life with her. I wanted to have kids with her. Then she was cancer-free for a while and we thought it had gone away and then she made it to Year 12 and at the end of Year 12 it came back and it was much worse.'

Reuben starts tapping the pavement anxiously with the toe of his right shoe. 'Our plan was to go to the school formal together,' he says. 'And she didn't make it.' He breathes deep, hugging his iPad to his chest now. 'And the shit thing was my grandma died at the start of that year, Year 12, and Isis was always with me and I never felt like I was that important to anyone.' He shakes his head and tears form in his eyes. 'It sucked,' he says. 'Isis made me feel so important. I had felt like this one lonely kid in all the world and then she decided to care for me. She made me feel like the most important person in the world.'

Two days before she died, Isis was lying on her bed when she pulled Reuben close to ask him something important.

It was a request she needed to make and one only he could grant. 'Promise me you'll find someone else and be happy,' she whispered.

'And we'd always do this thing where we pinky promised,' he says, raising his right pinky finger. 'You know the pinky promise?'

I nod.

'The pinky promise meant a lot to her. I never broke a pinky promise I made to her. But that one's been *haarrrrd*, man. I'm still not ready to keep that one, you know what I mean?'

I nod.

'I keep her photograph in my car and I talk to her after each day like she's still with me in real life. I'm like, "Hey, how ya goin'? My day was busy today."' He laughs and fights back tears. 'People say to me, "You do know she's gone, right?", and I go, "Yeah, I know," but it's good to have that feeling, that feeling that she's still there.'

'Hey, Reuben,' I say, softly. 'It's not my place to say, but I think you gotta keep that promise. You know, be happy. That was the promise.'

'Yeah, I know bro, I know.'

He looks both ways along Adelaide Street, takes in his concrete surroundings. 'Sometimes I wish I could just live in a world where reality doesn't exist anymore,' he says.

'Yeah, I know what you mean, man,' I say.

And suddenly we're hugging. A brief man-hug, Compton gangster-rapper style, all chests and fists. It lasts less than three seconds.

'Sorry, man,' he says.

'Don't be sorry. I loved hearin' your story.'

He wipes his eyes and he becomes the shark again. Always moving forward. Never stop swimming, or you'll sink and die.

'See ya, man,' he says. He shuffles on down the street. 'Don't forget to write to Eric,' he says.

'I promise I will,' I say. 'I pinky promise.'

Dear Joni,

Everything you gave to us was the truth, and the
least I can do is give some back. The whole truth
and nothing but. I'm losing someone I love. He's
slipping away from me and it makes me so fucking
low, Joni, that I don't know if I ever want to get
high again. You ever felt that kinda low? The kind
you want to stay in? Wish I had a river, too, Joni.
I wish the Brisbane River would turn to brown ice
and I wish I had a pair of ice skates and I wish
that I could ice-skate because I'd skate away. Just
for today. I'd skate along that river all the way
to Ipswich, where I was born, and you'd be there
in your ice skates, too, at a corner of that river,
waiting under the shade of a hanging riverside
jacaranda. I had a batshit daft daydream about us,
Joni. Sitting right here on this corner of Adelaide
and Albert. I saw a scene with only us two in it.
We were talking on that frozen river.

'What's new, buckeroo?' you said with a smile.

'I'm low, Joni,' I said. 'Low as dirt. Low as
mud.'

'Hey, you need to slow down, teary clown,' you said. 'You need to stop, lollipop.'

Then we had one of our talks.

'What did you do, Joni, when you realised you were running out of time to fix the things that needed fixing?'

'I sang. I played piano. I cried some. I hurt some. I lost some. I loved some.'

'All that feeling that you gave us. All that heart and soul and pain you shared with us. You have been so generous to us. Why were you so generous?'

'That weren't generosity. That was just honesty. I was just thinkin' out loud.'

'I'm low as fuck, Joni, and I don't feel like getting high again.'

'Hey, why ya gotta swear, polar bear?'

'You can take the boy outta Bracken Ridge ...'

'You're still puttin' chicken salt on your hot chips, aren't you?'

'Yeah, can't stop.'

Then you skated in a circle out onto the frozen river and executed a perfect, Olympic-level triple axel, acknowledged the miracle leap with a humble nod.

'I lost it, Joni,' I said.

'What did you lose? And don't you dare say love, turtle dove.'

'Why can't I say love?'

'Because that was never yours to lose.'

'It sure felt like it was mine.'

'It wasn't.'

'I felt it. I held it. I kept it.'

'But you didn't own it. Love can be given and love can be received, but it can't be owned. It can be treasured and it can be worshipped and it can be kept inside the steel safe inside your heart, but it still can't be owned. Someone can choose to give you their love, but they can choose to take it away, too. They can do that because that love belongs to them. And that's what makes it the greatest gift. That's why we must treasure the love we are given for as long as we are given it. It's a gift that needs our work and our time and our care. If we get to care for and carry that gift for as long as we live, then right on, Donkey Kong! But please don't think for a second that it's yours to own, Pat Malone.'

I traced a triangle in the ice with my skate. 'Joni, why do you think they gave us love?'

'Who's they?'

'The masters of the universe, the forces of evolution, God, whatever you wanna call it.'

'Oh, they.'

'They gave us something so truly beautiful, but it's also something that causes us so much pain and confusion.'

'Well, they had to give us something to do. We couldn't just watch *Tiger King* the whole time.'

Then you said two simple words, Joni. 'Both sides,' you said.

'Both sides?'

'The low side and the high side of love,' you said. 'You're on the low side of love but that's still love all the same. Maybe you're lucky to have held a kind of love that makes you feel so low. Some folks feel no side of love at all.'

Then you gave my shoulder a warm and gentle punch. 'Look, cheer up, buttercup,' you said. 'You got more love stories to hear on that corner of yours. All those beautiful strangers you keep talking to, they know the answer as well as you do. They know how to get that love back.'

'How?'

'Just do the work.'

Then you said, 'Better swish, jellyfish.' And you skated away.

'Wait, where are you going?' I called.

And you stopped and looked back at me.

'I'm skating up to Fig Tree Gully,' you said. 'It'll be a long journey but I'm gonna find the source of this dirty brown river. I won't stop until I've found it.'

'Can I come with you?'

'Nah, you got more stories to write.'

'What do you think you'll find up there, Joni?'

'The same thing I find at the end of any long journey.'

'What's that?'

'The beginning.'

Then you smiled and skated away again. 'In a while, crocodile,' you hollered over your shoulder.

I dropped my head and frantically racked my brain for something nice I could say back to you. By the time I looked up again, you had disappeared up the river.

'Bye, bye, butterfly,' I whispered only to myself.

Yours by the river,

Trent

GOOD EVIL

He says he has a romantic little pet name for the love of his life. 'Lady Succubus She-Bitch Demon From Hell,' he says.

She, naturally, has a sweet little nickname for him. 'Evil Demon Spawn Imp,' he says.

In the interest of brevity I'll just call him 'Evil'. His head is shaved and he wears a black shirt over a blue and green tartan kilt because he's Scottish.

'Where did you guys meet?' I ask.

'I met her through one of my social clubs.'

'Which social club?' Rotary? Bridge club? Rebels outlaw motorcycle gang?

Evil smiles knowingly. 'It's more of a private thing.'

'What ... like ...'

'Like ... a *Fifty Shades of Grey*–type thing,' Evil says. 'My lover, my girlfriend, is currently my dom. She's a dominatrix.'

He keeps shaking a 600-ml carton of eggnog in his right hand. The carton moves as fast as his busy lips as he details the tricky love territory you have to navigate when you fall head over heels in love with your dominatrix.

'My phone is on charge right now in case she calls during the day,' he says. 'She can phone anytime and say, "I want you at my workplace by midday to get me lunch," and I go and get that organised. It's called servitude. She will often phone and say, "My friend and I will be home at 6.30 p.m. and I want dinner waiting for us," and I'll have to have that ready. I've got a hospitality background, so I do that stuff well. Then she'll come home and I'll be waiting in the kitchen with dinner and she'll point at me and say, "Go in the lounge room and chain yourself up until we want you again." That's true love and servitude. Sometimes that's good and sometimes that's a weight off my mind because I've normally got a busy mind and it's a relief to have a woman do all my thinking for me. I let her take control for a bit and there's a peace in that and that's the beauty in the dynamics of polyamorous–BDSM–kink relationships. She's on top with all the power and control, but the person at the bottom is in control, too, because we know it's relaxing for us.'

I take a moment to process Evil's breathless love monologue.

'Wow,' I say. 'I've never had it explained to me that way. I totally get that.'

Really not too different from me watching the Brisbane Broncos on the telly every Friday night. Time out of mind, man. Same thing everybody's chasing. A break from all the thinking.

Evil nods, but he raises a forefinger because I haven't heard the tricky flipside of it all. 'She's trying to change me,' he says. 'I'm forty-five and she's trying to make me a better person. I'm trying to change her to make her more relaxed and more tolerant of people's failings and imperfections. We can't all be perfect all the time. It's interesting, because she's very powerful in her day job, always in control and very focussed, knows everything that's happening. She likes to be the one in control. But I'm teaching her to realise she can't always be in control of me. I'm my own person.'

'Have you spoken to her about what you're searching for in that dynamic?' I ask.

'See, I go both ways,' he says. 'I'm a switcher. I top, I bottom. I let her be in charge of me in those intimate situations because it makes her happy and she feels love that way. But we need to set limits and rules and regulations that we do not cross, outside of an intimate situation.'

Fascinating love pickle. The dominant–submissive dynamic works well enough in the BDSM dungeon warehouse on Friday night, but it don't always play so well on Saturday morning in the pest control aisle at Bunnings Warehouse. Lately, it's been the lover, the carer, the partner he knows outside the dominant–submissive dynamic that he's been falling in love with all over again. 'It's not about sex,' he says. 'True love is the little things. It's dealing with all the "isms", all the imperfections that make us who we are. I leave my cup on the coffee table and she'll come along and put it in the sink and rinse it, and being me, somewhat of a male, I'll say I've left it there for a reason, namely that I haven't finished using the cup. I was going to go fill it up again and have another drink. But she's come along and washed it and I've come back to the coffee table, knowing where my coffee cup is and I've gone, like, "What the fuck?" So then I say, "Honey, do you realise I wasn't finished with that cup?" And she says, "I know," and I say, "Then why have you washed, rinsed, dried and put the cup away?" And she says, "Because it was there."'

'Oh man, I do that to my wife all the time,' I say.

He nods his head and shakes his eggnog. He raises his left forefinger and thumb, keeps them a centimetre apart.

'True love is accepting all those little things,' he says. 'But most of all, true love is just being there for her. It's not all about sex. Sometimes she wants to be at home on the couch with hugs and cuddles. It's not all about the physical thing. Sometimes true love is not saying a single word. Just being there. Sometimes that's the greatest love we can bring someone. Just be quiet. Just shut the fuck up and be there.'

HENNY AND DENISE

Two old friends in the morning sun. Henny, a retired nurse.
Denise, a retired primary school teacher. Something so serene
about the way they sit, their thighs almost touching, Denise's
right calf swinging back and forth with the flow of her thoughts.

'How did you work it all out?' I ask.

'Work what out?' Denise replies.

'You both look so serene,' I say. 'So peaceful. Nothing's
hurrying you. Nothing's bothering you. You look like you've
worked it all out.'

'I'm just happy to be sitting with my friend,' Denise says.

'And I'm happy to be sitting with mine,' Henny says.

*

They met twelve years ago through a craft group. Scrapbooking
and calligraphy classes. Lots of time to tell stories in classes like
those. Lots of time for love stories.

Like the one about Don and Molly, Denise's parents. Don, the
handsome Irish boy from Uki, northern New South Wales, one
of fifteen kids, who was pushing his sister's baby's pram down

94

the street one day, his sister by his side. Molly was watching Don from afar, spying on the young man whose face had caught her eye at a town hall dance. 'That's a shame,' Molly told herself, misreading the moment. 'He's already married.' A few days after that, a friend gave Molly the good news: 'Don's not bloody married!' A lot more days after that, some more good news spread across the village of Uki: 'Don sure is bloody married!' Better still, 'Don married Molly!'

They had four kids. Don worked as a banana farmer and a cane and cedar cutter. He built the family home himself. Their daughter Denise was twenty-one and studying teaching in Sydney when a priest knocked on the door of a Balmain flat she was sharing with some fellow student teachers. 'Your mother, Molly, passed away,' the priest said. 'She died of a cerebral haemorrhage.'

*

Henny was born in war-ravaged Holland at the end of World War II. One of Henny's earliest memories as a very young girl was looking at her dead grandmother through a glass-topped casket, like the one Snow White was placed in after she ate the poisoned apple. She remembers her father lifting her up in his arms so she could lean over and give her grandmother a goodbye kiss on her cheek. She doesn't remember being scared of her grandmother's cold body. She only remembers love.

Henny and her parents sailed to Australia in 1953, when Henny was eight years old. The first place the boat pulled into was Fremantle, Western Australia. A fellow passenger treated Henny to a lolly at a nearby café. Henny ate the lolly then quietly took her mother aside. 'Mum, we need to return to Holland,' she said. 'The lollies in this country are terrible.' Two years later, Henny was ten years old and staring at her father's dead body inside his coffin. He'd died of cancer.

'It wasn't awful, either,' Henny says. 'It just looked like he was asleep.'

*

'Why are we telling you these things?' Denise asks, smiling. 'I don't normally tell people anything.'

'Blame the pandemic,' I say. When the future is uncertain for us it feels nice to talk about the things we're certain of, like the past. Same reason I have a Martika song on my Spotify playlist.

'I guess anyone passing up and down this street has a story,' Denise says.

'You wouldn't believe the stories they have,' I say.

Sometimes when Denise is taking public transport and she finds herself frustrated by someone who's holding the bus up or earbashing someone in the seat behind her and, in turn, earbashing every other sorry passenger within a four-metre radius, she tries to remember that every person has a backstory, a series of events, often tragic, often joyous, that shaped them into the person they are at the precise moment they spin into her own storied orbit. She remembers the time someone in the city aggressively asked her youngest daughter, Jasmine, for some spare change. They weren't taking no for an answer and had they considered some of Jasmine's backstory they might have had some understanding as to why the usually unwaveringly kind and loving Jasmine turned this day with gritted teeth and spat out, 'GET FUCKED!'

*

Denise met her husband, John, when he lived in the same block of Balmain flats she occupied as a student teacher. He was blond, handsome and tall: Redford meets Newman meets a telephone pole. He worked as a technician for the Postmaster-General's Department, or PMG. They had three kids: Jason, Justine and Jasmine. One summer, the family travelled north from Sydney to spend Christmas at Tweed Heads. It was on that trip that John said the strangest thing to Denise. He said he'd been thinking about road accidents for some reason. 'He had a premonition that something bad was going to happen, so he decided we'd get the train back to Sydney and put the car on it because you could do that in the old days,' she says. 'You could go by train from Murwillumbah to Sydney and your car would be on the train.'

Nothing bad happened on that trip.

'But then we got back to Sydney and his mate said, "Look, I've got to take a load of bricks down to Port Kembla, do you want to come for the ride?"'

John had several days free and he welcomed the road trip.

'Well, on the way home from that trip, there was a car on the wrong side of the road. A Spanish guy. He had two little kids in the car. My husband said he could see the man coming towards them, so his mate, the driver, veered across to get away from the Spanish guy and they hit a power pole. John had multiple injuries from that.'

The year was 1974. The injuries from the crash meant John later had to leave his PMG job. 'He became a house dad,' Denise says. 'He used to ring me up and say, "I can't find the nappy pins." I'd say, "Well, they have to be somewhere, your daughter hasn't swallowed them."'

Denise howls with laughter at the memories in her mind. 'He was hopeless,' she says. 'He had a walking stick and if there was a noise in the house he'd hand me the walking stick and say, "Here, go and see if there's someone trying to break in."'

Then Denise stops laughing and sorrow fills her face. 'Finally, his injuries got worse and then he got depressed and the rest is history.'

She doesn't say exactly how John died and I don't feel like asking her because it's too good a day and the sun's shining too bright.

'That's what happens,' she says with a shrug.

John died in 2004. He was cremated, along with his walking sticks, in Brisbane, because local family members helped organise his memorial service, held in the Mount Gravatt Cemetery and Crematorium on Mains Road, Macgregor. Denise eventually moved up to Brisbane for good.

'I was so mad with him that when I would drive past Mains Road to go to my Probus meeting I would say, "I'm still cranky with you, John." I know it sounds heartless, but I am still cranky. He could have had a good life. But after the accident, he just went downhill. He didn't have that will. He was a terrific reader, for example, but in the end he wouldn't even get his glasses repaired.'

*

Henny always loved the smell of hospitals. 'I know that seems silly,' she says. 'It was that ether smell. I knew I was going to be a nurse when I was very little.' She began nursing at seventeen. She met a man and fell in love. They were married for twenty-two years, had two kids. Tracey is forty-eight now and Michael is forty-six. 'I met this man who was very nice, with dark skin and brown eyes, and he was just lovely and I thought I loved him, but it didn't work out,' Henny says. Henny threw herself into the job she loved. She says the last five years of her working life were probably the most fulfilling. She was working in palliative care in Redcliffe, the seaside peninsula community in Brisbane's north. People didn't always understand how she got so much out of it, nursing people at the end of life. She explained how she didn't fear the dying, just like she didn't fear the dead as a girl. Most of her palliative care patients were at peace with their lot. Time and time again, she watched those patients find a rare human grace, some profound acceptance that comes with stripping existence back to the only thing that matters.

'Love,' Henny says.

It was always the visiting relatives, the loved ones, who were hardest to deal with. She always had the good human sense to understand that it was love – true love and true grief – that made people so stressed in those moments. But most of the time there was so much good life stuff to learn from the dying that outshone the messy family stuff. One day a patient who was slowly dying whispered to Henny that she could see an angel at the end of her hospital bed. 'You probably think I'm mad,' the patient said.

Henny was gentle and sincere. 'I don't think you're mad at all,' she said. 'What's the angel saying to you?'

'I don't know,' the patient whispered, keeping her voice down as if the angel in attendance could hear her.

'Well, maybe you should find out,' Henny whispered back.

*

Almost six years ago, Denise was travelling through Vienna when her son-in-law, Matthew, phoned to tell her that her youngest daughter, Jasmine, had been diagnosed with a brain tumour. Jasmine's daughter was almost three years old. 'The tumour wasn't curable,' Denise says. 'She lived nine months.'

She takes a deep breath. 'It was tough ...' She pauses when tears well in her eyes. 'But ... I don't think about those nine months. I just think about the whole thirty-five years I had her.'

'That's good,' Henny says. 'That's good.'

Denise leaned on Henny through those nine long months. Henny brought every bit of her end-of-life care knowledge and understanding to caring for her friend.

'Jasmine had something about her, didn't she?' Denise says and Henny nods along with her. 'She was so full of life. It was like she knew she wasn't going to live long. She lived her life full-bore. And ever since all that happened, I've done everything just like Jasmine. Full-bore.'

Her son-in-law, Matthew, has found a new partner and Denise is glad about that. She saw how hard it was for him to cope with Jasmine's death. He wore her wedding ring permanently on a chain around his neck. He never moved a single piece of furniture in the house for years. Everything was kept how Jasmine had liked it, and Denise wasn't sure how she felt about that. Maybe true love is Matthew wearing that wedding ring around his neck for the rest of his life, Denise wondered. But maybe true love is also being strong enough to gently take that necklace off.

It looks like there might now be a wedding down the line for Matthew and his new partner. 'I've made a decision,' Denise says.

'I won't be going to their wedding. I don't think he needs Denise around at his wedding.'

And that's got nothing to do with how deeply she loves and treasures Matthew, and everything to do with Matthew writing new chapters in a beautiful new love story. Or, to put it another way, she's helping him take the necklace off.

*

Henny remembers walking back into that palliative care room occupied by the woman who'd seen the angel at the end of her bed. The woman was dying, but she smiled as she told Henny that she'd managed to communicate with the angel and she was delighted because she had worked out what the angel had come to her room to tell her.

'She was so at peace,' Henny says.

Henny lets her love story end there.

'But what did the angel tell her?' I ask.

'I don't know,' Henny says. 'I didn't ask her to tell me.' She smiles wide and shrugs her shoulders. 'I didn't want her to tell me.'

BURIED TREASURE

'Love stories?' says the lanky and twitchy man with a tattooed lizard running up the left side of his neck. 'How 'bout I bury yer fuckin' head in concrete?' Crew-cut hair, half-cut blood, high on something strong and strengthening that makes two thick blue veins move beneath the skin of his forehead as though two electric eels are trying to find a home inside his brain. I think he's misread my intentions, but here are a few other things to believe in. Peril. Danger. Death. The knowledge that one day, sure as winter, I must curl up like a fallen leaf and die.

I believe.

That's what this street does to me. It makes me believe in life and numbers. Numbers on the face of the Brisbane City Hall clocktower that rises above my right shoulder and keeps chiming to remind me I'm here to die and to live and why both those tasks are as serious and funny as each other. Numbers to tap into phones to call family members I love. Numbers for when they're down and numbers for when they're up. And who's to say when our number's up?

This street reminds me to look alive. Be alive. Be here now. I believe in this man with the crew cut and the Chicago Bulls shirt who tells me he's going to drive my head into concrete for no reason beyond the fact that my sign, my table, my existence caught his eye. He looks like he could probably do it — the concrete burial, I mean — so I best get busy appreciating these final few seconds of my life, these last few numbers I have left before he begins his aggressive grave work.

*

But I still haven't typed that letter to Hiedi Owen. The one about the day in high school English class, senior year maybe, when we were talking about the new Smashing Pumpkins record, then somehow we came to the merits of Valentine's Day because maybe it was 14 February, and maybe I said something try-hard cool and grunge-like about how Valentine's Day was a corporate scam for suckers and sellouts.

'I don't know,' Hiedi said softly, tapping the rubber on the end of her pencil against the brown school desk next to mine. 'It's nice to receive a rose.'

Hiedi turned to face me. 'Have you ever been given a rose, Trent?' she asked.

'No,' I said.

'Everybody should know what it feels like to be given a rose, at least once in their lifetime,' Hiedi said.

Then it was the afternoon and after school and summertime-hot, and our house in Bracken Ridge smelled like last night's spilt beer that made the peach-coloured kitchen lino sticky when I walked over it in my bare feet to check the fridge to see what was for dinner and there was nothing in that noisy rust-covered Kelvinator but a tub of Black & Gold margarine, a can of Powers

Bitter and a half-hacked Hans Devon roll that someone hadn't covered properly with Glad Wrap. Then it was 5 p.m. and *The Wonder Years* was finished and I was lying on my back on the lower bunk of the double bunk bed I shared with my brother, and my fingers were picking at the underside of his thin yellow foam mattress pressed against the sagging spring support base of his bunk. And I gave a grim half-smile because my single greatest achievement for that day was that I had picked the words 'SHIT' and 'HOLE' out of the bottom of that mattress. Then there was a knock at the front door and I almost fell out of my bed in surprise because nobody ever knocked on our front door. And I opened the door that afternoon to find Hiedi Owen standing on the concrete porch in her Converse sneakers and she was smiling, and when Hiedi Owen smiled whole fields of sunflowers bloomed in Egypt and penguins in Antarctica did backflips and mute ninety-year-old monks in Nepal ended their quests for meaning. She held a single rose in two hands and she gave a little chuckle as she handed it to me. 'I wanted you to know what it feels like to be given a rose,' she said.

*

And I still haven't typed that letter to you, Mrs D, that sorrowful, confessional letter I should have written when I was fifteen. The one about how I had that dumb, drunken teen-boy fight in the street with your son and how sick I felt when I found out two months later that your boy – *your beautiful boy* – had taken his own life. The letter about how much I wished I could hit rewind and go back and grab your boy and say, 'I get it, I fuckin' get it, man, how it feels so dark and it feels so black, but please don't

104

forget about the bells on the City Hall clocktower, man, because they keep chiming, because time ticking by is the one true thing you can always rely on, and if you just stick around long enough, man, they'll chime enough for you to be just as grown-up as all the grown-ups who keep making things black for you, and soon you'll write your own story instead of having them write it for you and the first chapter of that glorious story will be the one about you getting the fuck out of this shithole.' Or maybe, Mrs D, I should have just asked Hiedi Owen to hand your boy a rose.

*

Have I even told all the ones who matter the most why they matter the most? The girls. Yeah, every day. Fiona. Yeah, every night. Mum? Damn. Been a while since I called. She always says I don't need to call too often. She says she knows how busy things get, so don't sweat it, sweetheart, you know it's all good. Sure, she might be a hard-working single woman in her mid-sixties and a deeply loving grandmother who has lived three lifetimes in one and survived them all and a woman who spends her nights alone inside a small flat doing her best to stay off the damn durries, but it's all good, she doesn't need a phone call every week from her youngest son because she's got her *Midsomer Murders*, she's got her *New Tricks* to keep her company. She can cosy up gently on a lonely Saturday night to *Inspector George Gently*.

What the fuck is wrong with you, man? What book could you possibly be writing that's more important than calling up the woman who pushed your sorry arse into being in the first place? Note to self: if this crew-cut guy does not bury your head in concrete today, like you probably deserve for not calling your mum every second day, then you better call your mum, quick smart. *Ungrateful punk!*

This street makes me believe and I believe that if this man does not bury my head in concrete today then this is my lucky day and everything that happens from this moment forth is gravy, and I don't mean some cheap Black & Gold sachet gravy, I mean roast chook pan juice gravy with a splash of white wine and big chunks of tarragon and lemon stuffing that spilled from the end of a bird curled up dead and buried in olive oil and salt supposedly shipped all the way from the Himalayas.

*

'What a fuckin' story!' Crew-cut man smiles, lightning in his eyes. My head buried in the concrete footpath of Adelaide Street? Hardly *War and Peace*, to be fair. Flawed narrative development, lightly drawn characters, excessively violent. 'I'm all good, thanks,' I say, raising my open right palm above the typewriter.

And I want to tell crew-cut man what day it is. 'You wouldn't believe what day it is today?' I want to say. 'It's my forty-second birthday. What a day to have one's head buried in concrete!' But I don't say that.

'Would *you* like to tell me a love story?' I ask instead, gently, the way one might ask a fire-breathing three-headed dragon if it would care for a bowl of Coco Pops.

'Gyyyeeeerrrrrrrrrrrrrrrrr,' the man says, which I believe means 'Peace be with you' in drunk Russian. And he stumbles on his way, across King George Square, cursing an innocently waving Reuben Vui, the ChildFund Australia rep, as he goes.

*

I know what I want for my birthday. I want a Gray-Nicolls cricket kit. The kind of kit I dreamed about as a kid. The kind of kit those golden kids from Nudgee College used to have. A set of leg pads and a helmet for my thin skull, so that when my mate David Kelly bowls his in-swinging bouncers in the nets behind the local school I won't be killed and I will one day be able to see my children graduate from high school. I want a vintage Gray-Nicolls Twin Scoop Dynadrive cricket bat and a mallet to knock it in.

'But love's not about gifts,' says Magda Haj Gido, sitting at my desk. 'Love's not about receiving.' She's twenty-one years old. She's from Sudan. She came to Australia when she was four, fleeing a country in the grip of a war that would later be described as the first genocide of the twenty-first century. 'Love's about giving with all of your heart, giving all of your heart to the world,' she says.

'Who taught you that?' I ask.

'Myself,' she says. 'My mind, my thinking, my soul, my heart. All me.'

Magda's hands move wildly in the air when she talks. Rust-coloured lipstick. Her fingernails are polished in vibrant metallic blue and gold. Headphones pulled down over her shoulders. She's killing time in the city today because she's waiting for some money to drop into her bank account. She's killing time with me. When this money drops she will buy herself some lunch. She's hungry this morning but you better believe she's been hungry before and there are far worse things you can be than hungry. She says she's had a difficult life. She says she learned everything she knows by doing exactly what I'm doing here today. 'Just by sitting down and talking to people,' she says. 'I learned about life. I learned about love.'

And she tells me everything she has learned about love.

'You got to have patience with love,' she says. 'You got to mean it. You gotta put focus on love. You gotta put pressure on love. And then it's gotta have some magic on the side. And some romance, too. And when you love that person so much, you gotta call that person up and you gotta tell them, "Guess what? I love you soooooo much!" And then they will say, "Oh my God, this is soooooo good, I actually have somebody in my life who *loves* me."'

Guess what?
What?
I love you soooooo much.

And she makes it sound so easy and that's probably because it is. And then Magda Haj Gido shuffles on through the city, towards the bank, leaving this corner as quickly as she arrived, having given far more to me than she received from me.

I tap a bunch of words in ink on the white page loaded in the Olivetti:

```
I don't want a cricket set for my birthday.
I don't want a DeLorean that travels through
time when it reaches 88 miles per hour. I don't
want Princess Leia to pop out of a cake made
of Bubble O' Bill ice creams. All I want is
```

```
the same thing I wanted yesterday. All I want
is tomorrow.
```

The bells on the Brisbane City Hall clocktower chime and I tap a name on the favourite contacts page of my iPhone. *Ring, ring. Ring, ring.* Somebody answers.

'Hey, Mum, guess what?' I say down the line.

THE IN-BETWEEN

Sometimes when people ask about her parents she says her father was David Bowie. 'Yep,' she says. 'And my mum was Siouxsie Sioux.' She describes her childhood as something like growing up inside *The Rocky Horror Picture Show*. 'Except R-rated,' she says. Her mum was a heroin user who ran away from her father before she was born.

Her body is a thirty-five-year-old gallery of tattooed images stretching across her lean, yoga-teacher arms and legs, chest and neck, but if there is a single tattoo that tells the truest and deepest story of her life then it's the three-headed dragon breathing fire and surrounded by pink, orange and yellow flowers that Lei-iissa Celeste is progressively having inked across the canvas of her back.

'One dragon's head represents love,' she says. 'That's all the light, all the good stuff. Another dragon's head represents all the dark, all the shadow stuff.' The head in the middle is something more complex than darkness and light. This is something she calls 'the in-between'.

'I started getting tattoos when I was young,' she says. 'As a defence mechanism, like, "Stay away from me, I'm tough." I grew up very open, inside a dark world. If you've had a dark life, a lot of people shut down and close up. I did for a long time and then I realised I was so unwell because of it and then I opened up into it. I went introspecting into that dark world, and it has opened me up more than ever before. It's all about finding that inner love.'

No inner love. No outer love.

No outer love. No inner love.

Lei-iissa remembers reading something about ordinary love being just 'an almond-sized sliver' of an unseen extraordinary connection unifying every living creature on the planet. 'One infinite connection that draws all of us together,' she says, and she's not just talking about the bridge in 'Under Pressure'. 'Maybe we're feeling it for only a second, but what if we were accessing that same infinite connection that's so big and so far beyond our understanding? What if love is like the dark matter that's holding it all together?'

I remember talking to my father-in-law about dark matter over Fat Yak beers. My father-in-law is an entomologist – bug guy – but his interest in all science runs deep. We both agreed that nothing makes the human brain feel so acutely pea-like as quickly as the thought that the universe is comprised of sixty-eight per cent dark energy, twenty-seven per cent dark matter and only five per cent of anything we can possibly observe, such as stars, planets and Chris Hemsworth's abdominal muscles. NASA scientists call dark energy a 'complete mystery, but an important mystery' and that feels to me, today, like a fair description of what Lei-iissa is saying about love.

`Love is a complete mystery. Love is our most`
`important mystery.`

Lei-iissa and her partner have enjoyed a deep and loving relationship for thirteen years.

'We also share an open relationship,' she says. 'And it's been successful because we allow each other, through our love, to explore and to grow. For us, love is a connection. If you get to make many such connections in your life – and we allow ourselves to – then you get to feel more of that infinite connection.'

She laughs and shakes her head. 'I know I'm saying "connection" a lot, but that's what it's about. And don't get me wrong, I'm all for monogamy, as long as you're growing. People say, "I love you, I will have only you," but so often I see people in those relationships shutting off their love. So often the growing stops. Maybe a child comes along and that becomes your love, but the intrinsic love between the two lovers sometimes gets replaced.'

I get it. 'Sometimes my wife and I are so busy bringing as much love as we can bring to our girls, we forget to bring it to ourselves,' I say.

'Yeah, for sure,' Lei-iissa says. 'You know it's always there, but it isn't always accessed, I guess, which isn't always helpful. All I know is the more you shut down to things, the more you shut love down. And the more we shut it down, the less love we experience and the less we can pass on.'

I tell Lei-iissa about Robert McCulley, the retired postman from Wales who has a theory that love follows his wife around. 'He said it was all around her but people just couldn't see it,' I say. 'A bit like dark matter, but this was light.' Light matter.

'*Yessssssssss!*' she says.

Then I say three or four awkward sentences about a book I wrote called *Boy Swallows Universe*, which was a fictional tale half-based on my real life in the 1980s and early 1990s, when

I gladly took and was gladly shaped by the deepest kind of love from people who were drug dealers and drug users and demon drinkers. Some nights were *The Rocky Horror Picture Show*. Some nights were *Rocky*. *Boy Swallows Universe* is the story of a boy wondering if good love is still good love when it comes from bad men. 'I think all of that stuff left me with very complex views on love, where it comes from and what it is,' I say. 'Where are you at in terms of love for those people in your life? The *Rocky Horror* people, I mean?'

'That's very interesting, actually, because recently I started talking to my mum, after once vowing to maim her,' she says. 'A really good and wise friend of mine said to me one day, "You know, your mum has been this way her whole life, and you know that change that you're waiting for, that moment where she fully recognises her wrongs, you know that moment may never come? But maybe you don't have to love her with every sense of what we know as love, and maybe you can just accept what she is and who she is. If you can do that, then that's all you need to do, and that would be acceptance itself." And I was like, "Shut up, I plan on hating her forever."'

She laughs, takes a deep breath, thinks for a moment. 'But I did want to have peace away from the hate that I had,' she says. 'I wanted to have peace from the hate. So I just started allowing her to speak to me, and it didn't make me feel worse. And knowing that she has some peace in me speaking to her again, that makes me feel better in a weird way, so I'm letting her in.'

And then, unexpectedly, all that good, unexpected stuff comes. All that light matter.

'Connecting to the female figure who brought me here has helped me to connect to other females, because I've always had a barrier up towards women because of my past, but in speaking to her again I've become more confident as a woman, as a yoga teacher. I can now connect to women with a level of softness that I didn't [have] before. I know what that is now.'

'What is it?' I ask.

'It's vulnerability,' she says. 'I was always afraid to be vulnerable because I always thought it meant I was weak.'

I get it. I mean, I really, really get it. I then bore Lei-iissa with my go-to quote about the power of vulnerability. I've been boring countless people with it across almost two years of Covid-19, and I always get it wrong, but it's that Hemingway line about how life is going to break all of us eventually and some of us will be stronger after the breaking, but those who refuse to let life break them, life sometimes kills. He's talking about the benefits of being like water sometimes and not always like rock. We can break sometimes and come back stronger at the broken places. I think that's kinda like the story of the three-headed dragon slowly emerging in ink on Lei-iissa's back.

'I've got so many tattoos now,' she says. 'It's about time I got something that's as beautiful as I would like to be all the time, inside and out, and it truly is a beautiful tattoo. It's an armour that I'll be proud to wear, not to be tough, not to protect myself, but to *be* myself. There's the light, the dark and then there's the in-between. And I know what the in-between is now, too.'

'What is the in-between?' I ask.

'It's me,' she says. 'I'm the in-between.'

YES

Chloe was eighteen when she travelled to Paris on a Contiki tour. She hauled herself 276 metres up to the Eiffel Tower's observation deck. She looked through a wire protection screen across the city of lights, the city of lovers, and behind her back she heard the gasps of travellers from across the world.

'I turned around and a girl was crying,' Chloe says. 'A guy had tapped his girlfriend on the shoulder and he was down on bended knee on top of the Eiffel Tower.'

Then that crying girl whispered a beautiful and dangerous and terrifying word that creates and ruins everything, a word that makes anything possible. The only word that matters for true lovers who dare to risk it all. A three-letter symphony. Small-word music for lovers in any language. *Hěi. Ano. Nai. Ken. Tak. Chi. Oui.*

Chloe thinks about the way her father proposed to her mother in the late-1990s. 'Dad proposed to Mum in a bar after a soccer game,' she says.

Chloe smiles wide and bright, and that's the way she knows her mum smiled in the bar that day as that perfect three-letter word found its way from her lips through the chatter of drunks and the rattly wail of a bullied corner jukebox and the crack of a hard-struck cue ball and fell on her father's wide-open ears. 'Yes.'

Chloe shrugs. Maybe not melancholy in that shrug, just acceptance. 'In Brisbane, you just don't see that grand type of Eiffel Tower proposal,' she says. 'Where would you do something like that in Brisbane?'

No Eiffel Towers in Brisbane, I say, aside from the replica one that was salvaged from the French pavilion at World Expo '88 and dropped in the heart of Milton's bustling Park Road dining precinct. 'But we do have Thurlow Street,' I say.

*

I proposed to my wife in the gutter of a quiet suburban street called Thurlow Street, in the inner-north-west suburb of Newmarket, Brisbane. I'd organised a surprise stretch limo to pick us up from our ex–housing department house in Darra, in Brisbane's outer south-west. The limo driver smelled of night-time bourbon and morning Winfield Reds. He had a loose mid-forties garage punk mystique about him that I liked. He wore a black hat like a pilot's cap and his jacket was tight and black, like he was the bass player for The Knack. He had one bottom flap of a crinkled white business shirt hanging out over his black driver's trousers. In all, he had the unmistakable and endearing appearance of the modern Australian working drunk.

'You know how to work one of these?' I asked, handing him an early model iPod, the commemorative one faux-signed by the members of U2. The iPod was primed to play my specially curated 'driving across town to Newmarket to propose to Fiona' playlist, a sweeping set of lovers' tracks starting with The Smiths and ending somewhere over the rainbow with Judy Garland.

The driver gave a heartening thumbs-up that turned into a fist pump, and I wrapped my arm around my increasingly puzzled future wife in the limo's backseat. Then we made our way across town to the gutter at Thurlow Street, Newmarket, outside an old share house I'd helped rent, where once upon a time we'd had our first kiss inside a white Toyota Corolla hatchback after watching Sting play a concert at the Brisbane Entertainment Centre in Boondall.

I remember getting down on one knee that day beside the gutter. I took time to note my surroundings and committed the scene to memory so I could bore my kids with the details one day over steak, peas and a potato and pumpkin sunshine mash. There was no Parisian skyline to speak of. No majestic Arc de Triomphe to marvel at in this moment. No Notre-Dame Cathedral and no Champs-Élysées and no Grand Palais and nothing twinkling like the River Seine at sunset. There was only a stormwater drain and an empty packet of Chicken Twisties.

When I bent my knee, I turned my head right to see an elderly woman in a thin and fading blue nightie standing at her front door with a broom in her right hand. She stared at me the way she might stare at a bear in a tutu skateboarding past her blueberry ash hedge. The limo driver saw my proposal as a good time to duck out of the car, light a dart and rest his arse on the front bonnet, while waiting for a response from the love of my life, who was adopting the kind of befuddled expression women normally reserve for boyfriends who set fire to their farts.

And that's when Oscar Wilde whispered in my ear: 'We are all in the gutter, Trent, but some of us are looking at the stars.'

Truth is, I've been kneeling down in that Thurlow Street gutter for twenty years now, not looking up at the stars as much as at a girl with green eyes, just praying she'll keep saying that beautiful word until the day I die. 'Yes,' she said. 'Of course. *Yes!* Just get out of the gutter!'

*

A young couple pushing a pram. Aaron and Carly Hall and their fifteen-month-old son, Alfie, who has a smile that could melt an iceberg. Aaron proposed to Carly in 2015 with a flash-mob surprise at Southbank, Melbourne. Carly was casually walking along a crowded riverside promenade when a woman stopped her.

'Are you Carly?' the woman asked.

'Yes,' Carly said.

The woman smiled and started dancing in front of her. Then a troupe of dancers joined the first woman and began twirling and twisting to songs playing on a loud speaker: 'The Way You Make Me Feel', 'Come and Get Your Love', and that earwormy pina colada song. Some two hundred passersby stopped and formed a circle around Carly because they could tell something magical was about to happen, and something did, right around the time when Aaron emerged from behind a wall of black umbrellas that the dancers were holding and approached Carly accompanied by the life-affirming wonder of Daryl Braithwaite singing 'Horses'.

Carly watched Aaron move towards her carrying a small emerald-coloured box. He was wearing a grey suit and Carly was wearing a denim jacket and an orange scarf. And Carly was already weeping when Aaron went down on one knee. 'I love you very much,' he said, opening the box to reveal a diamond ring. 'I want to spend the rest of my life with you. Will you do me the very great honour of marrying me?' Carly was already nodding before he'd even finished asking that question. Then she squeezed the word out through tears, just in case there was any doubt. 'Yes,' she said, and two hundred onlookers rejoiced because this was true love being sealed for life before their eyes, because that moment reminded onlookers of the time they were proposed to, or of the time they fell in love, or that one day in the future they might get to be the girl saying yes or the guy on one knee laying everything on the line – pride, hope, the future and the present and the past.

'Kiss!' someone shouted from the crowd, but Aaron already had that covered. A gentle kiss on Carly's lips and then he drew her into the centre of the circle of onlookers and they danced as Braithwaite sang about the way it was gonna be.

And, six years on, Carly says, that's exactly the way it's been. 'Halfway through the proposal I started spotting family members, friends I recognised,' Carly says. 'Once Aaron walked through the centre, it was amazing.'

Carly remembers hearing about her parents' marriage proposal. 'My mum said, "So, are you gonna propose or am I looking for someone else," and that's the way my dad proposed. It was, "We've been dating for three years now; if it's not happening, move on."'

Aaron's proposal to Carly was so perfect, so right, that they wondered for a moment, six years ago, what it would feel like to provide such an experience for others. Carly was a part-time nanny and kindergarten worker. Aaron spent his days writing grant proposals for non-profit organisations. They started a business based on a wild shared dream: working to help people create grand and unforgettable marriage proposals to their one true loves.

'The dream came true,' Carly says. Last year alone, their business, The Proposal Guru, helped orchestrate some ninety epic, once-in-a-lifetime marriage proposal moments for lovers across South East Queensland. A series of grand romantic surprises for brides-to-be and grooms-to-be: couples stumbling into gardens lit up like fairytales; entire string sections emerging from bushes; two hundred lit candles spelling out MARRY ME on a faraway hill at sunset; flash mobs forming love circles around future brides; future husbands crying because they can't believe it all came together so perfectly. 'Aaron and I live and breathe each proposal,' Carly says. 'There's such amazing energy around a proposal. Especially a flash-mob proposal. There's an energy you can feel in the space; you can feel everyone stopping and getting involved in it.'

'They're feeling the love, I guess,' I say.

'They really are,' Carly says. 'That's the thing about love, and even more so in this pandemic: people just want to get around those good feelings. That's why everybody stops.'

'We've just gone full-time,' Aaron says. 'We just quit our day jobs. We've got another baby on the way and we're taking a big risk career-wise, but we're so grateful we can do it.'

'I love that the business of true love is going so gangbusters in South East Queensland that you were able to quit your day jobs and help people propose,' I say.

'The love is out there,' Aaron says, 'even more in the worst of times.'

'You saw ninety moments of true love up close last year,' I say. 'What have those moments taught you about love?'

'I think life ticks along every day,' Aaron says. 'You don't remember the breakfast you had every day. But you remember every detail of the special moments.'

Aaron looks down at his son, Alfie, in his pram. 'I remember every detail of his birth. I remember every detail of when Carly said, "I do." What I'm remembering is the love in that moment. We don't get those moments every day in life, so we gotta make the most of those moments when they come.'

Alfie's getting restless in his pram and Aaron picks him up and holds him to his chest. Aaron tells me they're neck-deep in the process of planning one such special moment for a Brisbane couple. If I want to watch a love story unfold before my eyes, he says, I should get myself down to the Saturday morning markets at the Brisbane Powerhouse, New Farm, one month from now.

'You want to come down and join us?' Aaron proposes.

I've only got one word for Aaron in reply. A three-letter symphony. Small-word music in anyone's language. *Hěi. Ano. Nai. Ken. Tak. Chi. Oui.*

'Yes,' I say.

*

And that word reminds me to run an important errand at lunchtime. 'I need to get this engraved,' I say, handing a silver ring to Duncan Vickers, a gifted engraver, who's had his workshop for years on the upper level of the Brisbane Arcade. Duncan's workbench is covered in fine metal-engraving tools, oils and polishes, and an engraving visor to enhance his vision and shield his eyes. I tell Duncan how I lost my wedding ring years ago playing touch football. Then, in 2019, my wife and our two kids and I found a silver ring in a vintage curios and craft shop in Texas, etched with trunk-linked elephants, and my kids said it would make an excellent replacement wedding band because my wife loves elephants. I asked the store jeweller – a rockabilly cowboy who looked like a mix of John Wayne and Elvis Costello – if he would be so kind as to give my new wedding band somewhat of a Texan blessing. He immediately instructed us to stand before him as if before God and hollered loud enough that the other store customers were drawn in a circle around us, like guests at what suddenly felt like an impromptu renewing of our wedding vows. 'By the power vested in me by the State of Texas and the good people of the Uuuuunnnited States of Ammmmerrica,' the jeweller exclaimed like a southern preacher, eyes alight, his palm resting on the elephant ring that was resting on my palm, 'I bless this ring and I bless this marriage!'

'What wording would you like?' Duncan asks.

I think about this for a moment and I ask Duncan if he remembers the soppiest message of love he's ever been requested to engrave on a wedding ring.

'There have been plenty of really soppy messages,' he says, 'but there's one that I keep in a folder.' It's a collection of words, he explains, so syrupy sweet that to hear them is to immediately know the rare taste of belly laughter and vomit. 'I'm not going to tell you,' he says – what happens at the engraving workshop stays at the engraving workshop – 'but that one took the cake.'

I tell Duncan I may have a contender for the title. Three words that have come to represent the love I have for my wife.

Duncan raises his eyebrows, slides a notepad and a pen across his workshop counter. I nervously scribble the three words on the notepad. I take a deep breath and wince as I hold the notepad up to the engraver's unprotected and vulnerable eyes. 'Can you fit that on a ring?' I ask.

If Duncan's choking back stomach fluid, I can't tell. He smiles and laughs. 'Yes,' he says.

AMBIGUOUS GAIN

Fe Brown sells orchids in the markets every Wednesday at the top of Queen Street Mall. She's seventy-nine years old and has been growing and selling orchids ever since she retired from her job as an aged-care nurse. She tells me how easy it is for me to see true love in action any day of the week. I just have to hop in my car and drive ten kilometres across the city to her old workplace, TriCare Annerley, the respite residence where she provided dementia and palliative care for hundreds of Brisbane's elderly.

There was this one guy, she says. True love personified, she says. Day in, day out, year in, year out, he visited his wife who was living with dementia. He read to her. He talked to her. He brought her gifts. Then he started to feel what the doctors warned him about, a thing called 'ambiguous loss', a kind of grief caused by a loss that has no clear understanding. The man felt like his wife had gone missing. She was sitting on a lounge chair, smiling just like she always had, right there before his eyes, but somehow she was lost to him.

'I learned something about love from this man,' Fe says. 'And he learned something from me. One day he said to me, "I don't know why I come." And I leaned close to him and I said, "It's okay. It's okay if she doesn't know who you are because, you know what, *you* know *her*. She's your sweetheart. You come because you know your story together and that story is still going.'"

If we must endure the hell of ambiguous loss, then let us be comforted by the ambiguities of love – the mystery of it, the inexplicable endurance of it. Fe told the man the same thing she told any family member who regularly visited a resident living with dementia, a few simple words of wisdom she could not support with any scientific proof but had learned through years of working at the wearying and emotional coalface of aged care: 'You have to hold them. You have to touch them.' Connection in its purest form. 'Hug them, give them sloppy kisses, dance with them, sing with them, hold them. You feel their heart through that touch and they feel yours.'

But Fe knows that's not always easy for loved ones, and that's the trick of deep love. It was love that kept so many people away from the nursing home – the more we love someone, the harder it is for us to see them like that – and, in turn, that made it harder for Fe and the nursing staff, seeing a resident live in confusion for multiple years without a single visit from a loved one.

Fe says she's been caring for her husband of forty years, Lance, recently. 'He had a knee replacement three years ago and then he was supposed to have the other one done and then Covid arrived and it was cancelled and then he got depressed and then he got all these aches and pains and then he couldn't breathe and he was rushed to the Coronary Care Unit at Princess Alexandra Hospital.'

She says he's recovered, but matters of Lance's health are a primary concern these days. The more health issues he has, the more she loves him; the more she loves him, the more she worries for him. Her love for growing and selling orchids has become a form of therapy for her, a way to take her mind off the road ahead. Good listeners them orchids. You can tell an orchid your deepest fears, load them up with your heaviest burdens; they won't wilt under the weight of the hard stuff, but remain stout, vivid and beautiful.

'Life is an orchid, growing,' she says.

*

In the northern mountain country of the Philippines there is a municipality called Bontoc, home to the Bontoc ethnolinguistic tribe, whose traditional rites of passage required young males to embark on journeys into the wild in search of human heads. Fe and her two younger siblings were raised in the St Vincent's Sisters' Convent, Bontoc. Fe's father, a tireless mechanic and builder, was forced to leave his children to be raised in the convent after his wife died giving birth to Fe's younger sister.

'And then two years later, my father had an accident himself,' Fe says. 'Dad was driving his own work truck and he fell down a cliff.'

Her father was killed. 'I had to grow up in that convent.' She gives a half-smile. Memory in it, melancholy in it. 'And that's where I really learned about love.'

Tough love. Hard and brutal Bontoc love. Food was hard to come by, hugs harder still. Fe had a beautiful singing voice and she sang in the convent choir every Sunday. Three performances: 7 a.m., 9 a.m. and 10 a.m. From the convent nuns she earned a ball of hard candy for every performance. 'You want to know about love?' she asks. Fe remembers kneeling down in a Bontoc village street with a rock in her hand, ten years old, cracking a ball of hard candy in two. 'Three lollies every Sunday morning,' Fe says. 'I sold two lollies so I could buy my paper and pencil, and I would cut the third one in half for my brother and sister. Get a rock. Boom. If there's any little bits left over, that's mine. And then I'd use the paper and pencil to educate myself and then I could start doing homework for all the boarders in the convent with the rich parents. Too lazy to do their homework and so they pay me.' More pay, more food, more lollies for her and her younger siblings. It was business. Love business. She was a ten-year-old hustler, a twelve-year-old grifter.

Some days the nuns would let her break up the sacramental bread for communion. She asked the nuns if she could have the remnants of sacramental bread that worshippers left on the church altar. She would then hawk these bread fragments to local kids less familiar with the symbolism of the Eucharist. 'Would you like to have all your mortal sins removed in an instant?' she would offer, in the voice of a travelling shaman. 'Eat this and you will carry no more sin.'

Fe slaps her knee. 'I sold that bread for ten cents a piece!' she howls. The nuns in the convent had a strict rule when it came to learning English. No English, no dinner. 'If you don't learn your English words, you don't eat,' she laughs. 'They won't feed you if you don't speak English. Those nuns in that convent, they loved me very much. They knew the only way we could save ourselves in life was to learn English. I was starving at night. I soon learned those English words. It was tough love but it made us good. And it was my English that brought me here.'

*

She came to Australia in 1975. She met Lance Brown in the seaside town of Hervey Bay, four hours' drive north of Brisbane, where she made a living selling homegrown plants from the front gate of her yard and going door to door hawking fresh fillets of whiting she caught every day in the glassy and bountiful bay.

'If I caught three whiting, that would become six fillets that I could sell house to house for fifty cents a fillet,' Fe says. 'Any spare money I sent to my family back home.'

Love is a fifty-cent fillet of fresh fish.

Love is hard candy sucked for six minutes on a Sunday morning.

Love is touch, and turning up every day to see a wife who does not know you.

Love is knowing her.

I ask Fe Brown if she would sell me a nice orchid sometime soon. I know someone who would love to receive one of her orchids.

'Anytime,' she says.

'Then I'll see you again real soon, Fe.'

```
Love is a stranger stepping back into the past.
Love is a stranger stepping off to work.
Love is ambiguous.
Love is lost in the weeds.
Love is found in the stars.
Love is plain as day.
```

'Love is beautiful,' Fe says.

'I reckon your life is kinda beautiful, Fe,' I say.

Fe Brown shrugs. 'Life is an orchid, growing,' she says.

MAGIC HOUR

These are the quiet magic hours on this corner. After breakfast and before lunch. After all the accountants have shuffled down to Edward Street and all the lawyers have rushed up to George Street carrying their briefcases filled with case briefs and their skinny flat whites in Keep Cups that say 'Queen Mum', 'Cool Beans' and – a cup covered in dancing panda bears – 'Bear With Me'. After all the students from Kelvin Grove High and All Hallows' and Brisbane State High have flushed out of Hungry Jack's in the middle of Queen Street Mall. After all the rebel kids have flushed out of the Albert Street 7-Eleven with multicoloured Slurpee mixes in one hand and mango-flavoured disposable vape pens in the other. Before lunch, when everybody shuffles back into the streets again for bibimbap. Before lunch, when King George Square fills with book readers and Twitter feeders and midday lovers kissing on stone-block seats beside bronze statues of Australian pioneers who never would have dreamed of such things as FaceTime calls to loved ones. These are the hours on this corner of mine that fall quiet and magical. Less rumbling of the buses. Nobody rushing to secure parks, so there's no beeping of car horns.

This is when the city birds can scan for last night's pizza crusts and vomit carrots in the middle of Adelaide Street in safety. The brave pigeons and the bold ibises with their white coats stained with twenty-first century rubbish bin colours like those of Coca-Cola and pink doughnut icing and tomato sauce and mustard. In the magic hours you have enough time to study the way ibises take a morning drink from shallow rainwater puddles. They lean down low and turn their heads sideways and slash their long beaks through the puddle the way you might slash a sickle through wheat. Those ibis beaks are actually things of wonder, weaponised with miraculous cells that can help them detect the vibrations of prey beneath sand and soil, a superpower they can thank their dinosaur ancestors for. These ibises should be down by the banks of the Brisbane River, vibration-scanning for mangrove mussels and crabs, instead of scanning open school bags at bus stops for packets of Chicken Twisties. I always see my fourteen-year-old self in city ibises. Total opportunists. Anything for a free feed. They skulk around people snacking on croissants at city bench seats with a 'don't mind us, nothing to see here' nonchalance that reminds me of how I used to skulk around the exit aisles at my old high school tuckshop.

'Wow, Kylie, your hair looks radiant today. Ya got fifty cents I could borrow for a sausage roll?'

'Fuck off, scab.'

This is the quiet magic hour when thick clouds shaped like flexed biceps float above the white Lego-block Commonwealth Bank building across the street and the warm morning sun means the homeless people on Adelaide Street can slip off their night coats and set up shop behind cardboard signs scrawled in permanent marker: *Laid off last year during Covid-19. Please give generously.*

What a prick of a year and three-quarters. What a fat, throbbing arse-cheek boil of a year and three-quarters. Easy time to love and write about love, but it's an easy time to hate, too. Hate the hand you've been dealt. Hate the ones who are different. Hate the ones who are luckier than you.

I've been thinking a bit about hate lately, ever since I've been writing so much about love. I keep thinking about all the men I saw as a kid in pubs and football clubhouses and public housing kitchens who had the words 'LOVE' and 'HATE' tattooed across their knuckles, usually a home-kitchen ink job in my neighbourhood. The lesson a kid could glean from those knuckle tatts was that one of those words could not exist without the other. Those words went hand in hand. To love someone was to step to the precarious edge of hating them, too. Then I'd watch some bloke drive the fist he had tattooed with the word 'LOVE' through the windscreen of his wife's car and I'd know that everything I was learning from my studies of such men was bullshit. Hate's got nothing to do with love. In the realms of powerful four-letter words 'hate' belongs down in the slums with 'burp' and 'fart' and 'piss' and 'moan'. Hate's just another bargain-basement addiction, as useful to the broken-hearted as the smokes and the smack and the cheap red wine. Hate is a gallstone. Hate is puppy fat. Weight we don't need. Another boulder too heavy for most. The hateful want the hated to be buried by their boulders, but they can't seem to let their boulders go. Some rocks are just too fuckin' big to throw. So the boulders of hate only bury the hateful. Void spaces once filled with love will never be filled with hate. Void spaces once filled with love can only be filled again with love. Hate sucks people in deep, choke-holds them in a bucket of misery-loving company. And eventually hate chases every kind of company away. Misery loves company, but hate likes it best when you are alone. No company. No love. No hands to hold on to, just a hand forming a fist to drive through a windscreen.

*

Rosie O'Malley smiles when she meets me in the magic hour and her light obscures the darkness of her day job. Rosie is CEO of the Gold Coast's Domestic Violence Prevention Centre. A typical day in Rosie's life might start with organising emergency accommodation for a young woman with no wallet, no shoes, three kids and two black eyes. Her day might end in the centre of a rehabilitation circle session with twelve male domestic violence offenders, in which one man might try to justify and minimise the impact of the night he tied his wife up and locked her in the family car and doused it in petrol. Sometimes Rosie's job is to explain to such a man why comments like 'Yeah, but I didn't light it' cut to the heart of a national domestic abuse scourge that has bled into the homes of two million Australian women.

'Love can be dangerous,' Rosie says. 'So many women make those vows, "for better or worse". Sometimes it's only worse and sometimes those vows for life cost them their lives.'

The real bad days for Rosie are the ones when she's driving home at night and she calls her husband of three decades, Seamus, and says, 'Will you run me a bath?', and if you're asking Rosie O'Malley what true love is then you can be sure that it's got something to do with the way Seamus brings a cup of tea to her halfway through her bath and doesn't ask why she's so quiet or why she needed the bath in the first place.

'Sometimes what really troubles me is the entitlement I hear in the men's program,' she says, 'the complete blindness in terms of their needs getting met and to hell with everyone else around them. And then I come home to someone who actually does the complete opposite, someone who actually decentres himself and really cares about those around him.' Every few years, Seamus asks his wife a question she finds more romantic than anything that sparkles or comes with a liquid caramel centre: 'Is there anything I can do to be a better husband?'

'Damn,' I sigh.

'What?' Rosie asks.

'I've been with my wife twenty years and I've never come close to asking something so de-centred.'

Rosie smiles, understandingly, then sums her husband up in three words. 'Seamus is truth,' she says. 'Love is the privilege of being with someone long enough that you're gradually refining the truths that you tell each other. You feel safe enough to keep showing more and more of yourself to each other. To me, that's what love is. It's not the fireworks and the rainbows and the butterflies. We all keep pieces to ourselves. True love is showing up as yourself.'

And now I know what love is:

`Love is exposing all the pieces.`

The pretty pieces and the ugly pieces and that piece of us that always gets wedged in the floorboards beneath the kitchen table, because the thousand-piece puzzles of our lives are never supposed to end up perfect anyway.

*

Easy to hate in a pandemic. Easy to love, too. Easy time to do what Magda Haj Gido says to do, give your heart to the world, or maybe just give $10 to some bloke sitting on Adelaide Street who I know might spend it on a goon bag – or, just maybe, a bus ticket home to the ones he loves, to the good company, to the people who accept all of his pieces.

It's in these quiet magic hours that a seventy-three-year-old Melbourne woman named Patricia watches the city pigeons from a bench seat in Queens Gardens, outside Brisbane's Treasury Building. She's remembering the time when, some fifty years ago, she worked in a dress shop on George Street called Carmel's and she would leave her infant daughter, Holly, in the long-gone nursery school that was housed in the top of that old sandstone Brisbane City Hall building. At lunchtime, she would check Holly out of the nursery and walk her along George Street and spend an hour looking into her eyes while having a sandwich in Queens Gardens beneath the watchful gaze of a towering bronze Queen Victoria statue that still watches over us now. This was when she was married to her first husband, the father of her two kids, a man who, at that time, was a soldier serving in the Vietnam War.

'Sometimes I think I like places more than people,' Patricia says. 'Places where you can just sit and have a think.'

I tell her I've been doing just that for two weeks on the corner of Adelaide and Albert. I ask Patricia to have a think about true love for a moment. She says she's married to a former rugby union

Wallaby now. Patricia and her husband are visiting Brisbane from Melbourne, mostly because their long-time dentist, John O'Hare, is up here.

'He must be one hell of a dentist for you to travel from Melbourne to see him.'

'Everyone thinks I'm nuts, but I love John.'

She says John O'Hare's a legendary rugby tragic. He's written books about the game. It's not unusual for John to spend much of his valuable time with Patricia in the dental chair regaling her with his informed insights into why her husband was such a brilliant sportsman.

'Captive audience?' I suggest.

Patricia nods, theatrically rolling her eyes.

Patricia says she loves visiting the Brisbane CBD because the landmarks remind her of the story of her life, her dreams, her failures, her successes, her loves.

'What have you learned about love the second time round that you didn't know back in your first marriage?' I ask.

'I think you just grow up a bit,' she says. 'You learn to become a bit more tolerant.'

She says it wasn't easy for a lot of wives who had husbands who came back from the Vietnam War. She says it wasn't easy for the husbands either.

Patricia's granddaughter was married on the weekend in the Hunter Valley, New South Wales. At the wedding she found herself talking about love and marriage with Holly, the girl she took to that city hall nursery some fifty years ago. 'We had a heart to heart and I said to her, "I really did love your father. No one gets divorced easily. But then you find a different life. Your life goes one way, their life goes another."'

Patricia loves the North Queensland city of Townsville. Her family had a getaway tin shack on Magnetic Island, eight kilometres from town. 'Sort of place you used a stick to hold the windows open,' she says. Patricia did it tough through the peak of the Melbourne Covid-19 lockdowns in 2020 and 2021. One thought alone lifted her spirits during the most oppressive and stifling days: the idea of sitting on Stanton Hill on the coast of Townsville looking out to Magnetic Island. 'Most beautiful view in the world,' she says.

She remembers growing up in a house in South Townsville. 'It was the wharves area,' she says. 'There used to be forty-nine hotels in this one little suburb. Mum would kick us out after breakfast and we'd come back home in time for dinner at night. We had Ross Creek behind our house and my brothers and I would be knee-deep in mud. We never knew about the crocodiles. We'd go crabbing all day. We'd go to play basketball and there used to be a man who would pull up in an electricity truck at about four o'clock in the afternoon and flash himself at us, shaking his hips, and we used to laugh ourselves silly. We used to call him Elvis, but we never told our parents because they would have stopped us from going to basketball. My father would've gone up and murdered him or something.'

Then something seems to dawn on Patricia. 'It's really weird,' she says. 'I can't believe I'm this old.'

I tell Patricia one real nice thing I've noticed about getting older. 'Love grows with you,' I say. 'Like, I loved my wife twenty years ago, right. But what I never expected was just how much it all just gets deeper and richer the more you get older, with all the ups and downs, and I know that's the cliché but ...'

'Oh yeah, you become best friends,' Patricia says. 'If she's not your best friend, then it's all been a waste of time. My husband's my best friend.'

'Yeah, it's like it all works backwards or somethin',' I say. 'I think the idea is that you work your way back from being lovers and you reach the point of being best friends and then you're this strange mix of being best friends who are lovers, and I don't know what that mix is called.'

'Marriage,' Patricia says with a knowing smile. 'How old are your kids?'

'Fourteen and twelve,' I say. 'Two girls.'

She lifts her eyebrows as though I've just told her I'm raising Black Sabbath.

'Teenagers,' she winces. 'I swear my daughter just grunted at me for eight years. And my son: every thought that went through his head just had to come out, didn't matter how hurtful it was.' She drops her head back in recalled despair. 'You could not pay me a million dollars to go through all that again.'

The teenage attitude doesn't always disappear in adulthood. 'Even on the weekend, my daughter saw my outfit,' Patricia says, 'and she goes, "Are you really wearing that?"'

'Can I tell you a theory I have on that particular parent–child phenomenon?'

'Yes.'

'That phenomenon works in complete parallel and proportion to the love that you have for them,' I say. 'The more a parent loves the child, the more the child knows they can say whatever the hell they want to the parent because they know the love runs that deep.'

'My daughter is the only person in the entire world I'm scared of,' Patricia says. 'Honestly, I'm terrified of her. I'm scared she'll stop talking to me forever or something.' She laughs. 'But they were good kids and they didn't take drugs.'

'Job well done then,' I say.

'Yeah, guess so,' she says and smiles.

Then I tell Patricia how I informed my girls long ago over Weet-Bix that I have exactly three fatherly expectations: 'Be kind, don't do drugs, Beatles before Stones.'

Patricia laughs, then waves goodbye. She's got to go because it's lunchtime and there are still a few more places across Brisbane where she wants to sit and have a think.

'Good luck with those daughters,' she says.

'Thanks.'

And the magic hours are over in the CBD and the lunchtime workers take up their spots in Queens Gardens, eating sandwiches under the eyes of Queen Victoria, one of the all-time great heartbroken romantics, one of the truest lovers who ever lived. In 1840, Queen Victoria married her German cousin Albert. Bit gross, to be sure, but theirs was a love for the ages. 'He possesses every quality that can be desired to make me perfectly happy,' she wrote of Albert. They had nine kids. They endured their share of teenage angst and kids who felt the need to share every last thought that entered their busy royal brains. Word has it Vic and Al had only three expectations for their children: 'Be kind, stay off drugs, Mendelssohn before Mozart.'

But then Albert died of typhoid in 1861 and Queen Victoria's world was painted black, and there I go putting Stones before Beatles. She had a grand and melancholy mausoleum made for her husband, funded from her own private purse, at a cost of what today would be almost £20 million. She kneeled in sorrow and laid that mausoleum's foundation stone and she wept privately inside it, wearing the same mourning black she would wear every day until her death. A shrine in Albert's honour was also built inside a room in Windsor Castle, and she instructed servants to fill that space with regular fresh changes of clothes for a husband who wasn't there, and fresh water for a washbasin he could not use, no matter how many times she prayed for him to come back home and do so. She travelled with one portrait of Alfred and woke daily to another; she saw him when she closed her eyes and she saw him when she opened them. She died in 1901 and five years later her statue was unveiled in these gardens in the heart of Brisbane city. She's not shown smiling in the statue and that's probably because she found it hard to smile. Maybe to smile would have been to forget. But there's love in that melancholy face. She looks sad, no doubt because that was how she felt for the rest of her life, and she looks troubled. Not because the brave pigeons of Brisbane are always resting on her head these days. But because she misses her lover. And she misses her best friend.

THE BIG CHERRY TASTE

Macpherson Robertson was born on 6 September 1859, in Ballarat, the eldest of seven children fathered by a luckless Victorian gold seeker named Macpherson David Robertson. When his father left his family to seek his fortune in Fiji, young Macpherson Robertson left school to become the chief breadwinner for his mother and six younger siblings. By chance, he landed an apprenticeship position with the Victorian Confectionery Co., where he mastered the art of making chocolates and lollies. In 1880, the ambitious twenty-one-year-old Robertson constructed a confectionery manufacturing operation of his own inside the cramped bathroom of his family home in Fitzroy, central Melbourne. He made his bathroom chocolates Monday through Thursday and hawked them through the streets of Melbourne's CBD every weekend. By the late 1880s, the newly formed Mac Robertson Steam Confectionery Works was big enough to employ thirty workers. By 1900, it was the largest confectionery works in Australia. It was Mac Robertson who introduced Australians to the wonders of chewing gum, fairy floss, Old Gold chocolate, Columbines and Freddo Frogs. In 1924 the Mac Robertson Steam Confectionery Works created its masterpiece, a uniquely Australian chocolate bar, less a confectionery than a state of mind: a coconut and cherry filling mix covered in MacRobertson's existing Old Gold dark chocolate, with a name that stretched back to an old street trader's cry:

Cherry ripe, cherry ripe
Ripe I cry
Full and fair ones
Come and buy

In 2013, Roy Morgan Research conducted a survey asking Australians to name their favourite chocolate bar. These were, evidently, simpler times, pre-pandemic, when settling on our favourite choc bar seemed a matter of national interest. The results weren't at all surprising for the ten per cent of Australians – some 2.3 million people – who were gobbling up Australia's statistical favourite, the Cherry Ripe, once a month.

'Great bloody chocolate bar,' I say to the woman sitting beside me. 'Maybe the greatest of all.'

Dot Larkins nods her head in agreement.

It could be argued that it's because of Macpherson Robertson's Cherry Ripe that Dot finds herself in the city today. She flew into Brisbane days ago from Biloela, a grazing and cropping town 120 kilometres inland from Gladstone, central Queensland. Her daughter, Joanna, aged seventeen, is attending hairdressing college for two weeks in the city.

Here's a short love story. Dot passing time alone in the city for the next ten days between 8.30 a.m. and 4 p.m., waiting for her daughter to finish hairdressing school. 'She comes out at 10.30 a.m. for fifteen minutes,' Dot says. 'Then she comes

141

out again at 12.30 p.m. and we have lunch. At 3 p.m. she gets another fifteen-minute break and at 4 p.m. she's finished and we catch the ferry back to the apartment we're renting while we're here.'

Here's a long love story. Dot and her husband, Gary, a night-shift worker at a mine in central Queensland, have been married for thirty-two years. Dot met Gary when she was working in a Biloela service station. She was supposed to change a tyre on Gary's car, but she was inexperienced and she had to explain to him that she didn't know how to work the machine that fitted new tyres around old tubes. Gary was kind and understanding about this and he was so taken with Dot that the next time he dropped into the Biloela service station he decided to ask Dot to dinner. They have four kids now aged sixteen to thirty-two. They live, Dot says, to make their children and grandchildren happy. One simple, pure, reasonably achievable daily goal: happiness for every member of the family. They are, themselves, only ever as happy as their unhappiest child or grandchild. That pure goal is the reason Gary is now looking after two of their youngest grandkids back home in Biloela, having only just returned from working three draining back-to-back late-career night shifts in the mine.

'Do you think your kids have any idea how much you love them?' I ask.

'No, they don't see it,' Dot says. 'But we never saw it either, until we had children of our own. Then you start looking at it and thinking about it a lot. You go, "Oh *riiiiiight*."'

When Dot was a young mum, she suspected the reason she was put on this earth was to raise her children. Now, as a grandmother, she suspects the real reason she was put on earth was to help her children raise their children. Some people, she says, are lucky enough to live long enough to watch their children help their children raise their children.

'You ever think about all the things you've done for them over the years and where that comes from?' I ask. 'Devotion, I mean. Do you ever think about where devotion comes from, scientifically?'

Dot shakes her head then tells me about someone she's devoted to. She's been thinking a lot lately about all the love-and-devotion things she missed about her mum, Joanna. 'I lost my dad two years ago,' she says. 'For some reason we knew exactly what Dad liked and didn't like in life. But, you know what, when Dad died, we had to start wondering about the things that Mum liked in life, like, "What sort of cake would Mum like for her birthday?" She was so casual: "Everything is good, please don't make a fuss." And you realise, Oh, we don't even know Mum. Who is our mum? Because it was always, "What Dad liked is what Mum likes." Dad liked fruit cakes, so there was always fruit cake. Everything revolved around Dad. The love for the both of them was always there, but we didn't really know what Mum liked. And my kids don't see it either. But me, as a mother, I'm noticing everything. I know exactly what their interests are. They still love me, dearly ... but ...' She trails off.

'They don't realise that you are this incredibly complex person, with all these individual facets about you, beyond being Mum,' I say.

Dot laughs and nods.

'It's interesting that you did the same thing with your mum,' I say.

'Yep,' she says, shaking her head.

'Is she still alive?'

'Yeah.'

'Are you learning more about her now?'

'Absolutely.'

'Has that relationship evolved since the loss of your father?'

'Absolutely,' Dot says. 'We're very, very close.'

And to illustrate this point, Dot tells a love story about her parents and the wonders of a Cherry Ripe chocolate bar.

*

Peter and Joanna De Git were married for fifty-nine years. Peter – full name Petrus Jacobus Antonius De Git – died on 26 November 2018, ending but not really ending a love story that featured twenty adored grandchildren and twelve cherished great-grandchildren. That love story began in The Netherlands. Peter and Joanna were both children of Dutch migrants. 'Mum came out a year before Dad,' Dot says. 'There were two brothers, Mum's dad and her uncle. They were supposed to stay together but they split up. Her uncle went to Victoria and Mum's dad went to Rockhampton. Mum's family were on a property there and then they ended up in the People's Palace because they had nowhere else to go.'

'What's the People's Palace?'

'They had a People's Palace here in Brisbane,' she says. 'It was for bush people or homeless people who had nowhere to stay.'

Of course: that big building on the corner of Edward and Ann streets, opposite Central railway station, built in 1910. Young Joanna would recall that building as a Salvation Army temperance refuge and a travelling workers' hostel, where no gambling or alcohol was allowed. I remember it as a backpackers' hostel in the early 2000s, home to Brisbane's Down Under bar, notorious for its $3 steaks and zero-dollar wet T-shirt competitions.

'They eventually found home on a Biloela cotton farm,' says Dot.

And it was on a date in a canvas-seat Biloela picture theatre that Peter shared his first Cherry Ripe with the girl of his dreams, Joanna.

'Dad bought that Cherry Ripe and he shared it with Mum,' Dot says, shaking her head. 'You know, they didn't have any money, those two. And when you don't have any money, something as small as a Cherry Ripe can mean so much.'

Their love was true. Their love had a coconut and cherry centre. Their love was sealed and wrapped for eternity in rich dark chocolate.

'But then Mum's family moved to Victoria, where her dad's brother was,' Dot says. 'So then Dad went all the way down to Victoria and swept her off her feet.'

'That's a love story right there,' I say. 'He would have had to write her a letter before he travelled down there, right? He would have had to confess his devotion?'

'Yeah, and it would have taken nearly two weeks for him to get a letter to her and then another two weeks for her to get a letter back to him.'

I imagine the waiting. That good-bad sick love fever Peter must have suffered for a month. Two weeks of poor young Peter De Git trying to distract himself in the Biloela wheat and sorghum fields while all he can see in his head is Joanna reading his hope-filled and shaky longhand words on a creased love letter.

She read the letter and she replied in kind. And she waited for her one true love to come for her.

'That was so brave of your mum to follow love like that.'

'It was massive,' Dot says. 'For a young woman to leave her whole family behind in Victoria!'

'She was saying, "I trust this guy implicitly, I'm going with him."'

'Yep.'

'Did she ever talk about that? About how glad she was that she made that decision, that she took that chance?'

Dot nods her head, emphatically. 'She was *so* glad,' she says. 'She was always glad, but it was a hard life for them. The Queensland Government was allocating blocks by means of a lottery and Mum and Dad drew a block at Banana, which was two thousand acres. And yes, there was a township called Banana [now a shire incorporating the town of Biloela] and it wasn't named because of bananas. It was named because of a bull that was yellow.'

Peter and Joanna shared Cherry Ripes right through the 1960s, even after the MacRobertson brand was sold to Cadbury in 1967. They shared Cherry Ripes right through the Vietnam War and through the disco era and through the shoulder-padded, hair-sprayed 1980s, when the Cherry Ripe choc bar was featured in television commercials in which couples dressed in white sat on white chairs surrounded by white doves and somehow fell in love – such was the strange anything-goes logic of 1980s television commercials – simply through a shared appreciation of the 'big cherry taste' of Macpherson Robertson's chocolate masterwork. Then the twenty-first century arrived and Peter and Joanna watched grandkids arrive with it and Cherry Ripe ice cream came, too, and so did white chocolate Cherry Ripes and dark berry Cherry Ripes and packets of bite-sized Cherry Ripe Minis.

Dot's dad was in his early eighties when he first suffered the blood and body infections that put him in hospital. 'His body was just worn out, I reckon,' she says. 'We nursed him to the very end. We ended up looking after him ourselves at home. We were able to hire a bed and a proper air mattress. We had to do training at the hospital before we could bring him home. Blue Care came and showered him once a day and we did everything else to make him as comfortable as possible. We never regret anything around that. It meant that we could love him so much, right to the very end.'

And she cries now, remembering those days. 'He was on that air mattress at home for eight days,' Dot says.

So much love in those bedside days. So much intimacy.

'What do you remember of the intimacy of that time?' I ask. 'Were there times when it was just you and him?'

'You bet,' she says.

'What do you say to your dad in that time?'

'Well, it's really hard when he can't talk back. He was too weak to talk back. But he could still get a message across. We had another bed set up beside him so somebody could always sleep beside him in the room. One night it was my turn to sleep beside him and I remember getting up during the night to help him with something and he just grabbed me.' Tears running from Dot's eyes now. 'He just grabbed me and gave me the biggest hug he's ever given me,' she says.

We sit in silence. Dot wipes her eyes.

'He was making sure you knew.'

'Yep.'

And she knew. She knew everything he was trying to say in a single embrace. A lifetime of love he could never put into words, even if he'd had the strength to. No words louder than Peter De Git's actions that night. No Shakespeare, no Keats, no Dickinson could write a love story as powerful as the story Peter De Git wrote for his daughter, Dot, with that deathbed embrace in the middle of a silent Biloela night.

'Sometimes you don't have to say anything, you can just feel,' Dot says. She takes a deep breath. 'Dad always said, "Dead is dead, just forget about it." But I don't believe that. I actually believe that so much of him is still helping us with daily life. And, sometimes, he's the strength I need to keep going.'

Then Dot shakes off her grief and sadness and she smiles because she wants to say one more thing about those bloody great Cherry Ripe chocolate bars. Here's the thing. Here's the sweetest thing about those sweet cherry treats. Her mum, Joanna, gets so sad sometimes. She misses the love of her life and she cries sometimes to herself. And when Dot knows her mum is doing it tough – because loving daughters know these things – she often slides a simple gift across the kitchen table to her mum. A coconut and cherry filling, wrapped in smooth dark chocolate. And it makes her mum smile and it makes her mum cry good tears.

'The Cherry Ripe has become this special thing for Mum,' she says. 'Sometimes love is just the little things.'

Just the other day she dropped in to see her mum and she was already busy with visitors. Dot had bought a Cherry Ripe to share with her mum, but there were lots of people around Joanna at the time and Dot had somewhere she had to be, so she simply slipped the chocolate bar quietly to her mum as she left. And Joanna received the gift with a silent and knowing smile that she reserves only for Dot. Nothing had to be said between them. Sometimes you don't have to say anything. Sometimes you can just feel.

SURSUM CORDA

Zak Frost needs to tell me something about her high school sweetheart. Zak – short for Zakyra – is a shop assistant in the Myer Centre, a short lunchtime walk from my corner. We've been connecting for maybe fifteen minutes this afternoon over a sprawling house we both love in Auchenflower, inner-west Brisbane, called Moorlands House. Zak fell in love with Moorlands House when a customer brought a haunting and framed painting of the grand home into Retro World Collective, the antiques and collectibles store she works at. Zak has been diving down the rabbit hole that is the chilling history of Moorlands House, the former home, built in 1892, of the pioneering and infamous Mayne Family, who generously donated vast chunks of their family fortune to help create the University of Queensland and sustain some of the oldest churches across Brisbane. For 150 years, rumours have spread through this city, suggesting that the family's patriarch, a butcher named Patrick Mayne, murdered an ex-convict named Robert Cox in 1848, at a Kangaroo Point bloodhouse named Bush Inn, and used the £350 he stole from Cox to establish the business that created his fortune. Inside Moorlands House is a majestic internal staircase with balustrades bearing Patrick Mayne's initials, and these balustrades rise up to a supporting pillar in which the Latin words *Sursum Corda* have been etched into the wood. Some believe these words, translated, relate to the freeing of Patrick Mayne's soul: 'Lift up your hearts.' Another reading of those words, of course, is an encouragement for all residents of Moorlands House to raise their hearts high, closer to God and the memory of loved ones lost. Lift up your hearts to the ones who have gone and the ones you're still committed to. Lift your heart up to love.

'Love is commitment,' Zak says. 'I don't just mean commitment to a person, I mean commitment to making space for someone in your life and letting them grow and change inside that space and still loving them.'

Then she looks me in the eyes as tears fill in hers. 'My high school sweetheart passed away,' she says. 'I knew him since we started high school together. He lived just down the road from me. We were best friends all the way up until we finished school and then we got together after school. We were a couple for six months, until his depression got too bad for him and he committed suicide.'

She's silent for a long moment.

'I'm still committed to him in my heart,' she says. 'I have a new partner now and I know that he would be okay with me having a new partner, because we were both committed to what was best for each other. And the partner I'm with at the moment I'm just as committed to.'

She still lifts her heart up for her high school sweetheart.

`Love is lifting your heart up for the ones you`
`love.`

'You still have space in your heart for the one you lost,' I say.

'I will never truly fill that space in my heart,' Zak says. 'He was my best friend. From the moment we met we were inseparable. Even before we figured out it was love, we were best friends. We never went a day without talking to each other. He was always so kind and so giving and so willing to help everyone else.'

He told Zak about his depression. She tried to help him as best she could.

'One of the last things he said to me was that I gave him seven extra years of life,' she says. 'His last words to me were, "Forever and always."'

When he died people kept saying to Zak that it was okay to be angry at him, but she couldn't bring herself to be angry at him at all. She could only love him.

*

Zak grew up in Nowra, two hours' drive south of Sydney. Her dad is a musician who met Zak's mum when he joined Zak's mum's brother's metal band, which went by the name of Temptress. Music and fashion and art and books are big in her family. She loves that she now works in a place that sells old music and fashion and art and books to the people of Brisbane. But she says the best part of that shop assistant job in Retro World Collective is where the counter is situated. Standing behind it, she can turn her head to the right and enjoy an unbroken view towards her boyfriend, Max, working behind the counter of a café some fifty metres away, across Level 1 of the Myer Centre.

'Guess what we did?'

'What did you do?'

Zak laughs, embarrassed. 'We both learned sign language so that we could say "I love you" to each other from a distance.'

There are many beautiful Auslan videos online showing how to sign various words and phrases, none more beautiful than the one with the boy in the big blue woolly jumper saying, 'I love you.' Point your forefinger at your own chest, form a cross with your forearms while placing your palms over your heart, then point your forefinger at the person you love: *I love you.*

Sometimes that's the best kind of love, the love you feel from a distance. There's deep romance in love from a distance. Two long-time lovers at a party on opposite sides of a room filled with fifty people talking too loud. Then the lovers catch each other's eyes across the room and they're both supposed to be listening to the person talking to them but they're not because they're in a tunnel built for only two, a cylindrical tunnel with circular walls that can't be seen but can't be penetrated either. And they give each other a half-smile, and all their perfect private language is conveyed in a single silent look.

We've been here too long.
It's not so bad, especially when you're here with me.
I kinda want to make love to you.
I want to look at you like this when I'm old and grey.
I love you. I always have and I always will.

Cheesy as hell to say, but I love Zak and Max's shopping centre sign-language love so much that I have to tell her about 'My left shoe'. Just some dumb thing boys and girls mouthed silently to budding crushes in my wife's primary school, three words that could, in schoolyard logic, look like 'I love you' to the lip reader on the receiving end. I took that ball and ran with it. Mouthed those words silently for years to my wife at parties and across crowded rooms and said them over the phone when I was on the other side of the world. There have been times when I've been away on long work trips in some faraway hotel room and I've had some lonely B.B. King kind of blues about me and then I've pulled out my good black leather dress shoes from my suitcase to wear to some fancy function and found a note from my wife inside the left one: *My left shoe.* These days, I don't even use my lips to convey how I feel about her across a crowded room; I just slowly raise my left boot.

'So, tell me what you love about Max,' I say.

And Zak sighs, shaking her head, eyes as wide as the future. 'It's just so hard to put into words,' she says. 'Let's just put it this way: I love him and he loves me. That's it. That's what I love about him.'

*

And now it's night-time and I'm back home in my house in the suburbs with my wife, Fiona, and my two girls, and I'm in the kitchen chopping zucchini for a chicken risotto Fi is making and I'm telling her about the sign-language love between Zak and Max. 'It's like "My left shoe",' I say.

Fi smiles. 'It is,' she says.

'Do you mind if I write about "My left shoe" in the book?'

'Oh, geez, is nothing sacred?' she replies, sighing.

'I know, I know!' I say, squirming. 'I'm sorry. I can't help myself. You should hear the things people are saying. They speak with such tenderness and truth and heart and it makes me so frickin' grateful and the only way I know how to repay them is by sharing something from my own heart and soul.'

Fi scrapes chopped chicken fillets off a breadboard into a hot-oiled pan.

'I just realised something,' I say.

'What?' she asks.

'I've never asked you what love is. I think I've asked two hundred random strangers what love is in the past two months, but how ridiculous would it be if I didn't ask my own wife?'

'No,' Fiona says.

'I haven't even asked you anything.'

'Good. The answer's no.' Fi pushes the chicken across the pan with a wooden spoon.

'I just had an idea,' I say.

'No,' she says.

'Maybe you could tell me a love story, too?' I continue, warming to my idea. 'Our love story is, like, the greatest story I know. It's, like, better than *War and Peace*. Maybe even better than *Back to the Future*.'

And Fi sighs, because I've been requesting personal things like this from her for twenty years, but then she gives a half-smile that suggests that behind the breadboard and the wooden spoon and the cup full of arborio rice and behind her long-suffering sigh there is a tireless working mother of two who, by some grand miracle act of patience and compassion, still loves me.

'Your warts and all insights on what love is,' I say, increasingly energised. 'Maybe a letter on Kath's typewriter? Your thoughts on the whole damn thing. The ups, the downs, the beautiful bits and the bits that drive you nuts, too. All of it. No holding back. Fiona's hardcore truths about true love!'

The chicken sizzles on the fry pan.

'I'll think about it,' she says.

And I nod in elation the way Marty McFly nodded when he saw his dad deck Biff back in 1955 to win the heart of the girl of his 'density', as he put it. His *destiny*. Then I remember that Auslan video I watched. And I point my forefinger at my own chest, form a cross with my forearms while placing my palms over my heart, then point my forefinger at the person I love.

LOVEBIRD WALTZ

The French have a word for this. A word for the way Lani and Ian Gibson take their weekly lovebird walks through this rattling engine of a city. A word describing the exclusively human art of strolling, of sauntering in no particular direction, with no specific destination in mind. A word that speaks of detaching oneself from contemporary life, with the sole purpose of acutely observing contemporary life.

'*Flâner*,' Ian says.

He says it's like what I'm doing with this book of love stories. He says this book will keep me young. 'You want to know the secret to eternal youth?' he asks. 'Stay interested, learn stuff, love stuff.'

Lani says she could swear she's only forty-five years old, despite the fact that the eldest of her two sons recently celebrated his fiftieth birthday, and despite the fact she's loved Ian for fifty-seven years of her life.

'You can't stop getting old, but you can definitely stop growing up,' Ian says, with a wink.

He remembers the first time he saw Lani's face. Clear as crystal and just as twinkly. It was 1964. They were teenagers. He was standing on a stage in a Brisbane ballroom dancing studio. Ian and his younger brother were handy and keen ballroom dancers who often led studio beginner classes, guiding newcomers through waltzes and foxtrots and quicksteps and rumbas.

'So I was standing up on the stage with my brother and there was music playing,' Ian recalls. 'And then my darling wife here walks in through the door. And I just thought, Ohhhhhhhh, gee. She had all the style. She had everything. And that was it for me.'

Ian elbowed his younger brother. 'Oh, my goodness, look at her,' he said to him.

It took Ian less than ten seconds to settle upon his next unequivocal thought: That's the girl I'm gonna marry.

'Now there were a lot of people in that studio that day,' Ian says. 'All these boys and girls dancing. Well, she just stood out from them all. And that was it. And it's always been the same since.'

For fifty-seven years, Lani has stood out from them all. Crystal clear and just as twinkly.

'Ian put his arm around me and asked me to dance that day,' Lani remembers. 'And the minute he put his arm around me, I knew I'd come home."

Love is knowing when you've come home.

Across the road from my writing spot on the corner of Adelaide and Albert is a retail store that Ian and Lani recently walked into.

'Oh,' a store staff member said, beaming, 'it's you!'

Ian and Lani gave a puzzled look.

'You're the Lovebirds,' the staff member continued. 'We call you two the Lovebirds.' The woman explained how her team often see Lani and Ian waiting at the traffic-light crossing outside the King George Square bus terminal they travel to each day, prior to another wander through the CBD. Apparently, the staff members love to look through the store windows and study the ways the Gibsons convey their undying love for each other as they stand at the crossing. Sometimes they kiss, sometimes they hug, and sometimes Ian grabs Lani's hand like he's about to lead her in a Viennese waltz across the grand ballroom in their imaginations.

'It's so beautiful,' the woman said, 'the love you have for each other.'

Ian worked most of his life in the automotive industry. He remembers talking to a long-time friend and colleague at work about his son.

'You ever told your son you love him?' Ian asked.

'No,' the colleague said. 'But he knows I love him.'

'But what if he doesn't know?' Ian asked.

Ian shakes his head. 'You've always got to tell someone you love them,' he says. 'You've got to say it: "I. Love. You."'

The way Lani figures it, they share an 'I love you' moment at least once a day. Sometimes three times a day, sometimes six times a day.

'Can I just do the maths on that for a second?' I ask.

Let's say they've said it just once a day, 365 days a year, for the past 57 years.

That's at least 20,805 times they've said, 'I love you.' Now let anything be possible for lovers and let us compile all those 'I love you' moments between Ian and Lani Gibson, and cut and edit them into a single unbroken reel of film, the most romantic movie ever projected onto the silver screen of somewhere quaint and cosy, somewhere warm like the Elizabeth Picture Theatre, just a five-minute walk from this corner. Grab a large tub of popcorn and one of Macpherson Robertson's Cherry Ripe chocolate bars – the old ones, like the ones Peter and Joanna De Git shared in the Biloela Picture Theatre – and let all those collected 'I love you' moments spill across the cinema screen.

Ian and Lani Gibson on small 1960s couches in small 1960s houses. 'I love you.'

On disco-era dancefloors. 'I love you.'

In 1970s maternity wards. 'I love you.'

In 1980s Italian restaurants. 'I love you.'

Beneath Christmas trees. 'I love you.'

By rivers across Europe. 'I love you.'

By suburban creeks and camping tents and in supermarkets and surgery waiting rooms and school classrooms on grandparents' day. 'I love you.'

And I still know when I've come home.

Canadian writer Malcolm Gladwell estimated that it takes at least ten thousand hours to truly master anything. Ian Gibson has been working on loving Lani Gibson since 1964. He has been learning the art of it, all its nuance, all its depth and complexity. He still practises every day, refining his craft, improving on his life's greatest work. He has now clocked up 499,320 hours. He is a Jedi master at loving Lani Gibson.

At loving Ian Gibson, Lani has gradually escalated in levels of expertise from rookie to warrior to ninja to samurai to queen, with more than enough love left over to shower it, rain it, upon her two sons and their families. 'I would have had twenty children if I could have,' Lani says. 'I couldn't have any more and it devastated me at the time. I wanted to have a big family.'

But her two sons love their mum with the force of twenty kids because Lani and Ian have always shown them how to. No handshakes in the Gibson household, only hugs.

'It's a family, not a corporation,' Ian says. 'You shake hands with the people you work with, you hug the members of your family.'

Lani wraps an arm around her husband's shoulder. 'Sometimes I jump into bed at night and I say to Ian, "I still can't believe we're allowed to cuddle for eight hours." I still can't believe it.'

'That's how I got a crook back,' Ian says.

Lani laughs, gently slaps Ian's thigh.

'I tell you what, though, all jokes aside, we're still madly in love,' Lani says. 'If we had another fifty-seven years, we'd still be madly in love.'

And, with that, accomplished *flâneurs* Lani and Ian Gibson press on with today's wanderings, drifting off into the crowds of mall shoppers and weekday workers. To explore and observe. To detach themselves from contemporary life, with the sole purpose of acutely observing contemporary life. And I realise it's the magic hour again in the Brisbane CBD, and from where I sit at this sky-blue typewriter I can now see the Gibsons detaching themselves from the very ground they walk on, because the Lovebirds have taken flight along with my thoughts. They float above it all, dancing, waltzing through a ballroom made of autumn air. It's a dance called the Lovebird Waltz. Crowds of people stop to lift their heads and marvel at the impossible dancers.

'How did you get so good at that?' one young man hollers up at Ian Gibson as he gently twirls the love of his life in mid-air.

And Ian looks down and says, with a wink, 'I just put in the hours.'

THE IMPORTANCE OF BEAR HUGS AND FALLING IN LOVE WITH A MARRIED MAN BACK WHEN TELEPHONES WERE STILL STUCK ON WALLS

'On-the-wall telephones,' Kathleen says. 'Remember those?'

Big cumbersome plastic communication devices fixed to living room and kitchen walls. Hard, club-like things that older brothers weaponised to crow-peck the skulls of younger siblings. Curled cords on them that 1980s teenagers twisted and wrapped themselves in when they were dizzy with love.

'I remember those.'

Kathleen remembers the constant on-the-wall phone calls from her husband during their courtship in the late 1970s. She'd met him at a dance at the University of Queensland. She says he was a gifted rugby player from Fiji. 'Isimeli Batibasaga,' she says.

'Your husband is Isimeli Batibasaga?' Legendary Fijian rugby scrum-half, father of legendary Australian women's rugby scrum-half Iliseva Batibasaga.

'Yeah,' she says.

'Holy shit,' I say.

Kathleen laughs and points to the handsome Fijian man leaning against a traffic light, out of earshot from us. 'That guy right there,' she says.

The thing she admired first about that guy right there was his persistence. Seemed like a phone call every two hours initially. I was a bit shocked,' Kathleen says. 'I never actually had anyone chase me like he did.'

They were days into their on-the-wall phone-call courtship when Isimeli dropped some news that he might usefully have divulged in their first brief encounter.

'He told me he was married,' Kathleen says, eyebrows raised.

'Oh,' I say. 'That's complicated.'

'Yes, it was,' Kathleen nods.

Kathleen knew the phone-call courtship had to stop. 'So what do we do?' she asked.

'It's too late,' Isimeli said. 'I've fallen in love with you.'

Kathleen turns towards her husband as she explains this, then goes silent for a long moment, as though memories she hasn't recalled in years are coming to her just now on this busy city street.

'So what did you do?' I ask.

'We followed the love,' Kathleen says. 'He organised a divorce, and that was very difficult for everybody, but he went through all that for us. We've been married for thirty-seven years now and I love him more than ever.'

Sometimes when Kathleen watches her daughter, Iliseva, on television, weaving through opposition defensive lines in her Australian rugby jersey, tears fall from her eyes. She's usually thinking about when she saw Iliseva's face for the first time, in the labour ward of the Mater Mothers' Hospital in South Brisbane. She remembers Isimeli's joy. He was scheduled to play rugby that day, was listed in the run-on side for an important game. 'If you go off and play rugby today, don't bother coming back,' Kathleen said. He didn't play that day. He spent that day the same way it seems like he's spent the last thirty-six years of his life, holding Iliseva in his arms. And now we're both looking at her husband, leaning there against the traffic light, looking back at us with a puzzled look on his face and not the faintest clue what we're talking about.

'I'm glad you followed the love,' I say.

'So am I,' Kathleen says. 'And so is my daughter.'

Kathleen moves away to join her husband. She's off to a midday gym class. 'There's one love in my life that I'm really not liking right now,' she calls back to me.

'What's that?' I ask.

'My love of food,' she says with a grin.

*

After lunch I see a man taking my photograph. The man smiles at my sign. 'I thought it was going to read, "The end of the world is coming,"' he says. 'But I like your idea. It's good to talk about love.'

His name is Harvey and he's in a camera club and today's assignment is to photograph interesting things he finds in the street. The first interesting thing he saw today was a man with snowy-white hair walking through Queen Street Mall holding a fistful of red balloons. Harvey felt there was something dramatic and artistic about the scene, and he politely asked the man if he could take his photograph. The man with the red balloons was happy to accommodate the request. Then, through the camera lens, Harvey realised the man he was photographing was Bruce Morcombe, father of Daniel Morcombe, the thirteen-year-old boy abducted while waiting to catch a bus and murdered on the Sunshine Coast in December 2003. Bruce and his wife, Denise, subsequently set up the Daniel Morcombe Foundation, which has since transformed the way Australian schoolchildren maintain their personal safety. Red was Daniel's favourite colour and he was wearing a red T-shirt when he was abducted. Thousands of red balloons have been raised to the sky in his memory.

'The light in his eyes, after what he's been through,' Harvey says. 'It was astonishing.'

'He's an astonishing man,' I say.

In 2014, I was among the reporters in court the day Bruce stood up and read his victim impact statement directly to the man who had killed his son. Might be the bravest thing I've ever seen a man do. Bruce spoke of family. Bruce spoke of love.

He was a great kid and would not hurt a fly. You have robbed him of seventy years of life. Our family's sleepless first night without Daniel on the seventh of December 2003 haunts me even today. That feeling of helplessness and unimaginable pain never leaves you ... I listen to Denise's broken sleep, punctuated by frequent nightmares, and look into the face of my younger twin boy who has lost his soulmate ... Our friends from 2003 are different because we are no longer the same people. We can be short-tempered and have a streak of bitterness and carry anger caused by your deliberate, selfish actions ... We could not return to regular employment because we were constantly distracted with disturbing thoughts. We were forced to sell all our hard-earned investments just to survive. But survive we did, because you made one monumental mistake that day. You picked on the wrong family. Our collective determination to find Daniel and expose a child killer was always going to win.

I remember a tweet Denise Morcombe posted on the day of her eldest son's wedding in 2018. It was a picture of Daniel playing in the snow with his two brothers as a boy. 'My boys are now grown up or gone,' she wrote. 'Enjoy your time with them.'

Harvey and I are silent for a moment on the street.

'You got any kids?' he asks.

'Two girls, fourteen and twelve,' I say.

'Amazing age,' Harvey says. 'Soon your oldest will be saying, "Dad, I love you completely, but you're so completely wrong."'

'That's already happening.'

'Give her a few years and she'll realise you were actually a wise man.'

Harvey's kids are now forty-two, forty-one and forty. He has grandchildren who call him 'Granga' and sometimes he has to stop himself from crying tears of joy when those grandkids hug him.

'What does it feel like to hug grandkids?' I ask.

'You'll find out,' Harvey says.

And that's a nice thought I hang on to for a moment.

'You ever do the bear hug?' Harvey asks.

He means the big, long bear hug he believes all dads should give their kids every time they cross paths in the kitchen.

'Not often enough,' I say. Probably still too many three-second hugs from me.

Then Kathleen stops in front of my writing desk again. She's finished her gym class. 'I just need to tell you that you swelled all sorts of bloody emotions in me during gym,' she says.

'Sorry, Kathleen.'

'No, it felt good,' she says. 'You've ignited something.'

'What do you mean?'

'Mate, you are dealing with something so powerful. Seriously, I was on the treadmill before and I was getting all emotional and I thought, Oh my god, what's he done to me? You ignited memories of all the loves in my life and it was beautiful. You just don't realise how powerful that word love really is sometimes.'

'Well, I'm starting to realise it's the strongest word we have,' I say. 'We had this huge, powerful thing that we couldn't understand, so we gave it a four-letter carry-all word to help us make sense of it.' Now the four-letter word slides so easily and unremarkably from our lips that we sometimes forget how remarkable 'l-o-v-e' actually is.

'Love is purpose,' Kathleen says. 'Love is meaning. Love is the reason to get up and if people don't have it then I understand why they don't get up at all.'

I point at Harvey. 'Harvey and I were just talking about giving bear hugs to the ones we love.'

'Oh, yeah,' Kathleen agrees. 'The longer the hug, the more meaningful. Go longer.' And she does the perfect bear hug action, right here on the corner of Adelaide and Albert. 'You gotta go right in there,' she says, seemingly hugging the rugby-playing whizz-kid daughter in her mind. 'Bring 'em right in and hold 'em until they say, "Mum, you can let go now."'

'They actually love it don't they?' Harvey adds.

'Yep,' says Kathleen.

Harvey nods at me: 'You go home and bear hug those girls tonight.'

Kathleen checks that I was following her tried-and-true bear hug technique. 'Did you get all that?'

I nod. 'I will be hugging them just like that this afternoon,' I say.

'Good,' she says.

And Kathleen and I hug across the writing desk, not quite a bear hug, but something longer than three seconds.

Then Kathleen walks off down Adelaide Street, and Harvey takes some more pictures on his camera. *Click, click.*

'So, I've told you something about me,' Harvey says. 'Why don't you tell me something special about you now? Why don't you tell me a love story?'

'Wow,' I say, put on the spot. 'That's only fair, I guess.'

And I think on this for a long moment.

'All right,' I say. 'We're talking hugs. I'll tell you a hug story. I'll tell you the story of why I reckon my old man was not much of a hugger.'

THE STORY OF WHY I RECKON MY OLD MAN WAS NOT MUCH OF A HUGGER

I hugged the Dalai Lama longer than I ever hugged my dad. It was a journo assignment, shadowing the foremost leader of Tibetan Buddhism during a three-day tour of Brisbane. That man knows something about love:

Love is a necessity not a luxury.

Remember that the best relationship is one in which your love for each other exceeds your need for each other.

We can reject everything else: religion, ideology, all received wisdom. But we cannot escape the necessity of love and compassion.

At the end of the three days I was granted a one-hour interview with the living Bodhisattva, during which I asked him two small favours: to bless the Queensland State of Origin football team and share with me the meaning of life. 'Why am I here?' I asked.

And you better believe the guy has a presence. That man glows the way fire glows in caves found sixty feet down in the dirt.

'Come closer,' he said.

I leaned forward.

'Closer,' he whispered.

The intention of the question was to access some of the many things he knows about the purpose of existence for all 7.9 billion of us. But he did something beautiful with his answer. He pointed to a woman in the corner of the room. Then he pointed at me. 'You,' he said, pointing at my heart. 'You are here to tell her story.'

Then he pointed at a man standing by the doorway who looked like Monkey from the TV show *Monkey*, which I loved so much as a kid. This man was the Dalai Lama's chief personal security officer, and he wore only expensive black suits over black business shirts and I swear he had ninja eyes and ninja fists and a ninja mind.

'You,' the Dalai Lama said. 'You are here to tell *his* story.'

Then he pointed to his own heart. 'You,' he said. 'You are here to tell *my* story. That is why you are here and that is all you have to do.'

And he was so perfectly correct. That was exactly why I was there. And I believe it is exactly why I am here on this corner and here on earth. And that is so truly useful to know. He took the biggest question of them all and reduced it, focused it and shaped it so that it applied only to the banana-bending chancer sitting before him. I don't know *the* purpose of it all, but I know *my* purpose inside it all because the Dalai flippin' Lama spelled it out for me in neon lettering that glowed like fire glows in caves sixty feet down in the dirt. Just tell the stories. Just write the stories. And that is all you have to do.

And we both stood that day and embraced and it was the kind of embrace that I didn't want to pull out of. Not to get all flighty here, but the closest thing I could compare that hug to was the time I hugged a four-hundred-year-old eucalypt in the Valley of the Giants, in south-west Western Australia. The guy was pure earth. The guy was oxygen. Or maybe it was just his story that made it seem that way.

*

A couple of years back I wrote a magazine story in which I joined a men's wellbeing group of thirty blokes in a secluded forest in Mount Byron, in south-east Queensland's glorious D'Aguilar Range. Every man had a reason for going. Some were dealing with childhood traumas, some were trying to be better husbands, some were trying to wind back the effects of three generations of that complex hot-button thing the world was calling 'toxic masculinity'. There was a wise man named Elder Blackburn who led us men through three days of self-reflection exercises while providing insights into why a lot of us weren't the best at giving hugs that lasted anywhere close to three seconds. 'My generation, the baby boomers, all the men in our world – our fathers, our uncles, our football coaches, our male teachers – were all ex-war,' he said. 'Their fathers were all ex-war, too. We had a whole generation of fathers up to about 1949 who had been traumatised, thousands of them. And we were the recipients of that. They didn't know how to father us and we were all under-fathered.'

Elder Blackburn's exercises were deeply funny and resoundingly useful. He had us flapping our arms through the forest, pretending to be coastal cormorants who were once too afraid to launch from clifftops but were now soaring through clouds across the oceans of our myriad fears and insecurities. Elder Blackburn taught us the 'Swapple Hug', which was kinda like the Gorilla Hug. Find a man you sense some connection with. Stand face to face, lean over and nestle your head into his shoulder; allow him to nestle into you. Transfer your weights, support each other, then wrap your arms around each other's back. Now gently slap your partner's back with a languid, rolling arm motion. That's the Swapple Hug.

Another elder showed me the nuances of the 'Pelvic Hug'. He pulled my pelvis against his pelvis so our thighs and our junk were touching. 'Place your hands at the base of my spine,' he said. 'Now lean back.' The Pelvic Hug: two strangers in the forest arching their spines back, kneecap to kneecap, pelvis against pelvis, penis against penis. It felt like we were playing tug-o'-war without a rope. That strange pelvic dick hug went on for at least twenty seconds, about eighteen seconds longer than any embrace I ever had with my dear ol' dad.

*

My old man wasn't a hugger and his old man wasn't a hugger before him. Dad showed his love in different ways. The care he took to thread a live worm onto my fish hook. Brief encouraging words on the way to footy training as a boy. Tender but rare notes in my letterbox when I became a dad. The closest I got to extended hugs from Dad as I was growing up was when he'd be having a lounge room bender while watching *The Outlaw Josey Wales* on VHS and I'd come out of my bedroom to turn the telly down at 1 a.m. and he'd wave me over to him with a series of messy hand gestures and mutter, 'Gimme ... [unintelligible pirate gibberish] ... hug.' And I'd lean down and wrap my arms around him and he'd smell of beer and beer nuts and Jim Beam and Champion Ruby rollies and he'd rub his right cheek against my right cheek and I'd feel the scratch of his two-day growth and then he'd always say something beautiful and tender, which was a welcome change from all the things he would say on the piss that were rock hard and terrifying. 'Everything's gonna be all right,' he'd mumble, and I was never able to tell if he was saying that to himself or to his ten-year-old son, the youngest of four boys he was raising on his own in a Bracken Ridge public-housing orange-brick shitbox.

Whoever he was saying those words to didn't matter, they always made me cry into the warm space between his neck and shoulder that smelled of Old Spice. 'I love you, Dad,' I'd say and he'd say the same thing back and then he'd always pull away from the hug before it got too close to something lasting and soft and gentle and true and transforming, and even when I was ten years old I knew why he was always pulling away. I knew he wanted me to know that life was not tender and soft and gentle. Life was rock hard and terrifying, and tenderness was folly. If you spend too long hugging your old man, kid, you might never want to let him go. If you start crying about all the things worth crying about in this life, then you might never stop crying. Best to not even start. Don't start crying, don't start hugging, don't start *feeling*, because you might never stop feeling. So now you know the great truth of the outer Australian suburbs, kid. Feeling is hazardous. Feeling is a one-way ticket to pain and madness. Feeling will break your heart.

*

My grandfather, Vic, was a Rat of Tobruk. He was a quiet and thoughtful timber-getter and cheesemaker from Queensland's Darling Downs. On 1 September 1942, during the interminable lead-up to the second battle of El Alamein, Grandad's 2/15th battalion was sent into a notoriously blood-strewn and barbaric diversionary attack south of Tel el Eisa, Egypt, codenamed Operation Bulimba. The battalion penetrated a German minefield and met the heaviest kind of battlefield resistance. Hemmed into a space surrounded by near-impenetrable concertina wire, they faced enemy mortar attacks and sweeping and catastrophic fire from German 88-millimetre artillery guns – the tank killers of World War II – which saw the 2/15th sustain 183 casualties and lose almost half of its fighting strength. Soldiers who ran out of ammunition during the prolonged insanity of it all were forced to club the enemy with their rifles and hack, bludgeon, stagger, stumble and crawl to reach respite back behind the wire. My grandfather, who was badly wounded in the attack, later recounted his memories of the battle for an official war history of the 2/15th:

> In the confusion of the noise and dust, some of us lost contact with our Sections, and I remember finishing up with another Section led by Bill Anderson. We blundered into an 88-millimetre gun which Bill immediately captured; whilst standing gazing at the tired-looking and dirty German gun crew, I was hit in the right

*leg. On recovering consciousness I found Bill Anderson wrapping
a field dressing round the wound, which bled fairly well. I was
helped through the wire by Johnny White and Reg Coyne. Reg
was killed outright but John got not even a scratch. After a short
wait some of us were picked up by a 17 Battalion Bren-gun
carrier in charge of a Lieutenant who sat on top of the carrier
directing his driver to where the wounded lay — all this time bullets
were whizzing around his ears like bees.*

That wound in Grandad's leg that bled fairly well was the reason
he spent the rest of his life hobbling around his beloved seaside
Sandgate, on Brisbane's north side, on a wooden right leg.
Grandad never waxed lyrical about the bravery of Reg Coyne and
Johnny White that day. Grandad wasn't all soppy and sentimental
like his grandson who would one day walk around Brisbane city
for two months asking people to tell him love stories.

My brothers and I lived with him for a year in the mid-1980s,
just before he died. I remember looking into his bedroom and
seeing the patience and grace with which he wrestled his wooden
leg onto the cold high white nub of his incomplete right thigh.
There were always whispers, as we were growing up, about what
those beautiful men, Reg Coyne and Johnny White, had done
to save Grandad's life. I remember first hearing about the strong
possibility that Private Reginald Andrew Coyne, aged twenty-
two, had taken a bullet and died while hauling my grandfather
to safety behind that German concertina wire. That made sense
to me. It helped me understand why Vic wasn't the hugging
type, why he was so silent all the time, why he seemed to walk
in shadow some days, why he could sit, mute like a ghost, in
his armchair in the corner of the lounge room, watching me

TRENT DALTON

and my brothers play around with *Star Wars* figurines, and we wouldn't even know he'd been watching us for two straight hours. I remember the day he let me see the wooden leg up close. I rested my belly on it like it was a pommel horse.

Three years ago, for a newspaper story I was writing for Anzac Day, I asked my aunties about the things Reg and Johnny did for my grandad. 'Did Reg Coyne die saving Grandad?' I asked my Aunt Joan, second oldest of Vic's four children.

'I definitely had a sense that Reg Coyne got that bullet helping Dad,' she said. 'Dad was hard to read. He was so close-mouthed, but one of the few things I do remember him saying about the war was that when he got back the first thing he did was visit Reg Coyne's parents and say thank you. I think he felt responsible for this bloke being killed.'

'I know he had the nightmares,' said my Aunt Monica, Vic's first child. 'I'd hear Mum in the night: "Wake up, Vic. Wake up." But he never spoke about it. Ever.'

Last year, a man named Gordon Wallace died at the age of ninety-eight. He was Queensland's last known living Rat of Tobruk. Gordon knew my grandfather. Gordon served in the 2/15th and knew, heart and soul, of the horrors of Operation Bulimba. Before he died, Gordon recounted his memories of my grandfather and of 1 September 1942. 'First of September,' he said, shaking his head. 'First of September, first of September. We got pinned down and held up in the wire and couldn't get through. We were supposed to have Pommy tank support but they wouldn't go in. With that Dannert [concertina] wire, the general way to get through it is either to have a tank go over the top of it, which we didn't have, or somebody's gotta lie down on it to make a path for the other bloke to walk over it. They flatten

176

it with their body weight and the other blokes walk over the top of them.'

Gordon said this was more than likely the method Reg and Johnny had used to haul Vic over the wire to safety. One Rat lying flat on the wire – razor-sharp barbs digging into his skin – and the other somehow shouldering or dragging Vic over the wire to a future where he gets to father four kids. And I have so much love and gratitude for Reg Coyne and Johnny White for doing this, because it's the only reason my daughters get to dance to Taylor Swift songs in front of the long mirror hanging on the inside of my wife's wardrobe door.

They weren't supposed to be so brave, Gordon said. 'You're walking into this mass of weaponry and you know blokes are falling alongside you, but you can't stop to assist them or see who it is. It could be your best mate, but you're not supposed to stop. You've just gotta go on. But these blokes did stop. They would've slung their weapons over their shoulder and they would have been there to assist your grandfather. Because he was their mate and he was injured badly. *They were mates.*'

That was a love story that Gordon was telling me. A love story of courage and humanity and friendship. I asked Gordon what he thought about the burden of survival, and he thought long and hard at his suburban kitchen table that was covered in photographs and diaries from his war years. And he told me a story about something that happened days after Operation Bulimba, when he was on a night post with an artillery unit that spotted a German ammunition transport at the bottom of a desert valley. He shot this German truck up with a long blast of anti-tank gunfire and one of its passengers was left lying in agony about twenty yards in front of his post.

'I went out and went through this bloke's pockets for his papers and he was crying for his mother,' Gordon said. 'He was an officer, but he was crying for his mother because he was in a bad way. If I'd have done him a good turn, I'd have shot him straightaway, but once you got him lying on the ground it was murder to do that. I went through his papers and there was a photo there of his wife and two girls with long blonde hair in plaits, probably nine or ten. The poor bastard. I've never forgotten him. I was out there two hours holding his hand until he died.'

Gordon was trying to illustrate with that story exactly how the bloody pool of war has its ripples. Gordon went home to Brisbane to raise four kids, just like Vic raised four kids. 'We weren't easy to live with,' he said. 'You can't do bloody nothing about guilt. I know how Vic felt. We all think the same way. You go over to that cemetery now in El Alamein and you look along that line of bloody gravestones and there's fifty-eight blokes – first of September, first of September, first of September, first of September – and this is where you think, Jesus Christ, I've had seventy-odd years since then, and these blokes were boys. A lot of those boys hadn't even been with a girl. They never had the chance. Too young. These are the things you think about at night when you lie back. I know Vic would've felt guilty to a certain extent. Reg Coyne got killed, and he came home.'

And Gordon and I had no doubt between us that the blood-pool ripples of war and coming home from war stretched for the next eighty years through my family, sure as they stretched through eighty years of Australian domestic and cultural and social life, generation to generation, husband to wife, father to daughter, father to son.

'But at the same time, he would have learned to live a decent life because he'd been allowed a second chance,' Gordon said. 'You learn to live a good life.'

My grandad was the best of men. A deeply pious man. He helped run the Sandgate RSL. He crunched numbers for the tax department for a living and on his days off he voluntarily crunched numbers for his local church. He made the most of every day that Reg Coyne and Johnny White gave to him. And if he was ever brought low some days late in life by the weight of Reg Coyne's sacrifice, then I never saw him hug his way through those days or cry his way through those days. I just saw him in the corner in his armchair, sitting silently for hours, smiling at his grandsons as their mouths made sound effects for the guns and the bombs of their make-believe battlefields spread across his lounge room carpet.

*

Grandad wasn't big on the hug and nor was my old man. That's just how it was. No big deal, to be sure, and generations of Australians know there are worse things in the world than dads who aren't big on hugs, like being left for dead as a baby under a tree in Rwanda for starters. So dry your eyes, princess, and put away the violin, ya sentimental git. Hell, the only reason I'm even mentioning it here is because it helps neaten the end stitches to one of my favourite love stories. The long one about me and my old man.

He died alone on his bed in his small bedroom, in the small public-housing flat he rented on Bribie Island, an hour and a half's drive north of Brisbane. I remember standing outside his closed bedroom door with my eldest brother while we waited for the people from the funeral home to come and take his body away in a bag. My brother said he wanted to go and sit with Dad for a bit, and I said I thought that was a good idea but I was going to give it a miss. I said I didn't want to see him that way.

Half an hour later I changed my mind. 'I think I might go in,' I told my brother.

'I think you should,' he said.

Don't start crying, kid, I told myself, because if you start crying you might never stop.

I started crying over him the moment I saw his body on the bed, and I've never stopped crying over him because I've never loved another man more than him.

Don't start hugging your old man, kid, because you might never want to let him go.

I started hugging him the moment I put my hand on his chest and I didn't want to let him go. I wrapped my arms around him and I cried when I put my head in the space between his neck and his shoulder. 'I love you, Dad,' I whispered. And, at last, this was a hug he couldn't pull away from, so I held him there for as long as I needed to hold him.

And it seems *so fucking tragic* and absurd to me now, and it hurts *so fucking hard* to confess through the tears that fall from my eyes, as I sit here on the corner of Adelaide and Albert streets in a busy world without him in it, that the longest hug I ever shared with my dad was the one we shared when he was dead.

FOUND UNDER TREE

He was born in Rwanda, but his accent sounds French. Somewhere in the early pages of Jean-Benoit Lagarmitte's adoption file is a space dedicated to the details of the place of his birth. Inside that space are the three typed words that are at once the most defining and motivating three words he's ever read in his life.

'Found ... under ... tree,' Jean-Benoit says, resting in the chair beside my desk, his right hand blocking each of those words out in the air. It feels like he's announcing the title for the tearjerker movie telling the story of his life, and maybe he is.

The Rwandan Civil War stretched across four barbaric and bloody years, from October 1990 to July 1994, and led to the Rwandan genocide, when extremist members of the Hutu ethnic group slaughtered hundreds of thousands of ethnic Tutsi and moderate Hutu people. The number of deaths was impossible to count precisely, but estimates suggest upwards of a million people died.

'I was born in the middle of that war,' Jean-Benoit says. 'They don't know my exact date of birth and they don't know my place of birth. In my adoption file it is just written those three words.

An old man brought me to the orphanage and that was literally what he said: "Yeah, what can I say, I found him under a tree." Just like that. No name. No date. No place. Nothing. I was very sick. I really don't know by what miracle I survived. I had double pneumonia. But there was a Belgian family in Rwanda at that moment, and they took me and they cured me. I stayed in Rwanda for four months getting better and then I was adopted by my Belgian family and I had the best childhood a person could ever possibly wish for.'

He's wiry and handsome and his forearms are made of iron from all that drumming on his fertiliser bucket that he does for coins in King George Square.

He speaks in broken but good English about how he grew up in a rolling green Belgian village not far from Brussels, which was populated with more cows than people. 'I used to joke, "If those cows can be smart, we fucked!"' he says.

And we both howl loudly for ten seconds and passersby on Adelaide Street wonder what's so darn funny.

Growing up, he rarely thought about the tree he was found beneath as a baby. He tried not to cling to feelings of abandonment or loss or thoughts of the genocide he'd so fortuitously left behind. He tried to cling to how warm it felt to know how hard his Belgian parents had worked to ensure he became their son. 'Do you know what it means to feel sooooo *wanted*,' he says. 'I love them so deeply for that. I don't feel grateful to them because they are my parents. They wanted me. But I love them so deeply for it. And I wasn't the best teenager. I showed them *alllllll* the colours of the rainbow, you know?' He grimaces at the memory of things that happened in his teens. 'I was looking for myself, you know. I think I was just pushing them to the limit of their love. It was stupid. It was, like, are you still gonna love me if I do this? And you know what? Yes, fuck yes, they loved me unconditionally. They proved it. Every time. But adoption has its scars, you know. Like, you can have a fear of abandonment. I think, unconsciously, I was testing them. And, yeah, in the end, they just loved me. And I know I'm the luckiest man in the world to have parents like that.'

Jean-Benoit was studying to be a funeral director back in Belgium when a burning wanderlust brought him to Australia two years ago. He came with $1000. He met a girl.

'We broke up a month ago,' he says. 'We'd been together one year, but it was for the best, in the end. We were 24/7. We love each other, like, *as fuck*. It's just crazy. We broke up because we love each other, but we just cannot stay together because we just ...' He slaps the topsides of his hands together. 'We're too intense. We started destroying each other, so we broke it off.'

He drums his forefingers on the side of my desk. 'But do you know what she just told me today?'

'What?'

'She said, "You are my twin flame."'

'That's what she said? "Twin flame"?'

'Yeah, man. That's what she said. I just broke up with my twin flame.' He shakes his head in regret.

'Well, sometimes twin flames burn too bright,' I say, trying to be consoling.

'Yeah, man,' he says. 'A lot. A lot. A lot.'

Then Jean-Benoit explains something complex that his ex-girlfriend told him about how we all have a twin flame, a fire that burns inside just one other person on this planet and is the exact same size and colour and gives off the exact same heat as the fire inside ourselves. These twin flames, she said, cannot be extinguished and they burn through lifetimes as we all move from one lifetime to the next and to the next and to the next.

'So, yeah, we just broke up,' he says. 'But we'll see what happens next lifetime, you know?'

I nod.

'This relationship was unconditional love, too,' he says. 'She could scream at me, she could do whatever she wanted to do to me. She literally broke a plate across my face, but I still loved her.'

'What had you done to warrant a plate across your face?'

'I deserved it,' he says. 'Niggle, niggle, niggle, then, *bam*, plate across my face! "Okay, I'll stop. And I still love you, twin flame, twin flame!"'

Two punk girls pass us with their shoelaces tied together so their inside legs walk as one. They look like a circus act and they raise a thumbs-up to us and we give our enthusiastic thumbs-up back.

'You put a lot of love out into the world, Jean-Benoit,' I say.

I've seen this myself for a week and a half now. People from all walks of life gravitating to his Osmocote fertiliser bucket drum. He teaches them how to drum and these total strangers play that thing he dug out of an industrial bin like they're playing with the toys of their childhood. Nobody ever leaves Jean-Benoit Lagarmitte's orbit without a smile on their face.

'I don't know, man,' he says. 'That's not on purpose. I think people see it when you love what you're doing. I love what I'm doing. I play music all day. I'm the happiest man on earth because people are always in a good mood when they come up to me.'

'I think that's because *you're* always in a good mood,' I say.

'Maybe, I don't know.'

I ask Jean-Benoit about his future. He tells me he's playing that Osmocote bucket every day in the street to make some spending money while he furthers his studies in humification.

'What is humification?' I ask.

'You know how when you're dead you have to essentially pay rent for your grave?'

I nod.

'Well, what the fuck is that? Paying rent when you're dead? Humification is when you turn a dead body into a tree. I want to start my own humification company.'

And I like the story of that possible future – a lot, a lot, a lot – for the great Jean-Benoit Lagarmitte, the boy left for dead under a tree, making his fortune by turning the dead into trees.

THE EVANGELIST

I told an old journo mate, Bruce, about what I was doing, sitting here on this corner writing love stories on Kath's typewriter, and he said it reminded him of the town-corner scribes he saw on his travels through Mexico. These professional scribes, once known as 'evangelists', spend their days sitting at desks in public spaces, typing letters for townsfolk who can't read or write but desperately want to send messages to the ones they love. The scribes can type up anything for you: dictated messages of abuse, injunctions, admonishments, tax returns, poems. For a hundred pesos, they can write you a love letter worthy of Napoleon. Bruce would float around these tireless public scribes, watching whole family units gather to bark suggested lines of love: 'No, Maria, you need to say that your heart rings out for him, like the bells of San Juan Bautista Church!'

That's what my corner feels like right now, a Mexican scribe corner, an evangelist post, and the locals have gathered around my desk to talk about love.

The Lovebirds, Ian and Lani Gibson, have stopped by again, on another one of their city walks. Harvey's still here with his camera, taking snaps of all of us talking. The Gibsons are talking to two young women who are best friends forever, Claudia, eighteen, and Brie, nineteen.

'Do you still get the butterflies after fifty-seven years together?' Claudia asks the Gibsons.

'Absolutely,' Lani Gibson says.

Ian nods. 'I stand at the front door before we go out and when my darling walks down the stairs I always get the little butterflies,' he says.

And the girls melt. '"My darling!"' they chorus, swooning.

Then Reuben Vui joins us around the desk, his iPad tucked under his arm.

'We met Reuben this morning,' Brie says.

'These girls signed up with me,' Reuben says.

'Good for you,' I say.

Reuben points at me. 'He signed up as well.'

I give a thumbs-up in solidarity.

'Will you just look at our little circle?' I say.

'A little pool of love,' Ian says.

Then Harvey, the Gibsons and Reuben drift off into the city, and Claudia and Brie take a seat beside my desk, Claudia resting on Brie's thighs.

'I've got an insane love story,' she says. 'Are you ready?'

I sit up in my chair. 'Yeah, I'm ready.'

'This is going to be a long story,' Claudia says.

'The best kind.'

And she speaks, seemingly without breaths and full stops, for three unbroken minutes. 'Okay, when I was fifteen I had a boyfriend and my boyfriend was friends with this girl and she was dating this guy and I'm just gonna say his name is Harry and I knew him since I was fifteen because his little sister went to school with me so I've sort of known of him and then when I was eighteen I was stripping and then his dad was always at my strip club, like, every night, and then this same guy, Harry, whose dad keeps coming into my strip club, starts talking to me on the phone and he doesn't know I'm a stripper until one night his dad takes Harry to a strip club for the first time and I'm just standing there and I'm like, "Ohhhhhhhhh", and then he was like, "Do you want to go get a feed?", and he was a bit weird about it all but I said yes to the feed and now we're just, like, really happy together and his family is, like, really good about it, and it began in the strip club but it's so good and the love I have for him is like we're best friends because I don't want all that sooky stuff in my life and I want a life partner and I want a best friend and this one feels different and he's a bit weird but he's cool and I think his brain is always on pending and I feel it's a brain that's been dropped a lot as a child but I love it also and I don't know if he's the one but I've also decided that tomorrow isn't promised and if tomorrow is not promised then, today, he's the one.'

And Claudia breathes and she smiles because she's deeply in love and it's almost as if she's just realised this and she wraps an arm around her best friend, Brie, who nods her head in elation.

'Yeah.' Claudia nods too. 'Today he's my soul mate and that's what I'm deciding to choose. I don't know what's going to happen tomorrow and I'm not going to hold on to a love until, like, someone bigger comes along. This is my person right now and this is the love of my life. Today, this is it.'

'What is love, Claudia?' I ask.

'Love is magic,' she says. 'Love is the magic that can change the world.'

*

Ashish Sood serves the best takeaway Indian food in the Brisbane CBD. His shop is called Ginger and Garlic Indian Cuisine and it's about twenty shopfronts to the left of my writing desk. I follow Ashish on Twitter. He posted a pic of his daughter, Soha, on her bicycle this morning with the words 'You are my life's most beautiful gift. Thank you for making me so happy. My dear daughter, you are the reason why my life is so much happier. I love you always and forever.'

Ashish has a heart the size of the Indian subcontinent. There's always a sign stuck to the window of his shop: *Free meals for the homeless. Every weekday after 10.45 p.m., Saturday & Sunday after 9 p.m.* He's been feeding Brisbane's homeless this way for almost four years.

'The real story behind it is that I was homeless myself,' he says, seated in the blue chair beside my writing desk. 'Thirteen years ago.' He points up towards Ann Street, beyond King George Square. 'I used to sleep on the bench. That was when I first came to Brisbane. I came to this country as a student. I never had money. Those times were hard.'

He was twenty-two years old. Lying on a bed of concrete, with an empty stomach, Ashish would stare up at the stars and make himself promises he wasn't sure he could keep: 'One day I will have my own restaurant and nobody will sleep hungry in the street.'

'And slowly, slowly, slowly, I get a job, I make some money and I bought this business in 2017,' he says. 'Now so many people aren't hungry. It makes me feel complete when the food doesn't go in the bin.'

Ashish rattles off a list of homeless regulars. 'Josh, Rick, Rachel, Ryan, Michelle,' he says. 'I've got Keith who doesn't have teeth, so I keep just the curry for him, no meat. I got Robyn, who is vegan. I keep a chickpea curry for her. I got a mother with two babies. Her babies are getting older now, so I'm giving them chicken nuggets and wedges.'

Ashish believes there comes a time when God gives every person exactly what they need. This, he says, is what is known as 'enough'. 'When God gives you enough and you then don't give back to other people, then karma is gonna get back to you,' he says. 'But the more you give, the more you get. That's like love. The more love you give to anyone, you get double back. It's a circle.'

Ashish now runs a second Indian restaurant in Kangaroo Point. It's called Secret Recipe Indian Cuisine, he explains, because all the food is made with a single transformative ingredient that does magical things to his dishes. This secret ingredient can turn his goat curry into a life-changing experience. This secret ingredient, Ashish explains, can change his prawn jalfrezi from an affordable dinner dish into a reason to go out on a cold winter's night.

'So what's the secret ingredient?' I ask.

And he smiles and leans in close with a whisper. 'Love,' he says.

*

Ray is an older man, maybe mid-sixties, who says he's a singer-songwriter from Victoria and has been working on a song that he hopes to send to The Veronicas.

'It's called "Boys in Danger",' he says. He takes two steps back from my writing desk and breathes deep to compose himself. Then he sings:

Oh, the city's hot and I'm hot to trot,
There's men on my mind tonight.
I wanna have a man.
You know I have a plan.
It may be wrong, but I'm gonna make it right.
There'll be boys in danger tonight.

And Ray takes a small bow, slapping his knees.

'Awesome song, Ray,' I say. He nods.

'I think this is lovely,' he says, waving his hands over my desk and my sign and Kath's typewriter. 'Love is respect and love is kindness,' he says. 'If you can meet someone who is kind, then you're halfway there. Me, personally, I want to meet Annastacia Palaszczuk.'

Ray puts a hand on my shoulder. 'Now, do you need any money?' he asks, with a caring, parental tone.

'Money?' I reply. 'I'm not asking for money. I'm just asking for love stories.'

He leans in close. 'Can you sing?' he asks.

'Badly.'

He says he will email me the lyrics to his latest song. He thinks I might sing it well. It's called 'Postcards from Paris'. But he wants something from me in return.

'Can I get a picture of you in those blue jeans?'

And I laugh because I think he's joking. But then I realise he's not joking. 'Ummm, I guess so,' I say.

As Ray rushes off down Adelaide Street, he calls over his shoulder, 'Is that a deal?'

'Yeah, Ray. That's a deal.'

*

Genevieve is seventy-seven years old. That's not her real name. That's a fake name that will allow her to tell me a secret about love that's been weighing her down for about as long as this pandemic has been weighing on the world.

Her mother left her when she was ten. She was raised by an alcoholic father. Then she met a good man in Warwick, 150 kilometres from Brisbane, whom she married. That man cheated on Genevieve with one of Genevieve's closest friends.

But none of that relates to the secret she wants to confess.

She moved to Brisbane and got a job. 'I worked at Wallies for years,' she says, nodding at the shop across the busy street from my writing desk. That shop has housed a Bupa Optical store in recent years but, Genevieve explains, it was formerly a Wallace Bishop jewellery store, which opened in 1925 and survived for decades. Then she set up a café that led to her running her own catering business. She's done well for herself and has been able to devote the past two decades to regularly travelling across the world. She's been to France and Italy multiple times. Morocco. Norway. Germany. Japan. She stays in affordable places, learns all she can by immersing herself in the local culture. The catering business was all but wiped out last year because Covid-19 all but wiped out catered events across Brisbane. Genevieve now spends her working hours giving cooking lessons to children with autism. But none of that relates to her secret.

Until recently, Genevieve had gone without another man for twenty years.

'I was sorta mortally wounded in the love department,' she says. 'I never dreamed my husband and I would ever part. And then I saw this thing happening and I thought, Nup, I'm not putting up with this shit anymore.'

She and her husband had four children – all grown up with their own kids today – and, for their sake, Genevieve decided she wasn't going to be vindictive and angry over the betrayal. The strangest thing about the break-up is that her ex-husband, to this day, acts as though it never happened. 'He rings me twice a week,' she says. 'He never forgets my birthday or our wedding anniversary, which is even worse.' Every year, mid-June, a message from her ex-husband lands in her phone: 'Happy anniversary!'

Genevieve's eyes catch a presence over my left shoulder. It's Ray again, returning to my desk, holding a waterproof disposable camera the size of a fruit-juice popper. He asks me to stand and pose for a picture. He can't get the camera working, then Genevieve tells him he has to rotate the disc at the top of it. 'Counter-clockwise,' she says.

Ray rotates it once.

'You gotta keep winding it back until you hear a click,' I say.

'Then hit the yellow button,' Genevieve adds.

Ray points the camera at me. Clicks and winds and clicks and winds. 'Thank you,' he says.

'I'm glad you got your pic,' I say, not entirely certain what he plans to do with the images.

'Have a guess which song I wish I wrote?' Ray asks Genevieve and me.

'What song?' I ask.

'"Killer Queen",' he says.

'Great song!' I say.

'Have you ever seen *What Ever Happened to Baby Jane?*' Ray asks.

Genevieve, sitting in the blue chair beside my desk, is visibly puzzled by the random nature of Ray's questions.

'Great film,' I say.

'You know it?'

'Of course I know it. Bette Davis. Amazing.'

'Yes!' Ray rejoices. 'All right, I'm off to the Valley. Gotta meet some nice Valley girls.'

He scurries off down Adelaide Street, slipping his waterproof camera into a carry bag.

Genevieve scratches her top lip and shakes her head and continues her story. And this is when she shares her secret.

'I didn't even think about love for twenty years,' she says. But then the strangest and most ridiculous thing happened. She fell in love with a Catholic priest. She says she met him in the lounge of Brisbane Airport in September 2019, just before setting off on a holiday through Japan. They shared a table in the dining lounge. They started talking and they could not stop. Then they started emailing and they could not stop. She says he might be the kindest man she's ever met. She says they've been intimate. 'It's very complicated for him.'

She says he told her that he has been attempting to separate the love he has for her from the love he has for God. He believes this is a separation he can sustain. 'I decided that's for him to work out, not me,' she says. 'I haven't got the problem, he has.' She shakes her head at the madness of it all. To find oneself in such a mess at seventy-seven years of age. 'It's ridiculous!' she says. She attends a church a short walk from where she lives in Brisbane's east. She knows and trusts the priest in this local church. She recently asked if she could chat with him, one to one. 'He rang me up and said he'd meet me at the coffee shop down the road,' she explains. 'A ten-minute cup of coffee turned into three hours. And I told him all about my relationship and he said, "Go gently." They were his words: "Go gently, my friend."' And Genevieve loved hearing those words because they didn't make her feel bad about what she was doing, they just made her slow down and consider what she was doing. The words made her go gently.

'So where are you at with love, right now?' I ask.

'I'm a bit conflicted at this particular minute,' she says. 'I woke up this morning and I thought, I'm sick of this, I'm over it. I woke up this morning and I thought, I'm just gonna let this be for a bit. He's a wonderful man and it's been a wonderful love story. But it's been a tough one, too.' She shrugs her shoulders. 'If it all ends, I'll be all right,' she says. 'I've learned to be resilient.'

*

Now it's 4 p.m. and I'm packing my desk away when a woman gently taps me on the shoulder. She tells me her name is Cinthya Lema Galarza and she's seen me sitting on this corner for a week now. She's been puzzled by the typewriter, by the people she's seen weeping in the blue seat beside my desk. I tell her I'm writing a book about love. Some days I'm typing letters to people I love. She asks me if I'm familiar with the notion that the loved ones we have lost remain alive in our stories. I nod.

'Can I please tell you a story about my grandfather?' she asks.

She's twenty-five years old and she was raised in Guayaquil, the largest city in Ecuador. She explains that in her family the children grew up calling her grandfather Papito. 'It's like Daddy, but with more love,' she says. 'Can I show you a picture of him?'

On her phone she swipes to an image of a handsome Ecuadorean man standing next to, Cinthya tells me, his wife of more than fifty years. Two days ago, at sunrise, Cinthya received a message from her family back home saying her *papito* had died. Yesterday, at sunrise, she tuned in to the online feed of his funeral service.

'When I come here, I wanted to stay for only six months to improve my English,' she says. 'But then Covid happened and I couldn't get back to my country, so I decided to stay for one year more. I wanted to be there for my mum, but it was not possible. I couldn't get back there.'

Cinthya says family is love and love is family. Family is everything. She has not known a grief like the grief she endures in this moment for her *papito*. She realises now that grief is the price she will willingly pay to have loved someone so deeply. She keeps thinking about a time when she was a girl and her *papito* taught her how to ride a horse. And she didn't think it was possible to ride a horse until he proved her wrong by lifting her onto a horse's back and guiding her through a ride. Then he suggested they ride up a high mountain that seemed like it reached the low-lying clouds and Cinthya didn't think it was possible to ride up such a mountain until her *papito* guided her all the way to the top. Atop her horse and atop that mountain that day, Cinthya Lema Galarza made a choice to believe anything was possible.

'I'm sorry,' she says. 'I want to cry.'

'Oh, please,' I urge, 'cry.'

The only cure for grief is to grieve. The only cure for hurt is to hurt. Every tear is a tribute. Every tear is a memory, every memory a treasure. So cry buckets, Cinthya Lema Galarza, and then when your bucket is full, pour your collected tears over your garden flowers and watch them bloom in all the sunrises of your grieving.

And cry she does.

'When I got the news, I was devastated,' she says. She had nowhere to put all her feelings, no place to focus her heartbreak and make sense of it. Then a friend told her to write a letter to her grandfather. 'Write every thought you ever had about him,' the friend said. 'Write about every memory you have of him, then set your letter on fire.'

She swipes to a video on her phone. Someone's filmed her holding up the letter she wrote yesterday to her *papito*. Tiny handwriting. Endless words. Two full pages, the front and back of a single page.

'You had so many thoughts,' I say.

'I told him everything I wanted to say,' she says. 'Like, sorry I wasn't there when you died. Thank you for everything you gave me. Thank you for your wisdom. Thank you for your love.'

She swipes to another video. 'And then I burned the letter,' she says. The video shows Cinthya weeping as her words to her *papito* catch fire. The paper shrinks in the flame to a jagged, black rock-like shape, then burns down to nothing but ashes and blue smoke.

'I'm feeling better now,' she says.

This morning was the third straight sunrise she woke up to see. Two days ago, she thinks, was the sunrise of his death. Yesterday was the sunrise of his goodbye. This morning she stared at the orange and pink sky as the sun rose up through the centre of it and she said something directly to her grandfather. 'You are there,' she whispered, and she felt as close to her grandfather in that moment as she had sitting on top of that horse on top of that mountain in the South American clouds.

'And now I have decided I will remember him in every sunrise I see,' she says. 'Every sunrise is beautiful and that's maybe how I will handle it. I will watch that beautiful sunrise and I will say, "You are there," and everything will be okay.'

She wipes tears from her eyes and gives an embarrassed smile. 'Thank you,' she says. 'I don't have any family here to talk to. Sometimes I just want to speak about him. Thank you for letting me speak about him.'

WE LIGHTEN

I'm discussing the myriad complexities of love with Kim and the rest of the externally gentle but internally tough-as-nails ladies from the anti-Chinese Communist Party petition group. Kim seems to be the group's unofficial team leader. I've been talking about how all our worries and fears so often seem to stem from love: the more you love someone, the more you worry about them. *I'll only ever be as happy as my unhappiest child.*

'What you worry about?' Kim asks, soft and concerned in her broken English.

'Whaddya got, Kim?' What now with this pandemic? What fresh hell waits around the endless bend for us? Will my kids be happy when they grow up? Am I doing enough for them? Do I do too much for them? Why did I never learn about the area of compound shapes in maths class? Did I leave the iron on? What is that pea-sized lump in my scrotum? Where will the intersection of climate change and global political instability leave Australia in the next hundred years? If China continues to successfully consolidate regional influence through a rapidly transforming foreign policy, will the United States seek to enhance geostrategic security and commercial interests by dangerously pushing back

against the might of Beijing? Will Britney Spears find the peace she deserves?

Kim says I need to stop looking at life from eye level. She says I'd be better served looking at life as though I was a wedge-tailed eagle way up high in the sky, looking down on it all. 'You'd let go of a lot of things if you saw life that way,' she says.

'I think I get my worry streak from my grandmother,' I say. She lived with polio, spent her life in a wheelchair. 'She loved so hard, Kim. She cared so much about stuff and the curse of that care was all the worry that comes with caring.'

Kim smiles. 'I also worried,' she says. 'We human beings, we love to worry.' She shakes her head and taps a finger on mine. 'You too heavy with thoughts.' She makes a waving-me-away gesture with her hand. 'You need to go love someone,' she says. 'You go care for someone. You unhappy, go love someone. You anxious, go care for someone. You stop thinking about self. All worries go away. You love someone, you lighten.'

I love someone. I lighten. We love. We lighten.

Thanks, Kim.

NAOMI

Jack Chester doesn't know where to begin. Then he realises he can't go past her eyes. She's got different-coloured eyes. One iris is green and one iris is brown. The condition is called heterochromia iridis, but Jack prefers to call it another one of her miracles, something that mesmerises him on an hourly basis. Then she has her humour and her kindness. You know that thing where guys say a woman has a good sense of humour, when all they're really doing is being kind enough to laugh at the guy's dumb jokes? She laughs at his dumb jokes. She makes him feel at home, and he's never really felt at home before.

They started dating a week before high school graduation and now they're about to celebrate their second anniversary. He asks if I've ever met the perfect girl. He asks me if I ever met that girl so right that she makes you believe in human purpose, that you finally belong to your own universally microscopic role in existence. He says he's met that girl. He says she takes the fear away. When you're eighteen years old, sometimes it feels like every move you make will have consequences, like every decision is a decision for life. Here's what Jack Chester wants to be right now: a businessman, a landscape gardener, a teacher and a filmmaker. He doesn't know which of those careers would be the most fulfilling for him. How does an adult possibly know these things until they know these things? Jack's life is a road that's meant to stretch on for eighty more years or so, but sometimes it feels like the world wants Jack to bitumen that road and paint white lines down the middle of it all in the space of the next six months. But that's all good because he knows love. That's all good because she's the girl on the side of his road with her thumb out, saying, 'Who the fuck knows where this thing goes, but let's just go there together.'

She has a Spotify playlist she calls 'Sparks'. I mean, can you believe the wonder in this girl? Who gives their playlist a name like that? Only a girl with the fire does that, only a girl with the burning inside her would do such a thing. And he reeks of the love he has for her. He stinks of it. Love is a new can of Lynx Africa and he's suffocating in the date-night bathroom spray of it. He'd die in that chemical cloud if he had to, if it meant he could take just one more breath of her.

He knows the very moment he fell in love with her. There's this song called 'Here It Goes Again', by the band OK Go from Chicago, Illinois, and one day she played it for him and he told her that song might be his favourite song of all time and he'd never met a single girl who knew or liked that song, and that moment made him think of the time his dad was six years old and he was living in New South Wales and his father – Jack's grandfather – flipped a coin and they said that whatever side the coin landed on would determine where the family moved to: north to far north Queensland or south to Victoria. Jack's dad's family moved north and Jack's dad met Jack's mum in far north Queensland and that's the only reason Jack was born. Jack always thought it was strange that he was essentially the product of a coin toss, but that all made sense when he heard his girlfriend play 'Here It Goes Again' by OK Go.

She's so fucking perfect that she makes him believe in fate and destiny and coin tosses and now when he sees that coin of his grandfather's flipping in mid-air in his mind, the only face he sees on either side of the spinning coin is the girl of his dreams with the green and brown eyes. And every single time that coin lands, it only ever comes up Naomi.

WAITING FOR THE ICICLE TO FALL

Jan Kubert is a retired secondary school teacher who was born in Michigan, in the upper mid-west United States, where the winters are unbearable and the front porches of suburban houses are deadly. He remembers a statistic that lodged in his brain as a boy and made him stay inside during winter. 'In the state of Michigan we would have eleven deaths per year, purely by people stepping out onto their front porch,' he says. 'There would be razor-sharp icicles hanging from the eves, some two metres long, and what happens during the night is the heat inside the house melts where the icicles are joined to the eve, and they become really unstable. People step out of their house and they get impaled by a falling icicle.'

He holds an orange and mango smoothie in his left hand and slaps my shoulder with his free right hand. 'Isn't that weird?' he says. 'That terrified me as a boy!'

Then he raises a forefinger because there's more to this story. 'You know what a snow shovel is? Big wide blade. A lot of people who haven't used a snow shovel think the idea of it is to put as much ice and snow on it as you can and then lift it up. Of course, people lift all that snow and it's too heavy and they have a heart attack. It's only a wide blade to give you the pressure to get under the ice on your driveway. You don't try to fill the thing up. Then there's the people from out of town who don't know to put ice chains on their tyres.'

Jan's dad, Ernest, worked in manufacturing, building lawnmower engines and such. He remembers Ernest driving to work each morning in winter and wiping his windscreen inside and out with a rag soaked in vinegar. 'A lot of people from outside of Michigan don't understand to do that, so ice forms on their windshield when they're driving and they go off the road and they might not be found again until spring-time.'

'Jan,' I say, 'Michigan sounds like the most dangerous place on the planet.'

*

Jan came to Brisbane in 1961 when he was thirteen. His mum was an Australian war bride who'd grown up in Nundah, north Brisbane. Summer in Brisbane was as unbearable to Jan as the Michigan winter. But there were no deadly falling icicles in the capital of Queensland. He worked at a brickworks after high school, and he worked at a funeral home, in the backroom as an assistant preparing bodies for burial. He remembers working alongside Mr Wade, the man the funeral home called 'the senior chemist'. Mr Wade had a series of embalming 'recipes' affixed to his workbench that he would use according to the size, shape and colour of the deceased. 'That man loved his job,' Jan says. 'He was an artist.'

Jan studied to be a teacher and then taught for thirty-four years in secondary schools across Brisbane. He taught maths, chemistry, physics and, later, computing.

'Have you ever been in love, Jan?' I ask.

'I sure have,' he says. 'In some ways I still am.'

Jan met Barb Woods in the mid-1970s. Love at first sight. Love at first smile. Love at the first touch of her perfect hand. Jan and Barb were engaged by 1977, when they pooled their savings to secure a deposit for their first house.

'And then she was killed in a car crash,' he says. 'It was late at night and she swerved and ran into a tree. A policeman woke me up that night. The only person available to identify her body was me.'

His head sinks into his shoulders. 'That was forty-two years ago last August,' he says. He sips on his smoothie, lost in his memories. 'I had to rethink everything about life. Grief and separation anxiety are two different things. But when you lose someone you love like that you end up having both. It's like being in a ring with two powerful boxers and they attack you either together or one at a time.'

Thump. Bang. Whack. Multiple-punch combinations. Rope-a-dope grieving. Down he goes. Knockout blows every night for years that leave a man crying on the floor of the first house he ever owned.

'I loved her and I still do,' he says. He sips the smoothie until the straw can't suck any more orange and mango juice and he seems surprised when he notices that the tall plastic cup is empty. 'But that's what happens,' he says. 'We lose people all the time.'

One day we're having eggnog inside a living room in Michigan, the next day we're stepping out onto the porch as an icicle falls from an eve. Sometimes Jan thinks about the life he might have had with Barb, had she made it home that night. He thinks about the kids they planned to have and how old they would be today.

I ask Jan what he thinks about the risk of love. Everything about love raises the stakes. Health suddenly becomes something of importance for a person newly in love. The future never seems more concerning. Global markets, wars in faraway places, pandemics on our doorstep. The safety and protection of the ones you love is suddenly as essential to you as air and water. Why would God or the universe or Mother Nature or fate allow Jan Kubert to love a woman as deeply and as cripplingly as he loved Barb Woods, only to steal her away from him on a dark road, late in the night, forty-two years ago last August?

'Everywhere we go, we will never know how many minor miracles occur each day that help us avoid calamity,' he says.

And now I know what love is.

`Love is never knowing how lucky you are to`
`have it.`

And that's what Jan was trying to get at with all that icicle talk. Love should not be about staying inside the living room and waiting for the icicle to fall off the eve, he explains. Love should be about knowing the icicle might fall, but stepping out the front door anyway because it feels so good just to stand on the porch.

TWO POETS

I just saw a man wave at a magpie. He looked genuinely surprised, and then sad when the magpie didn't wave back. I just saw a woman running to catch a bus, wearing a T-shirt that says, 'Your anxiety is lying to you.'

A young Aboriginal woman sits in the blue chair beside mine. She's been running from someone but she's not in danger. Just catching her breath. She's covered in water and she dries her bare feet with the towel she carries. 'Thanks,' she says, standing and hurrying on up Adelaide Street.

Then a young man with a bushy moustache, white-rimmed sunglasses and a grey and yellow hoodie sits in the blue chair. He's a poet who goes by the name Minus the Cynic – a big middle finger, he says, to all the cynics of the world. Fuck the Cynic would have been more to the point, but far less poetic. He's on his way to a free midday concert in City Hall, The Snake Gully Bush Band performing bush ballads like 'Click Go the Shears' and 'The Diamantina Drover' and 'Botany Bay'. 'The hardest love for humans to bring to the world is unconditional love,' he says. 'But the best love we can hope for is to love like a friend.'

He opens a large yellow JB Hi-Fi bag that's sitting at his feet. 'You own a magnifying glass?' he asks.

'I do.' My father-in-law, the entomologist, gave my wife and me a magnifying glass years ago to check our girls for head lice in their early primary school years. I now use it to stare into the faces of window geckos when I'm bored in the kitchen at night.

Minus the Cynic pulls from his JB Hi-Fi bag a book of his poetry that's two hundred pages long, its A4 pages bound together like something he had printed at Officeworks: clear plastic front cover, blue cardboard back page. He hands me the book as a gift. 'Legend,' he says. 'God bless you.'

Then he rushes away towards City Hall and I flip through the poetry book. There are exactly two hundred poems in the book, but the poems have been printed in a near-microscopic sub-eight-point font. The book feels like it would be six hundred pages long at a legible size. They are love poems, many of them beautiful, with long titles and breakneck sentence rhythms that speak of a man carrying a broken heart who perhaps tried to unconditionally love someone very special but had to settle for loving that person just as a friend. It's pure, heartfelt, heartbreaking writing. Minus the ego. Minus the fear. Minus the cynic. The tiny font size only adds to the mystery held within the poem titles.

Keep My Heart Locked in Yours and Throw away the Key

Just for Once Pretend That All I've Got to Offer Is More Than Enough for You

Turn On the Light of Love in Me and Let It Never Go to Sleep

Does This Actually Go Somewhere Other Than Pear-Shaped?

Our Words Always Made Love in Better Ways Than Our Bodies Ever Could

You Know How It Is When You Anticipate Break-ups Before They Happen So You Deliberately Sabotage Your Relationship to Save Face

That Number You Give When You Want to Get Rid of Someone Who Wants to Be Your Lover But You'd Rather Not Bother with Them (But Don't Want to Hurt Feelings)

*

Paul Gibson is a poet, too. He wears a Bunnings hat and a green and black flannelette shirt with black jeans. Packet of cigarettes in his shirt pocket. Paul says he's been in the mental health system for twenty years. He lives on the Sunshine Coast, but sometimes he just sits for days on trains travelling between the Sunshine Coast, Brisbane, the Gold Coast and back again. He writes poems on the trains.

'You got any poems about love?' I ask.

'Sure,' he says. And he recites:

Lady from France always loved to dance
And a night of lust without white dust is in my mind
Refine the time when love runs deep
Protect the weak
She's brave and strong and her life goes on
In her endless sleep.

'Who was that about?' I ask.

'A lady from France,' he says.

Paul's carrying a DVD copy of *Terminator 2: Judgment Day*. One of his all-time favourite films.

'Beautiful love story,' I say. A boy and his robot. I tell Paul how I cry every time endearing smartarse Edward Furlong begs Arnie not to lower himself into that molten steel pit. And here's my bad Arnie accent again: "'I know now why you cry, but it's something I can never do.'"

Paul grimaces, recalling the pain of the scene. 'You seen these robots they got coming out of America,' he says. 'You can get online and see 'em. They are so real. They're using a refined latex. You can program them based on your subconscious. There'll be a time when if your sister died ten years ago you can bring her back as a robot, be sitting with your sister again. The Jehovah's Witnesses in America are terrified of these robots. They're like, "God, help us all."'

'You ever been in love, Paul?' I ask.

'I've been in situations where I have been in love,' he says. 'I have also made many mistakes. I have lowered myself down to the cesspools, lower than society. Picking cigarette butts off the street, and I'm not proud of it. I drove myself into self-pity because of how my life turned out. I'm a really bitter person. Lotta hurt, mate. But ...'

And that's a long 'but', during which he looks to the sky and a light fills his eyes with some rare kind of peace or some rare kind of acceptance. 'Love,' he says. 'I think it can mend the broken things.'

`Love is mending the broken things.`

There might still be true love out there for Paul but he's worried he's spent too long on his own to know true love when he sees it.

'I'm a solitary man,' he says. 'You get to the stage when you can turn away from love, you realise you can be alone all your life and make it through.'

I tell Paul I think that happened to my father. He was alone for as long as I knew him and I knew him for thirty-six years.

I think he realised he could survive without true love, as long as he had cigarettes and books by Cormac McCarthy. I wasn't sure if he wanted more. 'I think we're supposed to want more,' I say. But more is a risk. More can break your heart again.

We sit in silence for a moment. Paul raises his *Terminator 2* DVD.

'Maybe I could find me a robot to love?'

Just a boy and his robot.

Paul stands and pushes on through the city, making another movie reference before he leaves.

'Well, get busy livin' or get busy dyin',' he says.

'*Shawshank*?' I reply.

'*Shawshank*,' he says, giving a thumbs-up.

And then I turn back to the Olivetti and type a love poem:

```
Love Can Mend the Broken Things but Nothing
Can Survive Being Lowered into Molten Steel


Love can mend the broken things
The beat-up plans and the wedding rings
Love can fix the broken hearts
The robot souls and the missing parts
Love can raise the poet's font
The need, the lust, the love, the want
Love can light the Brisbane sky
To let us know now why we cry
```

ARLO

That barrister wheeling a travel bag up to George Street. That Waanyi and Kalkadoon man. 'Josh Creamer!' I call, and smile. And he stops and smiles back, the way he stopped and smiled back the last time we saw each other. Six years ago. We were on the beachfront near the ferry terminal jetty at Palm Island, the Aboriginal Shire off the coast of Townsville. Josh was tirelessly collecting the evidence – traumatising oral history after traumatising oral history – that would lead to him and his legal team winning what was then Australia's largest human-rights class action, brought on behalf of 447 Aboriginal and Torres Strait Islander residents of Palm Island against the State of Queensland, alleging unlawful racial discrimination during the investigation into the death in custody of Mulrunji Doomadgee in 2004. In 2019, Josh was also a key part of the team that achieved what is Australia's largest successful human-rights class action, the historic Stolen Wages Class Action that settled with the Queensland Government for $190 million to compensate Indigenous workers whose wages were withheld or not paid as a result of legislation in effect from the late 1800s to the early 1970s.

We first met ten years ago. I was the young bleeding-heart journo begging Josh to let me write a newspaper piece about how much pale white arse he was kicking as a twenty-nine-year-old Brisbane barrister, then one of only four Indigenous barristers working in Queensland. He was the wise young lawyer wary of the journo's dubious sales pitch: 'Big page three pic! You in your wig and robes. "Bright young blackfella brings blowtorch to white man's law!" How inspiring would that image be for Queensland Indigenous kids to see?'

Josh didn't share my enthusiasm. 'Aboriginal man excels in chosen profession.' He wanted to live in a world where that wasn't newsworthy.

'It's funny,' Josh says, reflectively. 'I always run into you at key periods in my life.'

'I was about to say the same thing to you.'

I tell Josh about my book of love stories. 'Ya reckon you got a love story in you?' I ask.

And he thinks on this for a moment and the left edge of his mouth curls upwards and I know full well there are sixty thousand years of stories in that wry smile.

'Yeah, I got a love story,' he says. 'But you need to come to my house to see it.'

*

One day later and I'm standing in Josh's living room as a warm-faced young mum named Kara Cook emerges from her bedroom. A former gun domestic-violence lawyer. Current Labor councillor for Morningside, south Brisbane. Josh's wife. She holds a small miracle in her arms, only three months old.

'Meet Arlo,' Josh says. 'That's my love story.'

Job done. Story told. That's all you had to say, Josh Creamer, because I can see how beautiful that story is. A story that begins in that perfect little baby's toes and ends at the soft skin of his scalp beneath his scruffy black hair and in the smile that can't be removed from Kara's face. 'He was born just after that last three-day lockdown,' Josh says. 'So it was just Kara and me in the hospital. We weren't allowed to have visitors or family, none of that, not even his two big sisters, Eden and Rita.'

He shakes his head in wonder at his baby boy. 'I've just been taking time to appreciate what a little miracle babies are, the fact two people can come together and create something so beautiful,' he says. 'They're so perfect, they make *you* feel perfect.' He grips Arlo's fingers. 'Yeah, my kids are my love story,' he says.

And that's a story, he says, that goes back to 1898, and another sixty thousand years before that. He turns to a wall unit on the edge of his living room. It's covered in framed photographic portraits of members of his family.

'That's the whole story right there,' he says. 'That's where I come from. That's where Arlo comes from.'

He points to a grainy black and white photograph of an Aboriginal woman in the top left corner of the wall unit. 'It starts with Opal,' he says with a smile. 'My great-great-grandmother.'

Opal Maginmarm was born to a Waanyi family in the Northern Territory in the mid-1880s. When she was fifteen she was forcibly removed from her family by a party of men from the notorious Lawn Hill Station, who set her to work among white pastoralists who, according to a growing and damning accumulation of documented evidence by modern Indigenous historians, could potentially be linked to atrocities ranging from child molestation and rape to the keeping of Indigenous male body parts as trophies. Opal married a Lawn Hill Station cook named Sam Ah Bow, who had come to Australia from China to claim his piece of a dry southern land's gold-rush pie.

Josh points to another photograph. 'My grandfather, Moody Leon,' he says. There's also a framed certificate on Josh's wall, dedicated to Moody: *In appreciation to Moody Leon for his dedicated service of over 30 years to the battling Aborigines.*

'Grandad was always out there fighting for the blackfellas of North West Queensland,' Josh says. 'He had a house in Mount Isa that's been in the family for about eighty years now. That house had an open-door policy. Any Aboriginal person who was passing through and needed a place to stay, or food or whatever they needed, they stayed at Grandad's house.'

He shakes his head. 'That man showed me so much love,' he says. 'I see my grandfather in everything I do. Everything I do is part of a value system that he had and that our family has held on to.'

Then he points to an image of his mum, Sandra Creamer. Born in Mount Isa, 1961. The youngest of twelve children. Sandra's mum died when Sandra was six months old. She was asked to leave her school in Year 9 for no other reason than her Aboriginality. She became a mum to four kids. Josh, the eldest, remembers watching her endure vivid and disturbing scenes of shocking domestic violence. She raised her kids herself, holding down part-time jobs and saving every spare dollar she had, to give her kids a life she'd never had. Survivor. Warrior. Grandmother. Lawyer. Inspired by the work of her eldest child, Sandra enrolled in a law course at Melbourne's Deakin University. In 2011, she graduated with a law degree. In 2020, Josh had the distinct honour of moving the admission of his beloved mother – the woman he once saw pressed against a fibro wall with a man's hand around her throat – as a lawyer to the Supreme Court of Queensland.

'That's a pretty beautiful love story right there,' I suggest to Josh.

Then Josh looks again at the photograph of Opal and back across 120 years of family, all the way to the perfect face of his baby boy, Arlo. And he asks me directly if I can spot the common thread stitching all those people together through that story.

I knew the answer, from the first photograph he showed me. 'Love,' I say.

He nods his head. 'Love.'

He looks at his boy again. 'Fifty years ago, someone could have busted through my front door and said, "We're taking this boy." Can you imagine that? Could there be anything more traumatic than having that boy removed from us right now?'

Arlo, he says, is the product of a chain of ancestral love that has miraculously remained unbroken for more than a century. Arlo got lucky, Josh says. The story of love, he says, is so often overlooked when we examine the 230-year story of Indigenous Australian injustice and upheaval. Every child removed was another chain of love severed. Sustaining and empowering familial love – removed instantly from parent and child. Remove the child, remove the love, delete the love story.

'You can't think about what happened to a child in 1956 or 1986 or 2021 without understanding what happened to a child in 1905 or 1890. The same way I can't talk about Arlo without thinking about the people who came before him.

'Where did all this stuff come from? You've got a people who successfully raised their children for two thousand generations, across sixty thousand years. If they didn't do that efficiently, with love, how could they have sustained as a people for so long? They wouldn't have been able to sustain as a population if they didn't have young, vibrant babies, just like Arlo, who were healthy, nurtured properly and able to continue to build their community.'

Continuity of law. Continuity of custom. Continuity of love.

'That word "love" really resonates with me,' Josh says. 'Not only were kids removed and subjected to horrible things but, importantly, they weren't shown any love. They weren't shown any emotion. It was, "You are a number, you are a thing." We talk a lot about the physical nourishment that they were deprived of. But they weren't given any emotional nourishment, either.'

An unbroken love story stretching across sixty thousand years, then severed in the last 230. 'Just prior to European arrival there were probably about two hundred thousand Aboriginal people in Queensland,' Josh says. 'By 1860, that population had been killed down to about twenty-five thousand.'

He doesn't call such insights 'history'. He calls them 'evidence'. These are facts he has used to build cases in court, truths that do not collapse under the weight of courtroom cross-examination. 'In 1897, when they introduced the protections acts, they moved twenty-two thousand people to the missions. You're not allowed to practise your culture. You're not allowed to talk your language. You are, effectively, a ward of the state. You can't leave the mission without permission. You can't marry someone at that mission. It's like a prison. You're told what time you've got to wake up. You're told what you eat.'

Josh has lost count of the number of Indigenous elders – the ones aged seventy, eighty, ninety years old – he's interviewed through complex class-action cases who speak of flinching when their grandchildren and great-grandchildren hug them. Unbridled affection is not in their make-up. Touch is to be feared. Affection is foreign. Love is alien.

'If my family had been removed to Palm Island or one of the missions, it would have been fucking game over,' he says. 'My cousin's a doctor. I've had so many cousins go to university. All my uncles got trades in the mines. There would have been none of that. I'd probably be in jail, or maybe I'd be dead by suicide. It's sliding doors.'

In recent years, Josh has been journeying through Indigenous communities across Australia, recording oral testimonies for cases relating to contemporary governmental child-protection injustices. Same shit, different decade.

'I'm sitting in Cherbourg with a young girl, twenty-two years old, eighteen months ago, and she tells me about how she's sitting in the bathroom, breastfeeding a six-month-old baby, and a team of about a dozen cops and child-safety officers are ripping the baby out of her arms. That's what these cases are about. Her mother was subjected to the same, her children were removed the same way.'

True love, severed in an instant. Another love story broken.

There's a moment from the lead-up to the historic Palm Island class-action win that Josh can't remove from his thinking. Every Indigenous testimony he records seems to carry some form of trauma, but this moment seems to have clung to him tighter than most. 'I was up on Palm Island in one of the witness's houses,' he says. 'It's about 6 p.m. and we're sitting down, about to have dinner, and the family gets a call. Their daughter has hung herself. Time freezes, right? Like, literally, time freezes. I'm sitting there and there's a couple of adults there, and I'm like, "Fuck, what do we do?" For a moment, people almost start to continue what they're doing, but then I'm like, "Look, I'm going to leave." And I walk out of the house and I hear the wailing cry.'

A sound one can't unhear. The pain in it. That's the sound of 230 years of emotional upheaval. That's what a broken love story sounds like. Josh started thinking about his own family story, all the way back to Opal and the 1880s. He thought about the people in his own love story who fell through the cracks. The people who chose to bow out of the story because the pain was too much. The sound of that wailing almost broke Josh Creamer that night. But then something extraordinary happened. The wailing got him angry. The wailing got him strong. He phoned a senior member of his legal team. And he kept repeating the same words. 'I want to win this case,' he said. 'I want to win this case. I want to win this case.'

Josh Creamer won that case.

*

Now Josh carries Arlo in his arms as he casts his eyes back over the wall unit filled with the photographs of his family. 'I'm just a storyteller,' he says. 'When I think about where I fit into all this, I feel like I'm the storyteller. That's all I am. Whether I've got my robes on in court or whether I'm sitting down with my boots in the dirt hearing stories from elders, I'm just telling stories. That's all my role is.'

He can't wait to tell his stories to Arlo when he's old enough. All the evidence he has tirelessly gathered relating to where that beautiful boy comes from and where he's going. Evidence of pain. Evidence of injustice. Evidence of hardship. Evidence of hope. And the evidence of love Arlo will see every day on the wall unit of his home as he grows up and in the wide eyes of his tireless father, the bright middle-aged blackfella bringing a blowtorch to white man's law.

GYPSY STUFF

Love is a blown kiss through a car windscreen. Love is the way all the old guys who walk past my writing desk know how to be tender to their wives. The gentle holding of a hand. The stroke of a shoulder. The holding of a jacket. They are love-seasoned. Love is two high schoolers falling for each other over a shared high school musical script. They are love-raw.

Love is two young women resting their foreheads against each other on a metal table outside Starbucks. They block out the world and stare into each other's eyes over tall plastic coffee frappé cups. They look so truly in love. This love moment lasts ten seconds and then it ends, but I know what I saw. There are three people in the world who know what just happened between those young women, and I'm one of them.

'Excuse me,' I say, like an interrupting douchebag stranger with a notepad in his hand. 'This is going to sound totally ridiculous, but are you able to describe for me what just happened between you two when you were resting your foreheads together like that?'

And they laugh and they lean back in their chairs because they've been seen, because they've been found out. Their names are Ath and Sinead and they are, indeed, very much in love.

'I don't know where to start,' Ath says. 'It's impossible to put into words.'

But Ath really wants to put it into words because she cherishes the feeling and she agrees with me that it deserves description, so she thinks for twenty seconds on what that feeling is. 'Okay,' she says, settling on her words. 'When I put my forehead against hers, it felt like ... a little ... warm ... bowl. And inside that bowl is joy and comfort and I don't want to stop holding that warm bowl.'

And now I know what love is.

```
Love is a warm bowl. Love is joy and comfort
and two heads resting against each other for
a lifetime.
```

*

Love is Tony Dee singing 'Come Fly with Me' in the centre of the city. Black hat on his head. Sharp tie. A microphone in his hand, an amplifier strapped to his wheelchair with a bungee cord. Tony was born in 1969 with spina bifida. Tony remembers being part of the generation of special school students who were transitioned abruptly by the government into the state school system. 'That was different,' he says. 'I dropped out when I was fifteen.'

'Because there was too much difficulty surrounding that?'

'Socially, mostly,' he says. 'Kids. I copped a hard time.'

'Kids can be *real* arseholes.'

He shrugs. 'We hope there's a lot more understanding these days.'

Tony met his wife, Caroline, in an online chat room. They organised to go for a date. They arranged to meet in the carpark of Tony's church. Caroline is able-bodied but she suffers regularly from chronic fibromyalgia. She drove two hours down from Toowoomba, on Queensland's Darling Downs, to the church in Cannon Hill, in Brisbane's east. 'She later said she got to the carpark and almost turned around and went home, all the way back to Toowoomba,' Tony says. 'I was just some random dude she'd only talked to for a few hours online.'

He will never forget the way she greeted him that day. 'She just bowled up to me and kissed me on the cheek,' he says. He taps the wheel rims of his wheelchair. 'She completely ignored the wheels.'

They walked and wheeled along the Wynnum Jetty. They had lunch at Carindale Shopping Centre. Tony was so mesmerised by his date that somewhere during that lunch he unwittingly lost his wallet. Hours later, Tony received a call from the shopping centre's management saying it had been handed in and Caroline accompanied him the whole way through the laborious retrieval of the misplaced wallet. And then it was getting late and it was well into the evening when they drove back to the Wynnum Jetty, talking in Caroline's car as they watched the stars blink and throb over Pandanus Beach. Then Caroline drove Tony back to his place and they were sitting in his driveway inside Caroline's car, talking more, about life and childhoods and love and fate and faith and music and Frank Sinatra. And then Tony fell in love with Caroline.

'It was getting so late and then eventually she says to me, "So, are ya gonna get out?" And I said, "Have you forgotten about the wheelchair in the back?" And she had.' And Tony beams a smile with a twinkle in his eye like a star over the Wynnum Jetty. 'She completely forgot about the wheelchair.'

'The wheelchair stuff fell away?'

'That's right.'

'Nothing but each other.'

'That's right.'

No disabilities to consider in the story of true love. A woman and a man and a quiet night. Two friends who became lifetime lovers that night in the quiet car.

'That was the fourth day of the fourth month of 2004.'

Tony proposed to Caroline three months later, outside Myer in the Carindale Shopping Centre, where he'd lost his wallet.

'You know when you know,' I say.

'That's right,' Tony says.

And I know he knows I know who Tony is travelling with in his mind when he sings that song of Frankie's about packing up and flying away.

'When she's unhappy I want to be there for her,' he says. 'When she's happy I want to celebrate with her.'

Love is ignoring the wheels. Love is Tony parking his wheelchair beside my desk for the morning on my busy corner. And Tony's by my side when I see a man pass who looks a bit like me.

*

The youngest of my three older brothers stops in the street. He's off to buy some ink for his printer. And he laughs and shakes his head when he reads my street sign because he knows I know he knows I was always the cheeseball in the family. Of course he'd stumble upon me sitting in the street asking people for love stories. I was always the soppy one. I was always the one crying and he was always the one saying, 'Don't waste your tears on that bullshit.' We shared bedrooms across Brisbane for close to fifteen years. I love him with that sacred kind of love that floats eternally in the disembodied, lights-out bedroom voices of childhood siblings who refuse to go to sleep until they're old and have kids and beer bellies and live safe and secure lives in the suburbs of the inner city.

I introduce Tony to the man standing next to me. 'He's my brother,' I say.

He ain't heavy. He's the guy who bought me *Vitalogy* for Christmas. He's the guy who turned me on to Kate Bush and David Lynch. He's the guy who dived in without a second thought when a thug meathead four years my senior blindside-crash-tackled me at a high school party in Brighton. He's the guy who got a beer bottle smashed across his face for his trouble. He's the guy who plays Scattergories and sings Taylor Swift songs with my kids. We hug for less than three seconds but I could hug this guy for three days if we had the time. Never enough time for the ones we love. Where did all the time go, bro?

Don't waste your tears on that bullshit.

'You hungry?' he asks. 'You need something to eat?'

Still looking after me after all these years. 'I'm all good, bro. Thanks.'

And we hug again and he drifts off into the city as my attention is taken by the man on Adelaide Street who is staring at the sky through a telescope made from a long Australia Post mailing tube.

*

'I look up at the sky and through that little blue circle it's just me and the universe and I love what I see,' says the man with the tube. 'There's no one to tell me in that circle that I need to go to work or that I made mistakes or that I need to find some money to buy another drink.' He tilts his head back. 'Ha!' he says. 'Another drink. Now there's a love story.'

His name is Nick. He wears an Adidas jacket over an AC/DC T-shirt with a picture of Angus Young and the words 'For those about to rock'. He wears black socks stitched with the words 'Mr Cool'.

'I need to get me one of those telescopes,' I say.

He passes the telescope to me. 'Have a look,' he says.

And I stare up at the universe through his cardboard telescope from my desk chair and I see a perfect circle of blue sky. So much peace and quiet in that circle. 'Wow,' I say, 'the focus.'

And Nick nods, looking up at the sky with his arms raised high and wide. 'That's too much sky to take in for one person, hey?' he says.

'Man, you're right, you gotta make it smaller to take it in. Make sense of it in bits.'

'That's gypsy stuff, man,' he says and I have no idea what he means by that. Gypsy stuff?

He points at Kim and the girls from the anti–CCP petition group. 'They're lovely those girls, aren't they?' he says.

'They are.'

He looks at my writing hat, a brown fedora, not unlike the one Indiana Jones wears. 'What are you, Steve Irwin?' he asks. 'Actually, you know who you look like?'

'Who?'

'Vince Sorrenti.'

Then he tells me about his other enduring love, something he often considers with the same awe and wonder he applies to the sky and the universe. 'Boobs,' he says.

*

Funny day at the office. Funny peculiar. Funny ha ha, too. An hour later, around lunchtime, my brother returns to my desk and hands me a curried egg sandwich in a takeaway storage box. And I know what love is. Love is two boys in a bedroom at midnight trading riddles. Love is two boys weathering the storms of suburban drunks. Love is knowing curried egg is your little brother's favourite sandwich.

CUMULUS PEOPLE

Love is risk. Love is cost. Love is what NASA scientists say about failure: how there's no such thing, only early attempts at success. Love is R Sculptoris, a red giant star that is slowly dying 1500 light years from earth. Love is a group of astrophysicists and astronomers using radio-wave data emitted from R Sculptoris in the throes of death to form a gentle musical melody. Love is a requiem for a dying celestial miracle. Love is a river with rapids and waterfalls and calm little bits you can row on and terrifying dark bits you can drown in and it's flanked by tall trees and leaping deer and tigers wanting to eat you alive and if you make it far enough along the river you eventually come to the bit that runs into the ocean and that's when you've learned enough about boats to be able to fix your sail and catch the wind and meet every one of your impossible horizons.

*

Love is Stephen Dibb not taking 'nut' for an answer. He wraps an arm around his wife, Lisa, at my desk on Adelaide Street. Stephen and Lisa run a custom-jewellery store in the Brisbane Arcade, a short walk from my writing desk.

'We see love every day,' Lisa says. 'We're making their wedding rings and engagement rings. We don't ever get over seeing it. We've had the business for thirty-three years. Love never gets old.'

The Dibbs have made jewellery for three generations of the same family. They'll make a girl's christening bracelet, then her engagement ring and then her eternity ring. They've made countless rings for brides and redesigned countless rings for defiant divorcees.

'We do mourning jewellery,' Lisa says. 'We did a beautiful piece recently for a man whose sixteen-year-old son had died. His son was a gamer, so the dad got a little golden game console made, with stones, so that he could wear it every day. It was beautiful. I remember one customer came in and she just said, "What happened to my beautiful life?" She had lost her whole nuclear family in a very short period of time. And some people turn to jewellery as part of their mourning. It's all about emotion. It's all about love.'

Stephen and Lisa went to the same primary school in Mount Gravatt East, in Brisbane's south, and then to Mansfield High School, in the 1970s. They knew of each other in school but not well enough to talk to each other. Then, out of school, after Lisa had travelled around Australia, one of her friends was hosting an engagement party. Lisa had no decent clothes to wear to the party, having spent all her money on travel, so she told her friend she would simply help prepare food in the kitchen all night and not mingle with guests. Stephen was at the engagement party and saw Lisa breeze through with a tray of food. He remembered her from school, but there was something different about her in adulthood. Something mesmerising. He nudged his best friend at the party. 'I think I'm gonna marry her,' he said.

'I was dating somebody else,' Lisa says. 'And I'd been married and that hadn't worked out. Then we went out together and then he asked me to marry him. He asked me three times, publicly.'

'What do you mean by "publicly"?' I ask.

'In front of family, three times, he just put it out there,' Lisa says. 'I was, like, "What is wrong with you?" And three times I said, "Nut." It wasn't even no. It was "nut". I'd been young and married before. I had decided at the ripe old age of twenty-five that if you're not good at something, don't do it. I was good at many things, but maybe just not marriage. So, he'd keep asking me and it was almost, like, "Hell no." He wasn't getting it. Like, "Stephen, this is not going to happen, let's just be happy, let's just choose every day to be together and not make anything formal." So, anyway, this backfires on me.'

'How did it backfire?'

'Well, then we decided to have a family. And then we discovered we couldn't have a child. Stephen's got no sperm. He's azoospermic.'

'And that's something that happens to me, but Lisa is the hero in this story,' Stephen says. 'She did the IVF, she took the drugs, she did the whole journey.'

'And that can be an awful journey,' Lisa says.

Gut punch after gut punch after gut punch.

'So we decided to try adoption because we'd always had it in our hearts,' Lisa says. 'But then we discover we can't even apply to adopt because we're not married. So then there's the guilt and the guilt was awful and then there we are getting married in the registry office with me crying because I feel so bad and so guilty when I should have just said yes and stopped mucking around. I loved him. We were always going to stay together.'

The adoption process took six years in total.

'But then we adopted two of the most divine Ethiopian daughters, Gedarm and Tarik. The most divine little girls in the world.'

Then Lisa started working in the adoption community and realised how few boys were being adopted by Australian mums and dads. 'Then we got a heads-up that the department was going to close adoption for eight years and process only ten files a year, so I helped organise four hundred people to protest on Brisbane's Goodwill Bridge and we stopped them and we got a promise of one hundred kids being processed for the next two years. Just ordinary people seeing something wrong and doing something about it.'

Then they adopted an Ethiopian boy. 'Yared,' she says. 'The most divine little baby boy. Then we meet Yared's birth family and we stay in contact with them and over the years they ask us to adopt his little brother, Amenty. And talk about love stories, they are all love stories, because then we find the girls' birth parents and grandparents and that was a love story, and we get to know the boys' grandparents and that's another love story. All these people who made these impossible decisions for their children. When we're in Ethiopia we all sit together as a family and we all make decisions together. We all think about what's going to be best for the kids, collectively. And that love story between all of us goes on.'

A perfect love story, all because Stephen wouldn't take 'nut' for an answer.

'All these things that knocked on from that,' he says, smiling. He holds up his iPhone and swipes to a family portrait. Six of the happiest people in the world. Lisa looks at the image for a long moment and she mentions a song she loves by Don McLean.

'"Perfect Love",' she says. It's a song about how everything going perfectly right in our lives means missing out on all the things that go wrong and lead us to perfect love in the process.

'So, what did you learn about love all through that journey?' I ask.

'Well, here's an original Lisa Dibb quote for you,' Lisa says. 'Love makes you a mountaineer. Love makes you climb mountains you never thought you'd be able to climb.'

```
Love is a river.
Love is a mountain.
Love makes you a mountaineer.
```

*

Memories of love from the life of Stephen Page, the Brisbane surrogacy lawyer sharing a sandwich with me over lunch. Some memories belong to the swamplands of human hate. Some belong to the sky. 'I remember one night my husband, Mitch, and I were out in Fortitude Valley celebrating my thirtieth anniversary as a solicitor,' he says. 'We'd had a lovely dinner at our favourite Chinese place, five minutes from our home back then. We're walking home and I'm on top of the world and I'm with the love of my life and it's been a perfect night and then a stranger calls out to us. "Faggots!" he shouts. That's happened to us in the centre of Melbourne. That's happened to us in Sydney. We've been blessed with a daughter, Elizabeth, who, as of tomorrow, will be twenty months old. We were at a park the other day, pushing Elizabeth on a swing and there's another guy there with his son and he starts giving us the stare. You know, the death stare, the one that's trying to say so much about how he feels about us.' Stephen sighs in his seat. 'True love still has some downsides in 2021.'

He remembers the day he met Mitch. It was Christmas, 2013. 'It was a Sunday afternoon and it was hot and I was wearing a red shirt, green shorts and foam reindeer antlers,' he says. 'We agreed to go on a date. We sent emails to each other to arrange the date and I was very busy at the time, so I speed-read Mitch's email where he said, "I'll bring my three-year-old daughter." I'm a surrogacy lawyer, so I know there are different ways to create a daughter and I was all for it. Then he turns up with his dog and he says, "Didn't you read my email? It said three-year-old *hairy* daughter."'

He remembers the surrogate who brought Elizabeth into this world. That woman made Stephen reconsider what he knew of human kindness. That woman rewrote his book of love. Elizabeth almost died during the birth. 'What do you say to a woman who endures all of that for you? How do you possibly thank her for giving you the gift of life? We can't imagine a world without Elizabeth in it now. We call her our jewel. Our surrogate gave us our jewel. Surrogates are magic women. To ask someone else to be a surrogate is a big ask, but she actually asked us. She said to us that she'd had a daughter, that she didn't want to have any more children. She said her uterus wasn't being used and she said she loved both of us and she wanted to be our surrogate. At which point, Mitch and I cried. Genuine tears of joy.'

Stephen nods his head and smiles. 'So true love still has some upsides, too, in 2021.'

*

A stocky man with a friendly face inspects Kath's typewriter. 'Can't make any mistakes with these,' he says. 'Hard to go back and change your mistakes.'

'Yep,' I say. 'Really got to know what you want to write before you write it.'

His name is Stephan Swart. He's just turned fifty. He says he makes and sells homemade greeting cards and invitations. He has a learning disability. 'Can't read and write,' he says. But that hasn't stopped him from selling some 750 homemade greeting cards in the past seven years.

'Love!' he muses, shaking his head in what seems like a mix of wonder and exasperation. He's been advertising in papers to find the right partner. 'I want to settle down and have kids,' he says. 'I want someone who will love me for who I am and not for who I'm not. It has been hard, but I haven't given up hope. I'll keep fighting till the end.'

A car brakes hard in the street, caught in a kind of no-man's land, the driver having gone through a red light but not wanting to cross a second red only fifteen metres away.

'Look at this guy!' Stephan says, laughing. 'Where are the cops when ya need 'em?'

Then a Mercedes Benz pulls up at the lights in front of my writing desk. 'Here we go,' Stephan says. 'Mercedes Benz. You know how much a single pump costs for one of those?'

'I don't,' I say.

'I had McDonald's once with a man who owned a Mercedes Benz. He showed me the receipt for a pump he'd just bought.' Stephan leaves some air in his speech for effect. 'One thousand dollars!'

'That does seem excessive,' I say.

*

It's 2 p.m. now and a woman in an emerald dress lets a woman in a blue dress rest her right arm on her shoulder while she slips a high heel off and then back onto her foot.

Then a woman named Jo Carlin brings me a coffee. A strong flat white in a takeaway cup. 'Thought you might need it,' she says.

She says she once lived next door to Sinatra crooner Tony Dee. They're great mates. She often buys Tony coffees when he's busking on Adelaide Street, so she thought she'd buy me one, too.

'That's incredibly thoughtful, Jo,' I say.

'It's nothing,' she says.

'No, it's really something,' I say. 'Buying a coffee for a total stranger. There's humanity in that.'

'Love is humanity,' Jo says. She scans the street. 'Love is in the air,' she says. 'I look around and I see beauty and love. I see it on people's faces. I see it in the birds. I see it out the window of the bus I catch into the city.' She's seventy years old. She wears a grey cardigan with a plastic frangipani flower pinned near its top button. She suffers from severe arthritis and she buses into the city most days to walk around and study the world and move her joints and muscles. She has hair like Judi Dench and she has a Dame Judi kind of warmth. She carries a shoulder bag filled with stories and books and things she's collected on her travels through the city today. She hands me a short story she's been working on for years. It's a love story about two peregrine falcons from Brisbane, Frodo and Frieda, who meet and fall in love and endure great hardship before marrying under a wattle tree in Brisbane's New Farm Park. The birds raise four baby chicks and live happily ever after. 'Frodo and Frieda,' she says and sighs. 'That's a beautiful love story.'

Jo was a sailor. She met her first love, Mark, a marine engineer, in Gisborne, a surf-beach city on New Zealand's North Island. When she was young and beautiful and weighed fifty-three kilograms, Jo and Mark sailed all the way from New Zealand to South Africa on a yacht. 'A thirty-foot sloop,' she says. 'I was twenty-five years old. Took us thirty days to cross the Indian Ocean. You could pull up in a port and trade what we had on the boat – salami, pumpkins, onions – with the locals for a bit of water. We followed our hearts and the dolphins followed us across the ocean.'

Years later, Mark and Jo split. She loved Mark, but she loved something else even more. 'Moving on,' she says. 'Travelling.' She boarded a container ship as a working passenger and sailed to America. From America, she flew to Europe, where she got a job in a chocolate nougat factory in France. 'I loved that nougat,' she says.

A young man named Ben stops by my writing desk, breaks Jo's train of thought. Sunglasses, blue shirt, green pants and black shoes. A necklace with a star-shaped woollen pendant. He carries a smooth pure-white rock in his left forefinger and thumb.

'I keep finding these white rocks,' he says. 'They say if you find a white rock it means God has tested you and you have passed his test. I'm not really religious but I keep finding these white rocks in front of the church. I think someone leaves them there intentionally for people to find.'

'I've not heard this,' I say, confused. 'What is this?'

'This is the second white rock I've found in front of the church.'

'You find enough of them you can play knucklebones,' Jo says with a smile.

Ben laughs. 'Well, I went and researched the meaning of the white rock and there's, like, a religious context to it.'

'It is a beautiful rock,' I say.

'It's very white,' Jo says.

'What I'm saying is, if someone is intentionally leaving them for people to pick up outside the church, then that's kind of a loving thing to do.'

I think I understand what he's saying. I guess we're all trying to pass our own personal tests of varying difficulty and complexity. How kind of someone, then, to place white rocks in obviously meaningful places to be found by those who might believe they are a sign they've passed a test.

'I think there's some religious person who wakes up and says, "I'm gonna sit this rock out there, just to put love out into the world,"' Ben suggests. 'And that might be a nice love story. I don't know … I know that's strange.'

'It means something to you, so that makes it beautiful,' Jo confirms.

'We can't be sure of anything,' I say. 'You have to take meaning wherever the hell you can get it.'

White rocks found in front of a church. Jesus images in your Vegemite toast. Love-heart clouds in the sky. The songs of Whitney Houston. Whatever gets you through the long and sleepless nights. It's all right.

'I can't be sure until I see the person planting the rocks,' Ben says.

After a brief discussion about what Ben will do with the smooth white rock he has found, he decides to keep it. 'I collect rocks anyway,' he says. He's going to place it in his garden at home. I tell Ben that the smooth pure-white rock, regardless of its origins, may now hold additional meaning for him as a reminder of a nice conversation he had with two random strangers on the corner of Adelaide and Albert streets.

Then Ben has an idea. 'Do you want the white rock?' he offers.

'I can't take the white rock,' I say. 'I think you were meant to pick it up.'

'I mean, it's just a rock, really,' he says.

'No, man, the more we're talking about that rock, the more meaningful the rock is becoming.' I tell Ben I'm going to start looking out for white rocks.

'Well, look for yourself, the big church down the road, you'll see them there.'

Ben walks on down the street, placing the smooth pure-white rock in the pocket of his pants.

Jo digs into her shoulder bag. She has some DVDs that she just hired from the city library. She holds up a copy of *Let the Right One In*.

'Pretty scary, Jo, brace yourself for that one.'

'I will,' she says, raising her eyebrows, more enticed than concerned.

She pulls out *Once Upon a Time in Hollywood*.

'Pitt at his very best,' I say.

'Is he?' she replies. 'I love Ryan Gosling.'

'So does my wife.'

For no particular reason, Jo gifts me an information page from the Bureau of Meteorology that she finds in her bag. It's a cloud classification sheet with pictorial examples of the various clouds in the Australian sky. She says I can enjoy myself each day here at my writing desk on the street by looking up and documenting the kinds of clouds floating above me.

Cirrocumulus: High level, small rippled elements, made of ice crystals.
Cirrus: High level, white tufts of filaments.
Cumulonimbus: Low level, very large cauliflower-shaped towers to 16 km high.

I look up at the clouds above me. Puffy individual clouds plopped into the blue like balls of cream dropped in coffee. Foamy balls of shaving cream in the sky. I scan my new classification sheet.

'Cumulus,' I say with confidence. And Jo gives a knowing and proud nod. She looks at the sky with me.

'It will rain Thursday and Friday,' she says. 'But not tomorrow.'

'Wow,' I say. 'You can read the sky like a sailor.'

'Nah, I just looked at the weather forecast.'

Now Jo shows me a deep cross-shaped scar on her leg. She says it relates to a story about one of the other great loves of her life. 'It was a car accident,' she says. 'My partner was dead by the time the ambulance got to him.'

It happened at Mon Repos, on Queensland's twinkling Bundaberg coast. She and her partner, Julian, had been on a field trip, studying birds. And if Mark was the first love of her life, then maybe Julian was the last.

'We were really, really involved with so much shit,' she says. 'He loved life like I did. We studied the birds together. We studied the clouds. We were crazy together. We used to go out looking for storms and everything.'

And she's sad now. She was a cirrus cloud only seconds ago, high and light. Now she's all nimbostratus, dark and low. She runs her hands across the scar on her leg.

'I spent four months in hospital recovering from that accident,' she says. 'They put me in an ambulance and they sent me to the Princess Alexandra Hospital here in Brisbane. I was there for four months and then I went to rehab at St Vincent's Hospital. And I got by there because St Vincent's had a lovely little church and I used to go and sit in there and it was beautiful. And I had a bed in St Vincent's by the window and it looked down over these beautiful gardens and, every day, I would see two peregrine falcons soaring through the sky out my window. That's when I started writing the love story of Frodo and Frieda, two peregrine falcons who fell in love and got married under a wattle tree at New Farm Park and had some babies.'

And they lived happily ever after, because that's how love stories are supposed to end.

PAY NO WORSHIP TO THE GARISH SUN

He wears pyjamas. Plaid cotton winter jammies, vibrant pink and blue. His hair: Robert Smith meets a manga movie. Yellow smiley-face earrings, big as ten-cent coins, hanging from his earlobes. That's not a walk and that's not a dance. That's a dance-walk. That's a walk with beat and rhythm, as though Barry Gibb is singing in his ear, urging him to retain the wonder he clearly has in staying, keeping, being alive.

And then he stops on the spot to show me his Instagram account.

A grainy handheld video of a young man jumping the fence at State of Origin III before fifty-three thousand people at Brisbane's Suncorp Stadium, November 2020. A young man wearing red and black plaid pyjamas, dashing across the hallowed rugby league turf of Lang Park, weaving between game-weary and perplexed members of the Queensland State of Origin team, including stout-hearted team captain Daly Cherry-Evans, who watches the young man in pyjamas pause only metres from his grasp to execute a well-practised floss dance.

'That's me,' he says.

'That really is you,' I say.

'I love pyjamas,' he says. 'And I love flossing.'

Flossing, the man in the pink and blue pyjamas explains, is a rapidly dating dance move requiring participants to repeatedly swing their arms with clenched fists from the back of their body to the front in the same motion one might use when flossing an errant chunk of Scotch fillet wedged between two molars.

His name is Johnson Wen. He says he's twenty-one years old, which is older than the floss and younger than the bus stop, and I'm not talking about the bus stop where Jo Carlin is waiting for the 435 to Brookfield. I tell Johnson in return that my name is Trent Dalton and I'm forty-two years old, which is older than the moonwalk and younger than the moon.

'I'm writing a book called *Love Stories*,' I say.

'Book of the century,' Johnson says, unequivocally.

I immediately take a liking to Johnson's optimism.

'Anyone who stops, I ask them to tell me a love story,' I say. 'What does it feel like to be in love? What on earth is love anyway? What do we do when we lose it? What do we do when we're neck-deep and drowning in it?'

'Shakespeare is …' Johnson says, enigmatically.

'What do you mean by that?'

'In love,' he says.

'Yes, he is.'

Nobody more in love than Shakespeare. In it, beside it, on it, around it, within it, without it. Shakespeare is.

My bounty is as boundless as the sea
My love as deep; the more I give to thee
The more I have, for both are infinite.

It follows. Shakespeare knew how it follows. Love multiplies. The more of it we give, the more we get back in return. Basic business. Love business.

'I just love wearing pyjamas,' Johnson says. 'That's my love.'

Johnson only ever wears pyjamas. Day or night. Somehow he pulls off the look. He funks it up. He turns the humble jim-jam up to 11. It's the hair, the earrings, his multi-coloured sneakers. He lives in Toowong, in Brisbane's inner west. Four years ago he had some boring errands to run at the local shopping centre. 'I just decided to wear my pyjamas,' he says. 'A lot of people laughed and that made me laugh and, I don't know, I just decided to keep wearing pyjamas every day. I just did it for myself. I only wore them for myself. I didn't care a bit if people laughed or not.'

He was raised in Sydney and moved with his family to Brisbane. His father is Chinese. 'With a bit of American,' he says. 'Mum is Filipino with a bit of French.' Johnson was bullied in Sydney. 'Lotta fights down there,' he says. Johnson copped all the F-words in Sydney. 'Look at this little F,' he recalls, speaking softly now. 'I'm gonna F this F up. He's such an F-head.'

Johnson shrugs his shoulders then flosses on the spot.

'I wore these pyjamas in a stadium of fifty-three thousand people,' he says. 'I did not care one bit. I just rocked up to the game and I was like, "Screw it." I went to buy a packet of chips and a drink and I went down the stadium aisle and as soon as I got close to the field I literally slam-dunked the food on the ground and everyone in my section looked at me like, "What the F is this guy doing?" And as soon as I looked up, I'd jumped the fence. Then I just ran.'

'What did it feel like running around on that field in your pyjamas?' I ask.

'I felt free,' he says.

Love is not love
Which alters when it alteration finds
Or bends with the remover to remove.
O no! it is an ever-fixed mark
That looks on tempests and is never shaken

Johnson's Instagram account is filled with videos of him flossing in public places across the Brisbane CBD in his pyjamas: the Myer Centre food court, the Queens Plaza intersection on Adelaide and Edward streets, in the middle of Queen Street Mall. Early in November 2020, Johnson was fined $250 for dangling himself from the Museum and Cultural Centre footbridge at Brisbane's South Bank. He says he was on Xanax at the time and can't remember the incident. The presiding judge said he 'behaved like a bit of an idiot'. Johnson said he would behave better.

When Johnson talks, his arms flap about wildly. Random dance moves. Nervous-reaction leg kicks and rolls.

A woman passes his left shoulder carrying a shopping bag. 'Put your hands down!' she barks, aggressively.

Johnson and I both know it's not the wild-moving hands the woman hates. She hates the fact a young man is standing in the centre of the Brisbane CBD in his PJs. Johnson shoots his arms theatrically down along his thighs like a military recruit on parade.

'What's with that?' I ask.

'People hate me,' he says. 'People want to kick me in the head. I would actually let them. Kick me as hard as you can.'

'Johnson, who do you love most in this world?'

'I literally love everyone,' he says. 'Equally. I love every single person the same as I love my parents. Every person in this city needs love.'

He flicks his arms in a rolling-wave dance move and casts his eyes across the city.

'People keep laughing at me, but I just don't mind. They say, "This guy sucks, stop wearing pyjamas."'

'They just wish they had half your courage.'

Johnson is brave. Johnson is rash and reckless. And young. Johnson is Romeo. Johnson is Juliet. Shakespeare is:

Come, gentle night; come, loving, black-browed night;
Give me my Romeo; and, when I shall die,
Take him and cut him out in little stars,
And he will make the face of heaven so fine
That all the world will be in love with night
And pay no worship to the garish sun

And I know what love is. The ones we love are the stars in our black skies, blinking every evening after dinner to remind us that the darkness stretches out forever but the darkness does not win this thing.

'I had someone in a restaurant laughing at me because I was wearing these pyjamas,' Johnson says. 'But I just thought, "Live life. Do something crazy. Live life up and keep rocking pyjamas."'

Pay no worship to the garish sun, Johnson Wen.

'Maybe that's the trick,' I say. 'Living life up instead of down.'

'It's going to be messed up one day when I go to my wedding dressed like this,' Johnson says. 'People will laugh.'

'Probably.'

Then a new thought seems to drop like a heavy bass beat into Johnson's mind. 'Would you freak out if you saw me flossing at the Superbowl one day?'

'I wouldn't freak out,' I say. 'I'd just say something like, "Yep, that's Johnson Wen. He loves to wear pyjamas."'

Johnson gives a high-five and he shuffles on down the street, his limbs flapping in all directions because there's only one F-word he ever hears now. Floss.

THE LAST OF THE ROWING WHALERS

Bob Stafford has two love-hearts tattooed on his right thigh. An exotic smoking volcano foregrounding a rising sun tattooed on the topside of his right hand. Bob's tatts remind me of my late father's tatts. My old man's tatts were homemade and cheap-tatt-shop jobs that reflected his passion for the sea and the unanswerable and therefore grim purpose of existence. *Moby Dick* whaling ships and skulls and crucifixes. His outlook on life could well have been summed up by the two words he had tattooed on the inside of his bottom lip: *Fuck off*. In the latter years of a rich but penniless life, he exposed this inside bottom lip tattoo reluctantly and usually only in response to a request from one or more of the four sons he raised for a long time on his own and loved even more than the Rolling Stones and Moreton Bay mud crabs. Or to deter particularly aggressive door-to-door salesmen who wouldn't take 'We're all good, mate' for an answer.

Bob wears a rust-coloured North Face cap over long rust-coloured hair and has a Viking beard so bushy a grandchild could lose a lollipop in it. Grey shirt, hard sun-cured skin. Denim shorts and a brown leather belt with a big gold buckle. The man is all bone and story. Sixty-eight times around the sun and a few love stories gathered along the way. Along the hard way.

'Check this one out,' Bob says, lifting his shirt up to his chest to reveal a smiling heavyset Buddha tattooed across his belly. Bob's belly is Buddha's belly. Buddha's belly is Bob's belly. It's a tribute, of sorts, to a mate he cared about and lost.

'This bloke was in the royal navy,' Bob says. 'Coming through Bangkok he got this tattooed on his belly. His was smaller than this one. I had a photo of it. Anyway, this bloke got himself into a bit of mischief with some bikies and he ended up being pushed off a bank.'

'Pushed off a bank?'

'Yeah, he got knocked on the head and pushed off a bank in his car.'

'Fuck, Bob.'

'Well, that's all beside the point. Point is, he got fuckin' killed.'

Bob slips his shirt back down. 'I took the photo in to a tattooist – bloke named Pete Davidson in Nowra, New South Wales – and I got this done up. Cost me $50.'

One pineapple for a permanent reminder of a lost mate. There have been worse trades in Bob's life. Love swapped for despair. Hope exchanged for a bottle of beer.

'I'm a bit bitter on this love fuckin' thing, Trent,' Bob says.

*

Bob dropped out of school early. He met Moira while he was working for the NSW forestry department in Picton, south-west of Sydney. 'I seen her at a party,' he says. 'One night stand.

I fucked off and when I came back she was pregnant. That kid's forty-three years old now.'

The family moved to Brisbane for the sunshine. Bob lopped trees for a crust.

'We had two more kids,' Bob says. 'Twenty years together. And then she left.'

Moira found another man. If a tree lopper's heart falls in a forest, does anybody hear?

'Does a heart ever repair after something like that, Bob?'

'I don't think so,' he says. 'Ripped out, mate. Just ripped out.'

'Were there dark times for you after that?'

'I hit the bottle quite severely, yeah. I was lopping trees by day and drinking far too much at night. Just beer. I didn't have a lot of money. Got a bit more now. But I turned into an alcoholic. I was quite bad. It's fucked me since, so much so that I can't drink anymore because I have one and I literally fall over. So that fucked that.'

We sit in silence for a moment. Bob strokes his beard. Sighs over life. Sighs over love. 'Sorry to unload on ya, Trent, but that's me and love.'

'Bob, I'm honoured that you gave me the true story. And that's just real life. That's just real love.'

'Trent,' Bob says, and I'm starting to like the way Bob says my name when he talks to me, 'it's probably not fair, mate, *buuttttt ...*' – and that's a 'but' that takes as long to fall from Bob's tongue as a Sydney blue gum takes to fall to a forest floor – 'I think I musta been an arsehole.' He nods his head, agreeing with the thoughts in his head. 'I blew it,' he says. 'She made my life so easy because she would do everything. She cooked, cleaned, made the bed, did the dishes. Then she'd go and make some scones or something.' Moira raised the kids right. Always well-dressed, always well-mannered.

'You gotta look at it right,' Bob says. 'I blew it.'

'Bob, that's kinda beautiful that you can see it like that.' Clarity takes time, I guess. So hard to see the old growth forest for the trees. All the fault lines and all the little earthquakes, the myriad ways that Bob could rile her.

'Like, her name was Moira, but I found that quite a mouthful of a word to say, so I always just called her Sue,' Bob says. 'When we separated she went around telling all of her friends, "I'm not Sue anymore. Don't call me Sue. My name is Moira. Sue is what that prick used to call me."' Bob laughs, turns his palms to the sky. 'Sue was so much easier to say.'

It was a woman named Glenda who saved Bob from the drink. 'Glenda' rolls off the tongue just fine. She ran job despatches at the tree-lopping firm he worked for. They lived together for a time.

'That woman saved my life,' Bob says. And he wonders now about miracle timing. The way the universe sometimes sends the right person to you at precisely the right time. 'Just that one person who says you're worth something after all.'

I ask Bob if he remembers the love his parents had for each other.

'I never saw my parents together,' he says. 'They separated before I was born. In fact, I think they separated *because* I was born.' Bob adjusts the way he's sitting, speaks softly now. 'I don't think I belonged to the man she was married to at the time.'

Bob remembers boyhood arguments between the adults in his world. A lonely boy in a bedroom and raised voices echoing down the hallway with the most traumatising of messages: 'He's not yours. You can tell he's *not fucking yours!*'

And now there's a hole in my stomach. The hole is filled with something warm and heavy and I realise it's taken less than an hour talking to Bob to feel deeply for him. 'I'm so sorry you had to endure that, Bob.'

Bob slaps my shoulder. 'It is what it is, mate. Just the way life was. I'm just glad you're listenin'. You're giving me time to vent.'

'That's what this book is,' I say. 'That's all storytelling is. Time to vent.'

Bob laughs. 'I saw you talking to pyjama boy,' Bob says.

'Yeah. Sweet guy.'

'What's his story?'

'He just loves pyjamas.'

Bob nods his head twice and then, maybe because he feels he's ready to, he tells the deepest love story he knows. The one about how his father was mean and angry when Bob was born and how his mother's father, a good man named Joe Timms, decided to take him in and raise him as his own.

'My grandfather had raised twelve kids of his own and still took me in,' Bob says. 'He was an old whaler out of Eden. He was the last of the old rowing whalers, if you know what I mean by that.'

Whales lit the world up in the nineteenth century. Whale oil powered lights and lubricated machines and gave all those tireless and underpaid industrial revolution workers soap to scrub across their coal-black cheeks. In 1814, a young English mariner named Thomas Raine sailed for Australia as a junior officer on the convict transport *Surry*. A typhus epidemic wiped out nearly every passenger on that ship and Thomas Raine was the only surviving officer. In 1828, he established Australia's first whaling station in Twofold Bay, off the coast of what is now Eden, on the New South Wales South Coast. A century later, Bob's grandfather, Joe Timms, hunted whales in the 1920s and 1930s during the slow and inevitable end of the Eden whaling industry.

'He used to row out there chasing giant fucking whales with harpoons,' Bob says, shaking his head at the thought of such a thing. 'I mean, you're rowin' out there and harpooning a whale and, you gotta understand, when you harpoon a whale it doesn't just curl up and die for you, sayin', "I've had enough, thanks mate."'

'Off you go,' I say, recalling the many months I listened to *Moby Dick* on audiobook driving to and from my first journalism job at the *Courier-Mail* newspaper.

'Yep,' Bob says. 'Just hang on for the ride. Then you gotta row all the way back, towing this ten-tonne fuckin' fish. He was a tough old bastard my grandfather.'

Kind, too. The evidence of his kindness couldn't be found in the décor of Joe's home. That was all teeth. Killer whale teeth and killer shark teeth nailed to old wood walls. The teeth had a smell: the scent of sea and adventure and death. The evidence of Joe's kindness was found in the year after year after year he guided young Bob Stafford through life. It was only when Bob got older, well into his late teen years, that he understood the burden his grandfather had taken on in guardianship.

'He was already getting on by the time he took me in, early sixties maybe, and he still took me in. He grabbed me right at the formative years of my life. He gave me my morals. I realise what that means now. You don't realise these things when you're two years old.'

Miracle timing again. Miracle kindness.

'Joe just came along at the right time,' Bob says. 'He showed me that somebody actually cared about me.'

'What happened to him?'

'He got a little bit senile and then he died,' Bob says.

We sit in silence for a moment as afternoon shoppers zip past us, grocery bags and shopping bags in clenched fists.

'Bob,' I say. 'I reckon that's a beautiful love story.'

'Yeah,' Bob says, nodding his head. 'Old Joe. I guess he's my love story.'

'Do you believe there's another love out there for you, Bob?' I ask.

He shrugs his shoulders, grimaces through his bushy beard. 'Well, I got two daughters and a son and I love them very much and that'll probably do me.'

I nod in agreement.

'Guess what name I gave my son?' Bob adds.

'What?'

'Joe,' he says.

LOVE AND THE INSTITUTE OF CHARTERED ACCOUNTANTS, 1913

Late lunch is always the same. AJ Vietnamese Noodle House on Charlotte Street. Combination egg-noodle soup with extra coriander and just enough chilli to make a man blow his nose once but never twice. Walking up Charlotte Street after lunch and Magda Haj Gido with the blue and gold fingernails is walking down Charlotte Street.

'Hey, Magda,' I say.

'Heyyyyyyy,' she replies, beaming.

'Did that money end up dropping into your account?'

She says the money didn't drop that day. But somebody kind bought her lunch. What goes around comes around. Love goes around comes around.

'See you 'round, Magda.'

'See you 'round.'

I stop outside Archive Fine Books in the old John Mills Himself building. Number 40, Charlotte Street. Look up at that blue sky above, that keen listener, and see the triangular pediment atop the brown brick building and the triumphant words picked out in the tall parapet, in raised rendered lettering: *John Mills Himself.* Could be my favourite building in Brisbane. I always wondered what those words meant as a kid. Why was John Mills so keen on announcing his aloneness? Or was he suggesting something more about how thrilling it is for the city of Brisbane to have John Mills himself – John Mills, the one and only – based here in this brick building in Charlotte Street? He was a printer and stationer who first traded under the business partnership Mills and Green. But by the time he acquired this building in 1918, Green had left the business and he was working by himself. Hence *John Mills Himself.* I guess that was a better building name than some of the obvious alternatives: Just Little Ol' Me, John Mills; John Mills On His Pat Malone; and Thanks for Nuthin', Green.

I wrote a short film once called *Glenn Owen Dodds,* starring the gifted and easy to love Australian actor David Wenham. It was about a mug punter named Glenn Owen Dodds who was, in fact, God, the almighty one, the big cheese, the thick-crust el-supremo, who happened to be overseeing the further development of the universe in between listening to the Flemington races on a crackling wireless inside a cramped office beneath the John Mills Himself building on Charlotte Street, Brisbane. In the film, Michael, a twenty-eight-year-old man hardly dissimilar to myself at twenty-eight, has a chance encounter with Glenn Owen Dodds, who is acutely aware of Michael's deepest fears and yearnings, highest among them being his desire to find his one true love. Over the course of a five-minute office conversation, Glenn Owen Dodds helps Michael come to terms with his past – not to mention his workmanlike and unremarkable penis – all the while orchestrating the film's climactic chance encounter between Michael and the one true love of his life. The moral of the film: what is for you will not pass you by. I based the character of Glenn Owen Dodds on my dear friend Greg Kelly, son of Kath Kelly, the very woman who gifted me the Olivetti typewriter that inspired me to start walking these city streets asking people for love stories.

*

Five or six people inside Archive Fine Books this afternoon, padding silently between the shop's deep and cavernous aisles of tall bookshelves stuffed with more than half a million second-hand and antique books exploding with stories of adventure, history, crime, horror, politics, philosophy, war, sport, music, motorcycle maintenance, quilt covering, crab catching, kite flying, dragster racing, moon gazing, Scrabble playing, glass blowing, cake baking and love. So many stories of love. People have had their weddings in this bookstore. There's romance in the walls. Desire between the dust jackets.

It's difficult for the shop's co-owner, Hamish Alcorn, to fully unpack the phenomenon here over the counter but he suggests there's something strange about those high and crowded bookshelves, something peculiar at the end of those long book aisles that comes over a particular type of die-hard book lover.

'Look,' Hamish says, leaning forward from his desk chair to shorten the distance between his voice box and my ears. 'Sometimes it makes people, how should I say this ... *stimulated*.'

Not uncommon to find lovers kissing down the back of the store. Not so long ago, Hamish and his wife and store co-owner, Dawn Albinger, were at home well after closing time when they received phone calls from Queensland Police. 'Every night before we close we call out just to check there's nobody still in here,' Hamish says. 'Before we had closed up that night, a couple had hidden themselves away in the storeroom at the back. I had to drive back into town and unlock the door to let them out. They might have been seventeen or eighteen and they were rooting in the storeroom. It wasn't just the police who were here when I arrived. Their parents were here and I walked in and I'd guessed what had happened immediately and I said straight up in front of their parents, "So you were having sex in my store room?"'

Some local Tinder users with a fondness for literature are now using Archive Fine Books as a romantic rendezvous point: *Walk to the back of the third aisle from the left. Look for me in the red dress holding a copy of* Lady Chatterley's Lover.

'We're not crazy about that,' Dawn says, laughing and resting an elbow on a counter stack of leatherbound antique books. 'By all means come here on a date because you love books, but not just to hook up and walk out!'

*

Dawn Albinger has one of those rare smiles you see regularly on anyone who has found the life that was for them and did not pass them by. She was good friends with Hamish as far back as the mid-1980s.

'I really liked her,' Hamish says. 'She was two years older than me and way out of my league. I was just a kid. We both went our different ways, had different relationships, both got married.'

And both those marriages ended. What is for you will not pass you by. What is not for you must be recognised as quickly as possible or a whole life will pass you by.

'We were the generation that first used Facebook to rediscover schoolfriends through social media,' Hamish says. 'Before that you just lost them. We found each other on Facebook and we went for a coffee. That was 2 February 2009.'

'I love that you remember the exact date,' I say.

'You always remember the day when everything changes.'

*

I remember the day everything changed for me: 10 January 2000. My first day as a working journalist. Many things happened that day. America Online announced it was buying Time Warner in a stock-trade deal worth $182 billion, then the largest stock-trade deal in corporate history. A scallop-dredging trawler named *Solway Harvester* set off on its final voyage from the town of Kirkcudbright, Scotland, only to sink the following day in heavy seas off the Isle of Man coast, killing all seven crew members. The armed wing of the Algerian political party, Islamic Salvation Front, disbanded after amnesty negotiations with the Algerian government. And at a table booked for eight journalists in a café in New Farm, Brisbane, at approximately 10.15 a.m., I sat down beside the woman I was going to marry.

*

Dawn was living in Perth in 2009 but on 2 February 2009 she was briefly staying at a friend's house in Brisbane. Halfway through the coffee catch-up, Hamish realised he didn't want the catch-up to end. He wanted the world to stop spinning and he wanted time to stop with it.

I reckon there have been maybe ten times in my life when I've been given the opportunity – the challenge – to be truly courageous. I'd say we get maybe ten or fifteen chances through a lifetime to be truly brave, to lay every one of our love and hope and fear cards down and find out who is courageous enough to pick them up. The sun was falling for Hamish Alcorn and time was nearly up. He fought the sickness in his stomach and his brain took a moment to temporarily shift its focus from Dawn's smile to matters of the future.

This moment was long enough for his brain to tell the salivary glands in front of his ears to lubricate and loosen up his mouth in readiness for speaking. This moment was long enough for his brain to engage the irritable construction-site foreman who exists in every man's head. This particular guy in Hamish's head was called Roger and he wore a hard hat and he was already overworked and overwhelmed by the task of building the towering scaffolding surrounding the cerebral megastructure that was Hamish's vocabulary, a permanently expanding complex formed across half a lifetime of book reading.

This moment was long enough for Roger to then bark his desperate orders at a lazy and well-rested guy in Hamish's head named Al, who was always sleeping on the job but was supposed to be in charge of constructing all potential sentences relating to human connection and true love: 'Listen, Al, we're gonna need somethin' special here. This poor bastard is in over his head and out of time. We need something brave, Al. We need something bold. We need something that will show Dawn

Love Stories

Albinger immediately how much he cares about her, how hard he's falling for her, maybe even how he's always been falling for her, tumbling helplessly, arse over tit, head over heels!'

Al sprang from his slumber and dived immediately into Hamish's vocabulary, emerging seconds later, arms filled with a jumble of mixed-up words that made little sense.

'What the hell's all this, Al?' Roger barked.

'It's not my fault,' Al said. 'He's not thinking straight. He's all love-addled. His thoughts are flyin' at a million miles an hour. These were the only words I could get my hands on.'

'All right,' Roger said, rubbing his chin. 'I guess they'll have to do. Load 'em up.'

Hamish turned nervously to Dawn in the café on 2 February 2009. 'Ummm ... look,' he said, cautiously. 'I know you've ... ummm ... probably got plans tonight ... but ... I haven't,' he said.

And what he meant by that was, 'You're the most incredible person I've ever met and so it makes perfect sense that you would have plans because I imagine every creature on this planet would like to spend some time with you tonight but, truth be told, not one of those creatures could possibly want to be in your company tonight as much as me and I have absolutely zero plans for the future beyond my rapidly developing plans to marry you.'

'Anyway,' Hamish says. 'She had to return to Perth, but we started a series of phone calls. And then it was Valentine's Day and I said, "Look, I've never been to Perth." Bought my ticket, got there the day before Valentine's Day. Before I went, I had organised flowers to be delivered on Valentine's Day. This was a big, bold risk for me. I was flying to Perth to see a girl I'd not even kissed before. By the time the flowers came the next day, we'd had our first kiss.'

261

'Are you normally the type of person who would do something so bold and so grand?' I ask Hamish.

'I guess maybe I am.'

I turn to Dawn. 'He flew four thousand kilometres across the country just to see you again?'

'I know,' Dawn says.

'That takes guts.'

'I know,' Dawn says. 'But I'd given him some encouragement. I knew from the moment we had that coffee that this was going to be serious. It was just an incredible sense of foreknowing. I felt it. Something fundamental occurred.' And Dawn's hands hover across her belly, trying to find the place where this feeling emerged from.

'I think you just defined true love,' I say. 'Something fundamental occurring. Did you know it was love, even that early on?'

She dwells on this for maybe two seconds. 'I was never in love with Hamish way back in the day,' she says. 'I was a bit older than him and I was involved with somebody else and it never crossed my mind, but I do remember having a moment once when he introduced me to his beautiful friend Brigita, who became his first wife. I was hit with this feeling that ... maybe I'd missed the boat.'

A clarity moment. A hit-by-the-emotion-truck moment.

'I was like, "Ohhhh, did I just miss a moment, did I just miss a beautiful opportunity?" I hadn't really ever thought about him like that until that moment. I thought about being with him at precisely the moment he wasn't available.'

'Dammmn,' I whisper. 'That's kinda beautiful. Kinda crushing, too.'

'Isn't that always the way?' Dawn replies.

But Hamish feels the timing was exactly right. True love and its miracle timing. 'We both agree that if we'd got married back then it wouldn't have worked,' he says.

'That's true,' Dawn says. 'We're better at relationships now.'

'What's the secret to good relationships?' I ask.

'The secret is shared values,' Dawn says. 'Find a project. Find something to do together.'

'We are together an insane amount of time,' Hamish says. 'Because we work together. Love is about building up trust. You build and build and build, and one mess-up in terms of just being straight with one another can put that growth back. Two people can trust each other a lot, but that takes time. It's about communicating your flaws as much as anything else.'

'Oh man, *owning your flaws!*' I say. 'Hamish, I swear I only realised the importance of that maybe five years ago and I've been with my wife for twenty.'

I swear I need to type the same message on a stack of one hundred palm cards and keep them stuffed in the third drawer down in the kitchen.

Please accept this card as my heartfelt apology. I am owning my flaws. I recognise the fact that this argument only started because I couldn't admit I was wrong. I got that one wrong, but I'm already working on getting things right. I should have just owned all my weapons-grade dickheadery in the morning because then we both might have enjoyed a

brighter day. We lost eight hours to anger
and frustration because I couldn't own the
mistake I made and I think I do that because
of ego and pride and maybe even because you're
so good and so right all the time and maybe
because you're wiser and smarter and clearer
than me and maybe because I'm terrified you'll
wake up one day and say, 'I'm so sick of this
motherfucker being wrong, I'm booking the
next flight to Los Angeles to be with Keanu
Reeves, who's more in my league.' And maybe
I just want to be perfect for you. I want to
be great for you, to show you how much I'm
grateful for you. And, yeah, it's probably
a bit related to that weird thing whereby I
think you're secretly comparing me to your
dad with whom I can't possibly compete because
he's goodness personified, wisdom personified,
kindness personified, and I don't know if I
have all that in me because I don't know what
proportion of being a good man is work and
what proportion of it is plain old blood, but
please know this: you are the love of my life
and you are the place my blood runs to. I'd be
bloated and dead without you. I'd be lost at
sea, literally. I'd be so lonely that, in an
act of incurable melancholy, I'd try to sail

solo around Cape Horn to find some semblance of
meaning to my life, and I would soon realise
that I'm directionless without you and would
be, thus, quickly sinking off the coast of
Easter Island. I've done the sums and I figure
I've only got roughly fourteen thousand days
plus half a winter, if I'm lucky, left on this
beautiful earth, and all I know to be true
in this world is how much I want to spend the
next fourteen thousand days plus half a winter
of my life with you and I'm so sorry I wasted
one of those days on my mistake.

Or maybe instead of palm cards I'll get a tattoo on my palm: *Sorry, I've been a dick.*

'Yes!' Hamish says. 'We can all be dicks sometimes.'

'I think it's about conversation,' Dawn says. 'Hamish has always been a fantastic person to have a conversation with. Right from the start. He was always reading. Always thinking. A conversation with Hamish is a journey.'

She smiles at her husband.

'And we've been having a conversation for twelve years now.'

I cast my eyes around the bookstore. All the greatest writers about love are in this room with us. Emily Dickinson. Emily Brontë. F. Scott Fitzgerald. Henry Miller. Virginia Woolf. John Keats.

You are always new. The last of your kisses was ever the sweetest; the last smile the brightest; the last movement the gracefullest.

'You have ready access to the greatest minds in history who attempted to define love,' I say. 'Has that helped you both learn any more about what that word means? Did any writers ever get close to the right answer?'

'Books are the greatest teachers, I think,' Dawn says. She turns to the bookshelves. 'There are many answers in there,' she says. 'But not every answer will work for you. The trick is finding the answer that works for you.'

And Dawn turns on her heels and runs her hands along a tall bookshelf filled with antique leatherbound books spanning the left side wall of the bookshop. She's finding an answer that works for her. She pulls an old hardback book from the crowded shelf. She reads the cover title. 'This book is called *The Institute of Chartered Accountants*,' she says. '*A List of Members, 1913*. Everyone needs to see this book.'

This book about accountants carries in it the meaning of love. Not in the words inside the cover pages. Not in the list of chartered accountant members from 1913. But in the black and white photograph that's been resting safely for precisely one hundred years between its front cover and opening page, an image of a young woman with deep eyes and a wide, loving smile. So much spirit in her gaze, so much fondness for whomever she's intending to take ownership of this portrait. Dawn flips the photograph over and reads a message from the woman in the image: 'With love, Gladys, 1921.'

'Even accountants have their sweethearts,' Dawn says. 'I hope he took the plunge after he received this photograph.'

'She's beautiful,' I say.

Dawn nods, wholeheartedly.

'Kinda girl you'd fly to Perth for,' she says.

Dear Whitney,

This is Trent from Queensland. Long-time listener,
first-time writer. Just wanted to say thanks for
the joy you bring to my house. Just a little place
in the northern suburbs of Brisbane, Australia.
A wife, two kids and me, the dad trying to get a
word in edgeways. The girls and I were watching old
music clips the other night. We went down a rabbit
hole of your videos. I remembered the first time I
saw you on the telly. You really wanted to dance
with somebody and I really wanted that somebody to
be me. Then we watched that clip of all clips, that
Moby Dick of love songs, that Ben Hur of ballads,
'I Will Always Love You'. The girls couldn't believe
what they were seeing. How long you held those
notes. In the time it took you to sing 'I', Sylvie
was able to go to the kitchen, fix herself a Milo
and sit back down on the couch.

  I told the girls about the first time I saw that
clip. Year 8, Tristan Tapuni's bedroom, on the last
day of the school holidays. We were scoffing potato
chips and watching music videos and we didn't want

that afternoon to end. Then you came on, sitting
on that chair in the snow, singing about moving on
and remembering and always loving. Like, really,
really loving. *Hardcore loving.* I turned to Tristan
Tapuni with a mouthful of Samboy Barbecue chips
and said, 'Dude, imagine being loved by someone the
way she loves Kevin Costner.'

When I was a kid I used to stare at music video
clips and imagine that I was the guy various
female pop stars were singing about in their love
songs. I wanted to be the guy that fell and was
caught by Cyndi Lauper, time after time. I wanted
to be the guy Madonna was reminded of whenever she
used the word 'cherish'. I wanted to drive away in
that fast car with Tracy Chapman. I wanted to be
Susanna Hoffs' eternal flame. I wanted nothing to
compare 2 me.

I was watching that video clip and damned if I
didn't start imagining a parallel universe where
I knew jiu-jitsu and semi-automatic pistols and
I was your bodyguard and we inexplicably fell in
love. If it was my job to be the guy who always
loved you back, then I woulda done that shit right.
I would have recognised the precious and fragile
global gift that was your voice box. Those notes
you hit were more valuable to the United States of
America than all the gold in Fort Knox and all the

nuclear bombs at the president's disposal. There should have been presidential launch codes for your singing voice. I would have made you cups of lemon-honey tea to soothe your throat. I would have made you minestrone soup to keep your vitamins up on tour. I would have had notepads in every room of our Los Angeles mansion so you could save your voice and just write me instructions on how much Vegemite you liked on your toast. I would have massaged your temples in our reading room after the Grammys.

How would you know that I really loved you? You would know it in the time I took to iron your Oscars gown. You would know it in the way I made you that You Am I and Powderfinger mix tape. You would know it in the taste of my freshly baked blueberry muffins. I would have danced with you anytime. I woulda been your somebody.

Anyway, that's what crossed my mind when I saw that clip. We moved on from your songs after that – what's left to climb after Everest, right? Just wanted to tell you it was a real moment for all of us.

And I know I said I just wanted to say thanks for the joy you brought to my house. But I guess what I'm really trying to say is this: fuck each and every last one of those people in your life

who didn't love you as much as you loved to sing.
And fuck all those guys who made you sad. I hope
somebody loved you, Whitney, the way you loved
whoever you had in your head the day you recorded
that song.

We will always love you, too.

Sincerely,
Trent

LATER RON

Wind blowing my writing hat off as I cross the Victoria Bridge. A young girl, maybe five or six, on a scooter speeding away from her father, who's telling her to slow down. 'Dad, I can't hear you,' she hollers back over her shoulder. 'Dad, I simply can't hear you.'

An information sign for tourists explaining how this bridge was destroyed in the floods of 1893. A memorial plaque for Hector Vasyli, an eleven-year-old Greek–Australian who worked as a newspaper boy and had so much love and admiration for returning World War I troops that he spent his earnings on cigarettes, chocolates and flowers to give to sick and injured soldiers. On 9 June 1918, he was handing cigarettes and chocolates to a procession of shell-shocked soldiers when a vehicle, swerving to avoid hitting another vehicle in the procession, struck him and fractured his skull. He died before he could receive hospital attention. *In his veins ran the heroic blood of Greece*, the memorial reads. *And in the breast of a child he carried the heart of a man.*

The 204 bus to Carindale and an ad for the movie *Black Widow*. The 160 bus to Garden City. The City Buzz bus making its rounds through the CBD. The blue building that looks like it belongs in Gotham City. The construction work being done for a new casino precinct by the river. Cranes across the city that look like long-necked storks picking insects from the tops of half-made buildings. Endless signs of the city. *Detour ahead. Local traffic only. Walk. Don't walk. No smoking. One way. Park here. Share the road. No skateboards.* The sign language of a city. *Buy two get one free.* The sign of the busker on Albert Street singing 'Baby Come Back': *Be the reason someone smiles today.*

I set up the writing desk and chairs on the corner of Adelaide and Albert. A teenage boy with long blond hair and baggy jeans speeds past on a BMX, bunny hops up the gutter of Adelaide Street, nearly clips a woman carrying a bag full of plush toy love-hearts.

An elderly woman with a smile like a sunrise over Uluru sits beside me. Emily Wellock sits so close we're nearly rubbing elbows. She has auburn hair and wears a gold watch on her left wrist. She looks up at her partner, Ron, who stands four metres away from us, in a striped white and blue shirt and grey slacks. 'See that smile on him,' she says. 'It means he's got the shits. He's getting impatient.'

Emily is ninety-one years old. That's old enough not to be rushed when you're telling a good story. She moves with a walker because she's had a few falls recently.

'Love stories!' Emily smiles. 'Mine weren't no love stories.'

There have been three men in her life.

'Richard the First.' She laughs. 'Roy the Second.' She points at Ron. 'And this is Ron the Third. They were all bloody Rs.'

That's a Lancashire accent. Emily tends to use 'were' in places where others would use 'was'. As in: 'It were 1963 when I came to Australia with my second husband.'

That's the sound of a town called Colne, north-west England, where, as a nine-year-old girl, Emily sold chopped wood to help put food on the family table at the beginning of World War II. She sold newspapers. She collected bottles on the streets. She sang Christmas carols door to door for spare change. Trudged from house to house with a coal-black face, cleaning out fireplaces.

Her father was a hard man and her first husband was a harder man, who died when Emily was twenty-one and left her as a widow with two kids.

'Do you know much about mills?'

'Mills?'

'Yeah, cotton mills,' she says. 'Well, he were unloading a wagon one day and he got caught in the machinery of the mill, took him round and round the machine.'

She met her second husband, Roy Wellock, at a fair in Nelson, a town seven minutes' drive from Colne. She was waiting in line to go on a sideshow-alley fun ride called The Caterpillar. 'Shall we go on together?' asked the man standing behind her in the line.

'I'm married with two children,' Emily said, promptly, which wasn't a lie because she never considered herself unmarried from Richard just because he was dead.

'So am I!' Roy exclaimed, and that was a bald-faced lie that he maintained just long enough to win himself a spot beside Emily on The Caterpillar.

'And then we sat on a park bench afterwards because Roy couldn't afford another ride,' Emily says. 'I fell in love with him when I met him.'

Roy rode her home on his motorbike and Emily can't remember what was more exhilarating – the wind in her hair that night or wrapping her arms around his stomach to hold on for dear life, or the kiss he gave her when they reached their destination. She was certain she would never see him again because he'd told her he had to ride to Blackpool the following morning. But the next night she heard a knock on her door. And she found Roy Wellock standing on her doorstep.

'I thought you had to go to Blackpool?' Emily asked.

'I did,' he said. 'But I had to see you more.'

'We'd only been here in Australia for twelve months when my husband had a coronary occlusion, which is a fancy term for a heart attack,' she says. 'He lived until 1995.' Emily sighs and gives a half-smile. 'I'm still married,' she says. 'I've been married since 1949.'

I ask Emily about finding Ron in her twilight years. 'Did you think you would ever find another love later on in life?'

And she laughs and points at Ron. 'Well, I call him my "Later Ron",' she says. 'I found him *later on*.'

And Ron hears his name being spoken and he sits beside Emily out of curiosity as much as concern. It was Emily's granddaughter who paired them up. They were both living in Redcliffe, seaside north Brisbane. They were having a drink in the now-closed Palace Hotel at Woody Point, where the Bee Gees played their first paid gigs as boys. Emily's granddaughter demanded Ron introduce himself to her grandmother. 'My granddaughter then told me I had to speak to him and I said, "I don't want to meet anybody. I'm happy as I am." She told Ron how old I was and he said to himself, "Bloody hell, I don't want an older woman."'

'How old are you, Ron?' I ask.

'I'm eighty-five,' he says. 'I'm her toy boy.' He playfully elbows Emily and gives a wink. 'She wouldn't leave me alone,' Ron says. 'She wanted to take me up to the clubs all the time.'

'Bullshit,' Emily says. 'He kept ringing me up, seeing if I was home.'

'Tell me honestly, Ron,' I say. 'Did you expect to find someone like her so late in life?'

'Never in a hundred years,' he says, dead serious. And he looks at Emily as a tear forms in his eye. 'I'll never find someone like her again.'

Emily squeezes Ron's left thigh and plops her head on his left shoulder.

'Come on, let's go,' Ron says. And Ron helps Emily to her feet and she pushes her walker on towards George Street.

See you later, Emily Wellock. Later Ron. Thanks for being the reason I smiled today.

SQUARE TWO

Jo Carlin was right. It's Thursday and it's raining. Heavy rain drops love on a city. A working mum at the crossing with her kid. Nobody loves like she loves, the way she holds the umbrella for her toddler son in the puffy jacket and yellow gumboots. The kid splashes in puddles as he crosses the street, splashes water across the bottoms of his mum's black business-suit pants, which look new and expensive. She sticks the umbrella out for the kid, who could not care less about getting wet, and she takes all the rain for herself.

`Love is taking all the rain for yourself.`

Love is the email on my phone from Stephen Dibb, the jeweller who wouldn't take 'nut' for an answer. Last week, I sent him a rough draft of the brief love story I'd written about him and his wife, Lisa, and their four kids.

Hi Trent,
Thanks for touching us so deeply with your writing. Let me
explain. When I received your story I was in a pub in central

Queensland after a week of freezing camping at Carnarvon
Gorge on a father and son camp. It was the first email I had seen
all week due to no reception. I was so surprised and delighted I
started to read it aloud to my mate and the four boys. The tears
streamed down my face as I got about halfway. My son, Amenty,
was worried, as he had never seen me cry. I couldn't get through
it so, at 14, without hesitation, Amenty picked up my phone
and continued to read to us with a hand on my shoulder. I guess
that's another example of love. Thank you for your ability to distil
emotion. Lisa will be in touch with a few typos.

Regards,
Stephen Dibb

That's the thing about real-life love stories. They don't end. They build upon themselves. New characters can enter the narrative, new events colour the meaning of the story.

An email lands from Ben Stafford, sailing on another cargo ship that's taken him far away from his wife, Sarah, in Perth and his boys, Finn and Will. He's just read a draft I sent him of his story, which blended with the tale of the mighty Reuben Vui with the gold-flecked cuspids.

Thanks so much for sharing part of your book with us. It took me
a few days to get through your email, as I was initially reading it
whilst in a training centre, proving I could drive a crane, among a
bunch of rough sailors, and had to stop when I began to tear up.
Now it's 21.00 and I'm sitting alone in my cabin, with a mug of
rum, on board a dredging vessel in the North West, reading the
second half and Reuben's beautiful story has made the tears come
even more.

Love is a Facebook message that pings on my phone. A totally unexpected and random message from the best and scariest fighter in my neighbourhood of Bracken Ridge and Brighton, outer north Brisbane, when I was growing up. 'I had a disagreement with your brother, which involved myself and [insert name of equally lethal scrapper who may now have bikie connections],' he writes.

That 'disagreement' was a bloody and brutal fist fight in the dark pedestrian tunnel that ran underneath busy Bracken Ridge Road. This guy was dangerous with his fists when he was fourteen. By the time he was eighteen or so, when the 'disagreement' occurred, he was Mike Tyson meets Mad Max meets a meteorological phenomenon. 'I never knew the situation you guys were in,' he writes. 'My sincere apologies to your brother.'

Another message from him pings, seconds later. 'Might not make sense, sorry. I read *Boy Swallows Universe*.'

And now I know the distance between love and hate. It's the width of a five-hundred-page love story.

There's an email on my phone from a man named Alex Wittmann. He's the husband of Rhonda Wittmann, the woman who helps her best friend, Rachele, so beautifully when she's lost deep in her head. Alex is a counsellor and educator who works in, among many areas, post-suicide support. He has written a number of academic papers about love and the misunderstandings of what love is and how it affects our relationships. He passes on what he calls a 'teleological' definition of love. 'A teleological definition is one based on what something *does* – its impact and purpose – not what it *is*,' he writes. 'The analogy might be that love is like the sun. We cannot look directly at it, but we see our world because of it, and experience its many life-sustaining functions. Essentially, the "teleological" definitions of love point to it nurturing, healing and transforming humans (and societies) into the best versions of themselves. Much like the sun, love *nurtures* and *sustains* humans. At the fundamental level, it seems, love's purpose is growth – the growth of self and others.'

Love is like the sun. Love is growth. And I can say with all of my heart that I have grown in ways I never imagined, just sitting here on this corner hearing love stories from total strangers.

*

Here's a man now passing down Adelaide Street with a wide blue and white umbrella that he is offering to complete strangers, one of whom, a grey-haired woman in a thin see-through green raincoat, is grateful to take shelter under it as they wait for the little green man to say it's safe to cross the road. Not far from those two is a tall eucalypt sticking out of a perfect circle of soil cut into the Adelaide Street footpath. This stout thing loves a drink of fresh rainwater. The tree has no limbs because its relentless branches were stretching out and scratching the sides of passing council buses, so now it resembles a yellowed stick of supermarket celery.

Not far from the celery tree, an old friend of mine, Dom, is selling *Big Issue* magazines under an awning this morning, by the entrance to an H&M fashion store. I met Dom when I was doing a writing project six years ago with the 139 Club homeless shelter in Fortitude Valley. I spent a month in the 139 Club asking homeless people to tell me about the loves of their lives. I still can't say why exactly I felt like that was something worth doing, but it turned out to be one of the most fulfilling things I've ever done. Dom was the shelter's pool champion. He and his partner in life and eight-ball, a woman named Kid, spent hours in the shelter's upstairs activities hall, crushing all-comers in endless doubles eight-ball games on a well-worn pool table, stopping only for a feed of meat and three veg in the shelter's ground-floor kitchen and dining room. Dom told me over a game of eight-ball that true love is just another game of eight-ball. 'You gotta be patient,' he said. 'Some days, every ball will drop in the pocket for ya. Some days, you can't even reach the cue ball! You gotta be patient. You just gotta keep racking up.'

`Love is racking up. Love is reaching the cue ball just when you think it can't be reached.`

'Slow day,' Dom says, holding a *Big Issue* up to his chest. 'Rain.'

Dom wears a red polo; long black hair tied in a ponytail. By his feet is a backpack filled with his lunch and other belongings. On top of the bag is a portable EFTPOS pad that's made things easier than ever for Dom to sell his *Big Issue* magazines.

'How ya been, Dom?' I ask.

'Honest?' Dom says. 'Covid-19 came March 2020. I was doing well up to that March. Then the city shut down on 29 March 2020. Automatically, this place was a ghost town. Nobody didn't wanna know nobody.'

Dom stopped selling magazines in the city. 'Then we all came back around June 2020. After that we had to wear masks. My mind was working over and over and over. Too many thoughts in my head. I was watching too much news. All these people around the world who we lost. Italy, France, America.'

'Same,' I say. 'Read too much Covid news. Fucked with my head.'

'I brought a transistor radio in here with me and I had an earpiece in my ear, tuning in to all this horrible news,' Dom says, shaking his head like he's wondering why he was such a glutton for bad-news punishment.

Dom lives in a small unit in Nundah, on Brisbane's northside. He caught the 6.31 a.m. train in to Central this morning and was on his selling post by 7 a.m.

'I like this spot,' he says. He looks up to a CCTV camera fixed to the awning outside H&M. 'Cameras. Good security.' He points across the street. 'Big brawl over there a while back,' he says. 'I see it all.' He looks up to the CCTV camera. 'So do the cameras.'

I remind Dom what he told me about love six years ago in the 139 Club. Love is a game of eight-ball. 'Where are you at with love these days?' I ask.

'Love is helping others,' he says. 'You see someone sad, you lift them up. Buy 'em a cup of coffee. That's what I do. Don't leave someone at square one.'

Love is taking someone to square two with you.

Love is everything that happens at square two.

He's still in love with Kid. They play eight-ball now at a Red Cross community centre in Bowen Hills, two train stops from the city, where Dom is a volunteer helper. '139 Club hasn't got a pool table no more,' he says.

'Bummer.'

Then a young woman with blonde hair gently interrupts our conversation. 'Excuse me,' she says. 'We're just ducking into H&M, could you please mind this bike? We won't be long.'

No problem. The woman says her boyfriend just needs to buy a new shirt for an appointment he has today in the city. The young woman wheels an expensive mountain bike between where Dom and I are standing, leans it next to us against a shopfront wall.

'Nice bike,' Dom says, raising his eyebrows. 'Look at the wheel rims. That's quality.'

I make some notes in my notepad and Dom takes an interest.

'So, what are you writing about now?' he asks.

'I'm doing a book about love,' I say. 'I'm just jotting something down now about how this city is a million interconnected love stories. These stories are moving past us every hour of every day.'

I ask Dom about the people he's loved most in his life. He talks about a local man named Gary who taught him everything there was to know about eight-ball. Gary died in 2015 and Dom still misses him dearly, thinks about him often when he's out on this street selling magazines. He thinks of him on rainy days like this one.

'He taught me how to hide the white ball in a game,' he says, 'how to shut a good player down by snookerin' him for an hour. He showed me how you stretch one game out to three hours if you need to. Play the mental game. Snooker the livin' daylights out of 'em.'

It was Gary who showed Dom how eight-ball is like life. Be patient. Be happy with what you got. Don't always go for the quick win. Don't always go for the glory play. Hide that white ball behind your ball on the cushion. Don't be afraid to play it safe but know when you gotta go for broke, and if that means a jump shot over the blue 10-ball to drop that burgundy 7-ball in the corner pocket then you better fucking go for it, son, because life is short and games of eight-ball don't always go for three hours.

Dom watches people pass. Most smile when he gives them a thumbs-up and some don't react at all and only a few quicken their steps.

'I've had people scream at me, swear at me,' he says. 'One woman called me a bastard for selling the magazines. I just burst out laughing. I had one bloke get right up in my face and scream at me. I told him to have a nice day.'

Breathe in with the love, breathe out with the hate. Dom nods to a homeless man across the road setting up a cardboard sign asking for gold coins. I tell Dom how I did that myself once, when I was twenty-seven years old. I was writing a longform journalism feature about homelessness in Australia and I'd settled on the flawed idea of actually living homeless and penniless for a week to fully know what homelessness feels like. That's a flawed idea because I always knew, in the end, I was lucky enough to not know what it felt like to be without a home and, worse, without love. I was another lucky suburban bastard with love on tap. That said, I still felt every bit of the shame and sorrow that came with sitting behind a cardboard sign asking for gold-coin donations in front of the Tiffany's jewellery store in Queen's Plaza, some thirty seconds' walk from where Dom and I are now. I'll never forget the look in the eyes of a girl who passed by me, maybe eight years old. 'Don't stare,' her mum said, taking the girl's hand. And something about the way that girl looked at me broke my heart in two, not because there was disgust or freak-show curiosity in her stare, but because there was only kindness and compassion and love in it. I made a total of $2.50 that day and I spent that money on a second-hand book I found in Archive Fine Books in the John Mills Himself building on Charlotte Street. I gave that second-hand book to a homeless woman in her late sixties I had befriended on the street. Her name was Irene. She slept each night on the long bus-stop bench seats lining Adelaide Street, just metres from where Dom and I are standing. Irene had told me there was only one man in her life who could be depended upon, day in, day out, to make her laugh and make her see the lighter side of life and, in turn, somehow make her want to wake up each day and carry on. That man was Hagar the Horrible, whom she caught up with every morning without fail in the comics pages of discarded *Courier-Mail* newspapers. And that's why Irene shed a tear or two when I gave her the Hagar the Horrible annual that I'd bought from Archive Fine Books.

'Someone asks me if I've got a dollar, I say, "Yeah, I got a dollar,"' Dom continues. 'Then I take him around the corner to the 7-Eleven and I spend my dollar to buy him a coffee. You should remember that.'

'I will remember that, Dom, thanks.'

I look down at the young woman's mountain bike resting on the wall beside us. We've been watching over it for almost half an hour now.

'Hey, Dom,' I say, 'you think this woman's coming back for her bike?'

'She's gotta come back,' Dom says. He inspects the bike. 'This bike's too expensive not to come back for.'

And, on cue, the young woman emerges from the H&M store.

'I'm sorry,' she says. 'My partner's still in there, shopping.'

Her name is Mia. Her partner's name is Troy. She says they've been together for just over a year. 'But I love him to bits,' she says. 'He makes me feel beautiful every day.'

Then Troy appears over Mia's shoulder. He looks about forty years old and fit and wiry. The bike is Troy's. He went for a long ride this morning through the city.

'I've just been telling this man how much we are in love,' Mia says.

Troy smiles and drops his head back, taking a breath. 'This woman saved my life,' he says. And here outside the H&M store on Adelaide Street, Troy leans on his mountain bike and gently tells the story of why he loves Mia and how she saved his life.

'I'm almost at the end of a childhood abuse claim in court,' he says, softly and carefully. 'We're suing the government for institutionalised abuse from back when I was in juvenile detention.' He says abuses he experienced as a boy inside Brisbane's notorious and now mercifully defunct Sir Leslie Wilson Youth Detention Centre caused him to become a heroin addict at the age of thirteen.

I tell Troy that I know about that detention centre. I've written journalism pieces about it. Brisbane's Shine Lawyers have been representing abuse survivors from Sir Leslie Wilson for years. Their website offers a brief summary of the widely documented abuses that occurred at the centre across a period of four decades:

Many victims who we represent speak of daily emotional, physical and sexual abuse. No schooling was offered, sedatives were readily administered to those who didn't require medication and organised violence was sanctioned. Solitary confinement was another regular occurrence and a paedophile known as 'Lurch' is known to have sexually abused dozens at Wilson Detention Centre as well as bringing other paedophiles into the centre.

'Feel like I been a heroin addict all my life, until not so long ago,' Troy says. 'I'm almost forty and I spent … *fuck* …' – he runs his right hand across his scalp – 'maybe sixteen, seventeen years in prison and detention all up.' Countless crimes over that time, he says. All junk-related. 'Anything, really,' Troy says, openly. 'From stealing to selling drugs to fraud. Anything to gain money in order to gain drugs.'

He says the abuse claim unfolding now in court is attempting to determine what percentage of Troy's multiple drug-related crimes and myriad punishments can be directly linked to institutional abuses he suffered as a child. He'll be the first to tell you he deserved every one of those punishments, but the trick of it all is tracing backwards to find the things he didn't deserve as a boy, which led to the crimes he committed as a man. Troy calls this the 'tug-o'-war' and it's a war that threatens to break him, daily. What he hates is the fact that a bunch of educated men and women in suits are reducing an incredibly complex existence down to a percentage, down to a simple mathematical equation. Abuse plus crime divided by punishment multiplied by time equals money.

'I found it hard to give a shit about all that when I was younger,' he says.

But giving a shit about child abuse in his adulthood is proving harder still.

'Put it this way, eighteen months ago my plan was to get my payout, use the money to buy heroin and kill myself with an overdose. Because it was just anger money. Hate money.'

He looks at Mia 'Then I met Mia.'

So here's another equation. Life minus love equals hate. Light minus love equals darkness.

'My mum gave me away when I was eleven,' he says. 'I was in foster care and there was some bad shit that happened in foster care, and then I ran away from that and then I did some bad shit to get locked up in the juvenile detention system, thinking it would be way better than foster care.' He raises his eyebrows, grimly. 'It wasn't,' he says. 'It was way worse.'

When Troy looks back on it all, he struggles to find a single period of any extended length, prior to twelve months ago, in which he was in love or, moreover, felt the slightest bit loved. 'Mate, if you don't have love at thirteen, you're gone,' Troy says. He tells me that half the boys inside that detention centre were just like him: motherless, fatherless, loveless.

'What do you think happened to all the guys you were in there with?' I ask.

'Most of them are still in jail, the rest of them are dead,' he says. 'If there's no love and nurturing in your life, then you will struggle to trust anyone. It's taken me ages even to trust Mia.'

They met through a shared friend. Troy was still in the grip of heroin use when they met. Then Mia asked him a simple question: 'Do you ever want to stop?'

'I do,' he said. 'But I've never really had anyone to support me through that.'

Mia thought on this for a short moment. 'Well,' she said, 'I'll support you.'

Mia smiles at this memory. 'I didn't even know him that well then,' she says. 'I just thought it was the right thing to do.'

Troy told Mia every detail of what kicking heroin entailed. Nausea, abdominal pains, cold sweats, agitation in the first two days. Mad, desperate, fibro-wall-punching pleas for drugs in the peak days – days three and four – then darkness and depression as the cravings ease over days five, six and seven.

'It's fucking horrid,' Troy says. 'And it's embarrassing. You lose your bowel control and whatnot.'

I don't dare ask about the 'whatnot'.

'But she did it,' Troy says. 'She got me through it all. I detoxed in Mia's bedroom for a few long days. She cooked for me. She brought me everything I needed.'

He had tried to kick before and he had failed every time, but there was something new driving him through those peak days with Mia, some unforeseen motivation that he couldn't put his finger on, and that wasn't just because his fingers were shaking like dry leaves.

'It was this feeling I had for Mia,' he says. 'It was love. I had that love inside me and it was so strong that all the other physical shit went away.'

'That's a pretty cool love story, Mia,' I say.

She shrugs her shoulders, beams a wide smile at Troy and me. She's an artist. She says she paints beautiful pictures that are bright and colourful. She makes beautiful things with her hands that are deep and emotional and so often filled with nothing but big love that has origins in places she's not always aware of.

'I just decided to show Troy all the beautiful things in the world,' she says.

And that feels like a good place to end the love story of Troy and Mia, and now, two hours later, it's the afternoon and the rain has stopped falling across Adelaide Street because love is like the sun and it can't be beaten by the rain and I'm back here on my corner under a full warm sun tapping mathematical equations into Kath Kelly's sky-blue Olivetti typewriter.

```
Life minus love equals square one.
Dom plus eight-ball equals life.
Mia plus Troy equals hope.
Life plus love equals square two.
```

THE FIND

Sharing a coffee by the river with a man from Perth named Ned. He's a good man and a friend who is seventy-four years old and grieving the recent death of his wife, Viv, a truly good woman I knew and treasured only through a series of letters we shared about the books I've written. Ned tells me about his old day job as an exploration geologist. I ask him if he ever made that one eureka find during his many searches, often on his lonesome, for rich mineral deposits in far-off and hard-to-reach landscapes across Australia and the world.

'I did,' he says, eyes wide. Then he opens a sachet of raw sugar and tips six grains of it out onto the table between our coffee cups and explains how he was once walking through rocky country in north-western Australia and his eyes, which were laser keen and crystal clear in those days, spotted from a metre away a clump of vibrant yellow dirt that indicated a valuable base-metal deposit buried beneath the rocky surface. This vivid clump of yellow dirt was only as big as the collection of six raw sugar grains that sits between our coffee cups, yet somehow he managed to zero in on it – some profound meeting of knowing what to look for and being struck by enough dumb luck to stumble upon something you know. He says spotting that metal deposit on that quiet solitary day was the find of his working life.

'What did it feel like, Ned, making a find like that?' I ask.

He smiles and sits back in his chair by the river, awe and wonder in his eyes. 'Mind-bending,' he says.

*

But then Ned shows me something he found only three weeks ago that's far more valuable to him than any mineral deposit, far more precious to him than the heaviest gold or purest diamond. He opens the iPad he once shared with Viv and his forefinger swipes to a three-minute video of his wife talking directly to camera. He plays the video for me and he peers over my shoulder as I watch it. His wife is speaking with unbroken eloquence and sublime diction, giving a note-perfect monologue to camera about, of all things, the impact of excessive taxes being imposed on short-stay rentals in the city of Austin, Texas. His daughter lives with her husband and children in Austin and his wife recorded the video, self-shot, in support of the many Austin short-term rental businesses struggling to survive under such heavy tax burdens, including the inn she liked to stay at when visiting her daughter. I don't understand why he's showing me a video of his wife talking about taxes. Then he smiles with water welling in his eyes. 'Marvellous, isn't it?' he says. And I realise now that his wife could have been reciting names from the phone book and he would have been just as enthralled.

'It's not about what she's saying,' Ned explains. What makes the video so valuable to him is the way the video was shot. Viv put some time and effort into setting up the camera. She got the lighting just right. Ordinary household daylight filling the frame, but the best kind of light and enough of it to illuminate the perfect bone structure of her face; to capture the regular sparks flashing in her eyes; to visually document, just in case anyone other than Ned was ever wondering about it, the way she did her hair when she was presenting herself for something important.

Usually, it was Viv taking videos of everybody but herself. Only rarely did she turn the camera to her own smile, which was wider than the Indian Ocean. When she died, Ned struggled to find any videos of his wife in which she wasn't standing on the edge of the frame or just a blurred flash of a figure as the camera panned across endless family members and friends. He wanted to find something where she was sitting still. Just her, just wonderful *her*, staring straight into the camera and talking about something, anything, everything.

So the world can have its base metals and its oil and gold and diamonds. He'll just have that video. Three unbroken minutes of the love of his life talking about short-term rental taxes in Austin, Texas. The find of a lifetime.

EVERYWHERE I GO

'When I was young I used to make love to strangers to survive,' he says.

'Whaddya mean?' I ask.

'Whaddya mean what do I mean? I mean I made love to strangers to survive.'

Marko left Croatia when he was fifteen, but his Croatian accent never left him. He spells it all out for me again because I'm still just a Bracken Ridge rube, a little too slow on the uptake.

'I. Make. Love. To. Strangers. And. Strangers. Give. Me. Money.'

'Like a gigolo?'

He pats my shoulder like he's a kindy teacher and I just cut a straight line with the safety scissors.

'Easy money,' he says. 'I worked across Europe, I work in Paris, I work in Sydney, Melbourne, everything.' He tells me he can speak English, Croatian, French, Italian and Russian. 'And a little bit of Spanish.'

'How old are you?' I ask.

'You tell me?'

I make a quick visual assessment of Marko. Grey hair. Neat blue and white striped business shirt, black slacks, brown sunglasses, real Omar Sharif vibe about him.

'Fifty-eight?'

'Ha,' he says. 'You'll go far.'

Marko is a single man and he likes it that way. He says true love means responsibility, so true love is just a one-way ticket to a factory line. He grew up on a farm near Zagreb with three brothers and three sisters. Marko studied the farm boys in his village and he noted how much the farm boys looked like their fathers and he then noted how much those farm-boy fathers looked just like the farm-boy grandfathers and then he noted that all the grandfathers seemed to do all day was sit in the sun and wait for their shadows to die.

He turns to me with a grave look on his face and he doesn't look like Omar Sharif anymore. He looks all grim and burdened, like Max von Sydow out the front of that house in *The Exorcist*.

'Doesn't matter what you do, in the long run, you will be by yourself,' he says. 'You will be alone, no mistake. Me and my shadow. When my shadow disappears, I disappear. Everything is time. When the time goes, it's over for everyone. Greed, race, religion, life ... time beats all of it.'

Young Marko refused to spend his time on earth on the family farm waiting for his shadow to die, so he set about shagging his merry way around the great wide world. He says he supplemented his early-twenties gigolo income with work as a writer. With his thick accent, the word hits my ears as 'vighter'.

'You used to write?' I ask, picturing a 1960s version of Marko, like a *Streetcar* Brando writing books in Parisian bars by day and making love to wealthy and grateful French widows by night in apartments like the one in *Last Tango in Paris.*

'No, I did not write,' Marko says.

A writer who does not write. Cool concept. Ripper contemporary art installation in that. 'You just said you worked as a writer.'

'No, *waiter!*' he says. 'Waiter! Easy job. You broke, you go work, you make a few bucks, you fuck off again. I liked moving around. I've been everywhere but South America.'

Marko waited tables and bedded his way around the world until he landed in the shimmering blue city of Sydney where he says he met the 'Hungarian sugar mummy' of his dreams. 'She looked like Sharon Stone,' he says. 'I was very young and she was thirty-eight. She said I looked like James Dean, then she took off with a billionaire to New York.' He shrugs his shoulders in a way that hints at the difficulties inherent in sharing love triangles with billionaires. 'High rollers,' he says with a sigh.

He points at me like he's Yoda. 'You must know this,' he says. 'Life was never meant to be easy.' He points at me like he's Obi-Wan Kenobi. 'You know this yourself,' he says.

'How do you know I know this?' I ask, like I'm Luke Skywalker and I'm still stuck on the space farm. 'Because you're right, Marko, I do know this.'

He nods, fixes a rolled cuff on his shirt, refuses to elaborate.

'Did you ever find the love of your life, Marko?' I ask.

He reaches into the back pocket of his pants, pulls out his wallet. There were three loves in his life, he says. He opens his wallet and slides three small, square colour photographs from the same slots he keeps his bank cards in. The photographs are frayed and very old, like they've sat inside his worn leather wallet for decades. Three pictures. Three women. One woman looks like *Hounds of Love*—era Kate Bush and the other two look like the back-up angels Charlie had on speed dial in case Farrah Fawcett copped a bullet. Marko says three names – 'Francesca … Julie … Karen' – but I can't tell who's who.

'They really are beautiful, Marko,' I say. 'You ever think about sharing a life with one of them?'

He stares briefly down this alternative road. 'I stay with them, I die,' he says. 'I go to work all day in the factory, see nothing in the factory, come home and go to bed, see nothing in my sleep. Wake up, go back to work, see nothing. Then I die. Still see nothing.'

I try my best to suggest there's a little more to nine-to-five life than that. He's clearly forgetting all the *Friends* reruns.

He slips the square photographs back into his wallet. Who needs to work for true love when you can just carry it around in your back pocket your entire life?

'Love is a beautiful song,' he says. 'The song comes in and out of your life.'

He asks me if I'm married. He asks me if I have kids.

'Two girls, fourteen and twelve.'

'Another couple of years, they'll fall in love themselves.'

'Don't remind me, Marko.'

'Look, life is full of surprises,' he says. 'You don't know what's coming tomorrow. You like your woman, you like your kids?'

'Very much so.'

'Then that's a good life.'

'Thanks for reminding me, Marko.'

'How old are you?' he asks.

'Forty-two.'

'You look younger than this, which is why I know you have good kids. You have bad kids, then your wife drinking all the time. Your wife becomes angry, so then you start drinking, too, and you suddenly look fifty when you're forty-two. As long as your kids happy, your wife happy, you'll never get old.'

He points at me like he's Darth Vader. 'You'll die, but you will never get old.'

Cool concept.

'How old, actually, are you, Marko?' I ask.

'I'm seventy-eight,' he says. 'And I'm not old.'

We sit back in our chairs and watch people pass by. Couples, singles, families.

'Hey, Marko,' I say. 'You said love is a beautiful song that comes in and out of our lives.'

'Yes.'

'Who's singing the song?' I ask.

He dwells on this question for almost thirty seconds.

'Neil Diamond,' he says.

SAKURA TOMII AND THE GOOD THINGS
Part 2

The three good things Sakura Tomii notes in her diary each day don't always have to be miraculous or wondrous or life-changing. They can be three perfectly mundane and boring things. A cloudless blue sky. The fact she woke up this morning feeling healthy. The taste of the egg she had for breakfast.

Caramel popcorn. Rain. Cute baby.

'The tiny things in life make you grateful,' she says. 'The tiny things are the good things.'

Sakura Tomii was married on 9 August 2005. 'My friend said it is a bad day, as the word "nine" in Japanese shares the sound with "agony",' Sakura says. 'Many Asians are superstitious.'

She and her husband moved into a unit in Moorooka, in Brisbane's south. They had a cat named Ruby. They had a fish tank containing a giant oscar fish that her husband cared for like a son.

Some months after the wedding, Sakura noticed hitherto unseen mood swings emerge in her groom. He took a demanding job in property valuation and set up an office in the garage beneath their unit. Some days, through the floorboards of the living room, Sakura heard him erupt in wild explosions of anger, swearing loud enough for the neighbours to hear, limbs flailing against furniture.

'Why do you do that?' Sakura asked gently over dinner.

'Do what?' he replied.

Found a praying mantis. Capsicums. Kookaburra visited my place again.

*

Years passed. Sakura studied accounting for a time and was offered a potentially lucrative and fulfilling job that would complement her studies.

'No,' her husband said. 'You should focus on your studies.'

Sakura began to feel as though she had no say in the big decisions about their future. Her husband made grand plans to relocate to regional parts of Queensland where he could pursue his passion for agricultural science, and Sakura would go to great lengths to prepare to adjust her life accordingly. Then, seemingly overnight, he would abandon his latest plan, swap it for another.

'Why do you do that?' Sakura asked gently over dinner.

'Do what?' he replied.

*

'I didn't know where we were going,' she says. 'Whatever he planned, nothing happened. What he told me was always different from what actually happened. He never thought about me. Everything was about him. I think I thought controlling behaviour was a sign of affection. It's not affection. It's just a sign of insecurity. Things got worse in 2011 and I started to pull away from him.'

The relationship became more complex when he began treatment for what he described as chronic nerve pain, which grew to be so severe he often spoke of euthanasia.

'He asked me to go to Switzerland with him to get euthanised,' she says. 'I couldn't believe what I was hearing. He was forty-seven years old. I was forty-three years old and he wanted to die. He started showing me euthanasia videos, almost every day. I couldn't cope with it.'

It was as macabre as it was surreal. Sakura wondered how on earth she had found herself trapped in such a strange suburban Australian nightmare. Did all Australian men behave like this?

'I was not prepared for any of this. He was always really angry. He always wanted to die and I had to watch these videos and I felt like I was going to die, too. He wanted me to support his decision to die. Our marriage was ending and he was in pain, but I wanted him to stay alive.'

Attended an online paper craft workshop. Tried vegan mince. Storm and lightning.

Her heart told her to run away but she stayed. She pushed through the pain.

'He started seeing a psychiatrist,' she says. 'Then he started to self-harm. He bought chemicals and he tried to take his life inside the car, parked somewhere. It didn't work. He kept telling me he was going to kill himself. He said, "I'm in pain, I'm in agony, why won't you let me die?" I said, "I'm trying to help you." We are designed to live, no matter what. Even in pain, aren't we supposed to try to live? I tried to take him to hospital. I tried to get help for him. He really was in pain. But I think it was emotional pain as much as anything else. Mental pain.'

One night, after a heated argument in the kitchen of their Moorooka unit, he took a drinking glass and smashed it over his forehead.

'Then he went to the bathroom and he had a hot shower and he bled more,' she says. 'He was trying to hurt me, I think. I realised that, maybe one or two years later.'

Sakura phoned the police. They arrived to find pools of her husband's blood spread across the unit. 'The blood smelled so bad,' Sakura says. She was in shock. She remembers looking at an attending police officer's name tag. 'Pepper?' she said, smiling. 'You're Sergeant Pepper?'

'You can't keep living like this,' the officer said.

Sakura shrugs her shoulders at the café table. 'I didn't have anywhere to go. I was still studying. I didn't have a job. My mind was in a cloud. I was so scared. I was not in a good condition. It was just too much. But I finally realised, I have to leave, I have to get out of this.'

Sakura Tomii followed her heart. She moved back to Japan. Weeks later, her husband took his own life.

Sakura returned to Brisbane. She worked through the emotional and practical daily-life aftermath of his loss. She joined a suicide survivors' support group to help unpack the intense emotions she felt about his death. Some nights the group spoke of the complexities of still loving the people who'd caused them so much pain.

'I don't know about the definition of love,' she says. 'It's so broad. People use the word "love" so casually. It's hard to define what love is. I might change "love" to "care". I talked about it with my dad. He asked me how I felt. I said, "I was married to him and even though it became such a mess, I didn't mind staying with him to support him and it's so unfortunate he couldn't see what he had."'

Her father, Keisuke, was also grieving the loss of a partner. Masumi had asked her husband to never place her in a care home, no matter how intense and debilitating her dementia became, so Keisuke had begun a different kind of painful care journey of his own. Masumi died three months after Sakura's husband died.

'My dad told me this: "He is not in pain anymore. He is at peace. So you should be at peace, too."'

*

Sometimes Sakura feels like she's lived three lifetimes already, when she's really only halfway through her first. She's been in relationships since those years with her husband. Nothing's quite worked out. The closest thing she has to a storybook love is the relationship she has with her cat. 'I still have Ruby,' she says. 'She's eighteen now. She's stuck around longer than any of these guys in my life.'

She grips the love-heart pendant on her necklace. She's got a close group of female Facebook friends, who often speak online of ditching the pursuit of long-term love altogether. She recently added a comment to one such discussion: 'I'm a good one,' she wrote. 'I won't be defined by the bad ones.'

'You just have to think about how lucky you are,' she says. 'Happiness is overrated. What is happiness? People say, "Oh, you must be happy." But happiness is a high that is hard to sustain. Life is boring and mundane and it's happy, too. But I am so lucky to have many friends. I love my friends. These people are nice people and they choose me as their friend, so that must mean I'm a nice person.'

She holds up her phone and shows me a slogan she posted on her Facebook page: 'Your value doesn't decrease based on someone's inability to see your worth.'

Elsewhere, her Facebook feed is filled with all the good things she has observed in her life. All the endless good things in the eventful life of Sakura Tomii:

Discounted fluffy slippers. Pilates. Restored the lemon tree. New second-hand bamboo steamer. Another pleasant tradie. Learned that cat's urine can be removed by using washing detergent that contains enzyme. Storm! Got free sourdough bread. Had a long conversation with a friend in Japan. Read a free manga. Tried winged bean leaves, at last I tried! Found lavender oil is not harmful to cats. Quick haircut. Got an email from Dad. A box of Home Ice Cream. Joined Clean Up Australia. Had an iced latte. Found a roll of rope, plan to make Japanese slippers. Trimmed hibiscus early in the morning. Dragonfruit tree has a flower bud. The electrician who visited next door said my yard looked good. Saw the crescent moon in the morning. Survived one more year and didn't cry or anything. Just glad!

BLOOD CHEMISTRY

Dr John O'Hagan is older than the cheeseburger, the traffic light, the convertible automobile, water-skiing, television and penicillin. He's one hundred years old, to be more precise, which is why, in a conversation that has so far lasted an hour and a half, he has been able to tell me first-hand what it was like to be a soldier defending Townsville in the Battle of the Coral Sea and then to witness Beatlemania in Brisbane and then to marvel at the earth-shrinking powers of the internet and still live long enough to find out what it feels like to be a century old and have someone sneeze over the supermarket avocado bay during a global Covid-19 pandemic.

We're now talking about one of John's most enduring and motivating loves: the thrill of scientific discovery. The bone-chilling, pulse-quickening, mouth-drying elation that comes with finding something nobody else has ever found. Otherwise known as something new.

'Discovery,' he says, raising his century-old eyebrows with the verve of a teenager. John O'Hagan is one of Queensland's most celebrated and diverse scientists. He wears a blue flannelette shirt and olive slacks. His feet move slow but his mind moves quick.

I ask him to tell me about his many scientific discoveries over the past eighty years and I ask him to describe these things as though he's talking to a ten-year-old boy, or maybe a small lemon, because that's the size my brain seems to inexplicably shrink to when I have the rare honour of being around him.

I ask him about the ground-breaking discoveries he made in blood chemistry. We talk of haemoglobin, myoglobin and prostaglandins and I remind myself to google each of those things as soon as I get home. He tells me about his World War II military service, how everything he learned in science subjects at the University of Queensland proved unexpectedly useful in battle. He showed diggers how to use and safely destroy explosives, taught men about the properties of poisonous battlefield gases. 'If I used words with more than three syllables, the men would quickly call out "bullshit", so that taught me how to explain complex science in simple terms,' he says laughing. He applied his deep passion for cartography to making maps for senior intelligence officers; he applied his deep passion for mechanics and the way things work to the development of cutting-edge in-battle and on-the-fly radar equipment. He tells me how heartbreaking it is to be a scientist sometimes, to give decades of your life to potential discoveries that are so close you can touch them, yet as far away from you as Neptune is from earth. And I won't even get him started on how he's the reason I can take my kids to the Brisbane Planetarium – John was a key lobbyist for its construction – where, together, we get to feel the thrill of being three simple carbon-based bipeds inside a universe that's 93 billion light years wide.

He tells me about the inroads he made in biochemistry, molecular biology and immunology. There's a gold-fever element to scientific research, but the prize of the find is never measured in kilograms or carats. It's measured in answers. The priceless answers to the perfect questions nobody thought to ask. But for all that, he tells me, for all the questions he has asked and all the answers he has been granted in a hundred-year life of scientific wonderment, in the end, there remains one utterly critical human question far more mysterious and enticing than all others, which is yet to be satisfactorily answered. 'What is love?' he says, smiling.

And then Dr John O'Hagan tells me a love story that's as close to an answer to that question as anything I've heard in the past two months.

'I once gave a presidential address to the Royal Society of Queensland called, "Recent Chemical Findings Concerning the Origin of Life",' he tells me. 'And near the beginning of that I quoted a very old piece of poetry that went along the lines of, "Despite all the things we have discovered through science, how do I prove that thou art so fair and that I am in love?"

'That's a wonderful question. Science doesn't go into those emotions. Likewise, science can't really speak to aspects of religion either. Perhaps science can prove where there are faults in the Bible and the writings of Christian philosophers, but it can't get to the absolute nitty gritty of what it is to have faith.

'Yet,' he continues, 'love is an absolutely marvellous thing when you analyse the chemical aspects at play when one is in love and also the very real chemical effect on the body and brain when love is gone.'

He pauses to consider his thoughts for a long moment. 'I've experienced that,' he says. 'Very badly once with my first wife, Kay. She was a healthy woman one minute and then, the next minute, she was very ill. The actual correct diagnosis of what was wrong with her wasn't found until the post-mortem. I had left her that morning in the kitchen to go to work, and she was cutting up some melon to make melon-lemon jam. About an hour and a half later I got a call from her saying, "I've just spat up some blood." I hopped in the car and raced home and ...' – he adjusts his glasses, turns his eyes to me – 'when I got home she collapsed in my arms. I got her to hospital and she died within a couple of days.'

It was a cancer that had caused clotting in her heart and lungs.

'It knocked the hell out of me, I'll tell you.'

He's quiet for a moment. 'We were a pigeon pair,' he says. 'She got the same type of pass as me with her junior exams. We both went into government service. We used to have our lunch together, overlooking Anzac Square on Ann Street. Then we were married and had two small children, the loveliest kids. And then this happened. I was a mess for quite a while afterwards. But there was one thing that helped me.'

It was the strangest, most unexpected thing. John was lost. He didn't know exactly how he was supposed to carry on into the future; he was worried about how well he would be able to raise his two girls – then aged five and three – alone, while managing the deep emotional wreckage of Kay's loss. He's convinced he was suffering something close to post-traumatic stress disorder. He sought advice on his emotional state from a doctor who told him to get away for a bit. 'I went south to Sydney and then I got on a ship in Sydney and went round to Adelaide,' he says. 'And I happened to visit Adelaide Zoo, and inside that zoo there was a male emu that I saw with two little chicks it was caring for. Apparently, the female emu had been killed, most likely by a car. And this male emu was there, looking after these two little chicks. And I thought, Well, jolly, that's it, isn't it? If he can look after two little girls, then so can I.'

Love is an emu dad nestling two baby chicks. Love is innate. Love is primal. Love is animal.

Love is fundamental.

John later married again. A beautiful woman named Mary, with whom he got to spend fifty years of his life. He fathered two more children. He became a grandfather to eight and a great-grandfather to five. And he loves all those people with a love that he says is better explained by poetry than science.

'One of my great-grandchildren can speak four languages,' he says. And he shakes his head now, awed as much by the wonders of biology and evolution as by the growing miracles that come from love.

Love is Dickinson and Keats and Kipling, he says. And love is Einstein, too. Love is all around us and love is inside the emu yards of Adelaide Zoo. Love is biology. Love is biochemistry. Love is blood chemistry. And love is discovery, otherwise known as something new.

THE CRADLE

The crib. The bed. The cardboard sword. The man with the drugs. The bicycle. The man in the moon. The falling down the stairs. The scar on the lip. The body. The ball under the arm. The thin skull. The concussion. The needle in the garbage bag. The picture of the face in the corner of the mirror. The ambulance. The fuzz. The dippy egg. The train. The smashed windscreen. The hailstorm. The piss on the floor. The spit in the face from the boy with the Bible. The hole in the door. The dartboard bullseye. The lawn. The money in the pocket. The blood. The loss. The pills. The burning. The tinman. The best and fairest trophy of them all. The prison bars. The prison bakery. The skateboard outside the halfway house. The nun. The apple juice. The telephone booth. The man in the van by the river. The rage. The hate. The fire. The sand. The night. The fur coat. The wolf. The bull. The 522 bus to the city. The punch. The teeth. The stains. The reaching. The breath. The colour red. The monster with the moustache. The face plant. The welfare every second Wednesday. The strangler. The coughing. The coffin. The shit. The vomit. The shakes. The wedding. The stick through the thigh. The kick in the guts. The axe handle. The riptide. The snake in the grass. The falling debris. The parmesan cheese. The bird on one leg. The drowning in the rapids. The ashes. The note from the boy in the letterbox. The rainbow on Christmas Day. The woman in the room on the day of the swimming carnival. The island. The limbo. The waltz. The graffiti in the tunnel. The lost. The radio song. The green eyes. The sinking. The looking down at the ceiling. The looking up at the ground. The havoc. The waste. The postman. The promise. The forest. The mountain. The sky. The grave. The love.

The love.

The love.

The love.

The love.

Trent,

Love is not for understanding.

That was my first thought when you asked me to write you something about love. How on this ungodly earth do you explain the unexplainable, unravel the unfathomable, demystify the mystifying?

I've seen this book come together; I've heard the stories, often relayed by you, to me, in the place we seem to find ourselves in at the beginning and end of most days, our kitchen. That's the place where we give each other the headline news of our lives and where I ask for updates on the latest adventures in 'Trent World'. But with this project, more than any other, you start talking before I can even ask the question, so enamoured, so *in love*, with the stories you've collected that you cannot wait to share them, to share the joy, and the heartache, and everything in between.

The tales you've told me — and the stories I've surreptitiously snuck a read of — made me think there was nothing I could say that hasn't been said a thousand times better by the people who

have beautifully and graciously bared their souls
to you. I wasn't going to write this letter - it
was too hard, and I'm not like you, I'm not good at
sharing my personal thoughts so publicly. But I
started to try and after a while I realised maybe
I did have something to share. Because there are
things - not many things, but some things - I know
for certain.

I know that love is the beginning and the end
of everything, at least of everything good. Sounds
too simple to be true, but it is. It has to be,
because surely it's what makes us human, what makes
our lives worthwhile, and, when everything else is
stripped away, it's the one true thing that keeps
us putting one foot in front of the other, that
keeps us trudging through the sometime-swamplands
of our lives, and other times has us flying through
the highest of blue skies.

Love is the answer to every question. I assure
you I've thought about it for a long time and that
is what I now know. When life brings you down, love
harder. When you've been unloved, give love. When
love is hard to find, give more love. Double down on
love. When the world throws unimaginable grief and
tragedy at you, throw yourself into loving.

I know stories of love from the most harrowing
and desolate of places. Places like the Burma

Railway. My grandfather Ken carried his desperately
sick mate Leo so he wouldn't be shot, or left to
die, in a wretched World War II prisoner-of-war
camp. What else is it but love that propels people,
in the bleakest of circumstances, to risk their own
lives to save others, like those boys did for your
grandad, Vic? Leo survived and, years later, repaid
that love by carrying a by-then ailing, bed-ridden
Ken down the front steps of my grandparents' post-
war home in Gaythorne, Brisbane, so he could make
it to a reunion with their old mate Weary Dunlop.

The love didn't stop there and neither did the
carrying. Mum has always told me how, when Grandad
was too sick to get down the stairs to the backyard
outhouse in the middle of the night, and Grandma
wasn't there because she was out working night
shifts at the pie factory just to make ends meet,
and the kids were too little to help, Mum would
have to call out to their next-door neighbour
George Godbold. And beautiful, quiet, caring
George, whose house was only metres away from my
grandparents' home, would get out of his bed, walk
over from No. 27 Mott Street, Gaythorne, to No. 29,
and carry my grandfather to the toilet.

There are big, life-saving gestures of love and
there are small ones. My grandmother Jacquie, wife
and eventual young widow of that POW, wouldn't

allow us to sit down to Christmas lunch until she
had delivered a plate of roasted meats, vegetables,
gravy and many, many trimmings to the wizened,
toothless, hermit-like woman, Jessie, who lived
in an almost-derelict house up the hill on Mott
Street. That little neighbourhood surrounding
the corner of Dunkirk and Mott streets from the
1950s to the 1990s is a whole epic story of love in
itself. All the untold gestures of love from the
Godbolds, the Marsdens, the Cullens, the Woolfreys,
the Grays. I was only around for the tail end of
it, but their names are ingrained in my memory and
in my heart.

Love breeds love. Big or little, every gesture
of love is as worthy and important as another. And
maybe the small is actually not so small after
all. Sometimes those little gestures are just as
life-saving. I think of them all as forming part
of a big crocheted rug covering the world, joining
together, bit by bit, piece by piece, little square
by little square, and if everyone contributed
just their one part we'd eventually join up the
ends and be blanketed in so much love there'd be
enough warmth to snuff out any cold, hard anti-love
completely. Can't blame me for dreaming.

I know why you're writing this book. I know
you're trying to join the rug together. I know that

holding on to the smallest glimmers of love has
seen you through the darker times. I know you've
gathered all those glimmers and held them tightly
together until they've become one big light, bright
enough to dispel any darkness you worry might
overshadow you. It's so like you to embark on
this quest to understand this thing called love —
forever examining and searching for the answers
to the biggest questions, never deterred by the
naysayers, the doomsayers, the love-slayers. They've
never bothered you anyway. They don't know what you
know.

There's one more thing I need to tell you, one
final thing I know for certain: loving you, and
your big cheeseball heart, has been the greatest
and most unexpected gift of my very fortunate life.

Love is not for understanding.

And that's the best thing about it.

Fi

GOOD TO SEE YOU AGAIN, FE BROWN

On days this perfect, it's important to stop and smell the doughnuts. And the German bratwurst and the Merlo coffee and the roses in the gardens of New Farm Park. It's 8 a.m. on a Saturday and hundreds of lovers shuffle through the Brisbane Powerhouse Farmers' Markets beside the Brisbane River. Lovers move north, east, south and west. Morning park runners rush by in single file wearing visors and sleeveless shirts. Lines of market tents form a square of grass where couples talk and families share morning crepes and elderly lovers hold hands and young lovers kiss. Artisan cheese tents and cured meat tents and curry tents and fresh fruit and vegetable tents. Butchers, bakers, pasta makers, jewellers, hat makers, juicers and doughnut makers.

In the centre of the grass square at the heart of the markets, Aaron Hall, the marriage-proposal planner I met with his wife, Carly, and son, Alfie, gives a series of meticulously considered instructions to a group of trained dancers and a team of audiovisual personnel lugging cameras and sound-recording equipment. The man who is popping the question this morning is Paul, the guy standing beside Aaron in a crisp white shirt and grey checked slacks and good black shoes.

'Everybody, this is Paul,' Aaron says. 'His heart's going a thousand miles an hour.'

'Hey Paul!' the dancers holler.

Aaron addresses the dancers. 'You will all be standing here and here,' he says, pointing to sections of the park space. 'Paul and I will sneak around the back.' He points to a row of sprawling and leafy trees on the far side of the park. Aaron guides his camera operator to the centre of the park. 'The proposal itself will happen here.' The cameraman nods. 'There's a lot of moving parts,' Aaron says. 'But it's going to be amazing.'

Paul is nervous. He loves his partner, Victor, with all his heart, but who's to say how a man will react when surprised with a public flash-mob marriage proposal unfolding to the sound of a song called 'Marry Me' by Jason Derulo.

Aaron receives a secret message from Paul and Victor's friend, Maggie, who has deviously and brilliantly guided Victor to the markets this morning under the ruse of a casual catch-up.

'Okay, everybody, they'll be here in two minutes,' Aaron calls. 'Let's take our positions.'

Aaron hides Paul behind a large black umbrella as they duck into the trees at the far side of the park, while another member of his team sends music through a large speaker placed at the entry to the park space. The music plays and Jason Derulo echoes across the markets, singing about wanting to spend the next 105 years with the love of his life. Market-goers in their hundreds hear the music and, just as Aaron predicted, are drawn in a circle around the park space because something tells them love is in the air this morning.

Some twenty dancers fill the circle and move with choreographed grace and verve, and Maggie and Victor enter this scene with Victor entirely unaware that the whole spectacle exists for him. Then the dancers form a V-shape, clapping their hands in unison and, by some miracle act of smoke-and-mirror distraction, Paul emerges suddenly in the centre of the dancers and walks confidently and proudly, straight to the man he wants to spend the next 105 years of his life with. And the whole grand and wondrous subterfuge suddenly hits home with Victor, and the power of the moment buckles his knees. He momentarily collapses under the weight of the love inside the gesture. And the circle of market-goers scream wildly because they now know for certain what is about to transpire.

Maggie ushers Victor forward and Paul meets his partner at the edge of the circle, where he drops down on one knee and looks up at his lover. 'Will you marry me?' he asks, beaming.

Victor weeps and can't speak, so he has to nod his head three times to give his answer. Then he pulls Paul up for a kiss and he hugs him so tight they almost lose their balance. 'Yes,' he says in Paul's ear.

Then he leans his head back and says it louder for the crowd. '*Yes!*'

And every last one of us in the crowd hollers and claps like a goofy cheeseball romantic because we either know what that feels like or we now want to know what that feels like.

Yes. A hundred and five times over, for a hundred and five years to come. *Yes!*

*

Back in the heart of the heaving city again, I pick up my wedding band from Duncan Vickers' engraving workshop. I read the three words he has etched into metal with the truest of hands: *Sway with me.*

'It's perfect, Duncan,' I say. 'Thank you.'

It's my last day at my writing desk on the corner of Adelaide and Albert. I've heard enough love stories to write three books, and I feel so good about this corner and all those beautiful storytellers that I might do just that.

Jean-Benoit sits beside me for half an hour and, together, we watch the world go by.

'Look at us, man,' I say. 'Look at our lives. We're the luckiest bastards on the planet. Just sitting here.'

Jean-Benoit nods. 'I made enough money to buy my new bongo drum today,' he says.

'Are you serious? That's so great, man.'

He's been given enough coins by the people of this city that he's now going to upgrade from the Osmocote fertiliser tub. 'I kept looking in the garbage for a better drum,' he says. 'Then I thought, "Well, I could just buy one!"'

He's going to miss that Osmocote tub drum. He loves that thing like an old friend. And speaking of old friends, Jean-Benoit says he's organised a catch-up with his ex-girlfriend. His twin flame. 'I don't know, man,' he says. 'There's something about her. Something way beyond comprehension. I can't understand it. I just ...' – he thinks on the right words – 'love her.' And those words sound good to him. 'I love her.'

He says her name is Lily. She has blue eyes. She loves his drumming. She loves him.

'What happens next?' I ask.

'Huh?' he replies.

'Where do you hope it all goes? You and Lily.'

He laughs and starts stomping his feet, excitedly. 'To the eternity, man!' he says. 'Beyond earth. Beyond everything! That's what I want. *Eternity!*'

*

After lunch, the sound of bagpipes echoes across the city. I follow the sound to the centre of King George Square, where Piper Joe McGhee is playing 'Amazing Grace' from the very core of his heart and soul and his hard-working lungs. I look around the square and the sound has frozen some fifty people in time. I look up at the black hands on the City Hall clocktower and I swear it's the magic hour again and that means the hands on that clock stop moving. That haunting and sublime collection of Highland notes has temporarily stilled the faces of young lovers and old loners and men in suits and women with kids and lunchtime smokers and all the rowdy drinkers at the bar in the corner of the square who have suddenly shut the hell up and listened to what the world is telling them. And it's so truly easy to imagine the stories being told and recollected in their heads. Stories of the past. Stories of friends and family, of the blind and the ones who can see. Stories of being lost and being found again. Stories of all the wretches like me and the ones with grace like my wife and my kids and my mother and my father and my brothers and my friends. Stories of doing the work for the ones we love. Stories of love.

*

I pack Kath's typewriter back into my travel bag one last time. Fold the legs of the BCF table, pack my makeshift writing desk into the red, white and blue striped jumbo zip bag that now has a ripped handle from too much use and carrying too much weight. I pad back to my car via the markets at the top of Queen Street Mall in George Street.

'Hey, Fe,' I say. 'Good to see you again.'

Fe Brown smiles wide behind her market tables covered with exotic potted orchids.

'Good to see you!' she says.

'Can you help me pick an orchid for someone?' I ask.

'Well, which one do you like?' Fe replies.

I examine the two display tables covered with orange tablecloths and crowded with red orchids and pink orchids and exotic orchids that look like wondrous deep-sea jellyfish and orchids that look like miniature frangipani trees. A yellow-flowered orchid leans over like it's crying, and what's flowing from its eyes are the most vibrant scarlet petals.

Then I find the one that feels right. Life is an orchid, growing. Love is an orchid, growing. 'Can I get this one, Fe?'

Fe says it's a Cattleya orchid from South America, the Dream Weaver. Two tall bright-yellow flowers with blotchy red petals that resemble Rorschach paintings. It looks to me like an orchid made of fire.

'Beautiful orchid,' Fe says.

And I think of my old schoolmate, Hiedi Owen. Everybody should know what it feels like to receive a Cattleya Dream Weaver orchid at least once in their lifetime.

Fe Brown boxes up the orchid. Wraps a ribbon around it.

'For someone special?' Fe asks.

'Yeah,' I say, 'someone special.'

*

I cross back over the Victoria Bridge. Over the dirty brown Brisbane River that runs in my blood. Take the twisting exit ramp that folds under the bridge towards the entry tunnel to the Queensland Museum carpark. A gang of labourers are still busy with roadworks in the tunnel. I approach a woman overseeing the work, in a high-vis vest and a hard hat and holding a two-way radio. 'Sorry to bother you,' I say. 'I'm just wondering if Moana is working today?'

The woman nods. 'Yeah, she's down the end there.'

I hold up Fe's fire-coloured Cattleya orchid. 'I just wanted to drop a gift off to her,' I say. 'Can I go down there?'

'Wait, I'll call her up.'

The woman in the hard hat speaks into her transceiver: 'Moana, there's someone here to see you.'

From the darkness of the carpark tunnel, Moana emerges in steel-cap boots and blue and yellow workwear. She's smiling when she sees me.

'What are you doing here?' she asks, laughing.

When she's close to me I hand her the orchid. 'I wanted to give you this,' I say.

She's confused, but there are tears in her eyes when she takes the orchid in both hands. 'What's this for?' she asks.

'You told me you love this city,' I say. 'I wanted you to know it loves you back.'

the corner of Adelaide and Albert, outside Wallace
Bishop. I got the impression that everyone met
there back then. I met my very few awkward dates
there because Mum said it was a good central point
between bus and train stops.'

I had no idea about that, Kath. I only sat there
because security moved me on from my original
writing spot at the bottom of Queen Street Mall.
Ain't life a peach?

Then Judy turned to a few thoughts she'd been
having about me writing this book. 'That poor
Olivetti has fervently typed facts for years, but
not always in the best interests of recipients,' she
wrote. 'How ironic is it that it's back typing facts
again, but this time about love? I have given much
thought since Christmas to our complex mum and her
lifelong, relentless pursuit of knowledge and fact.
The investigator of Jack Street. But I get it now.'

Then Judy left a little pause in the letter,
Kath. A perfectly timed little writer's pause to
convey the passing of time, the ticking of clocks
and the movement of thoughts in her head from
questions to answers.

'Mum's first and true love was the written word.'

I got my not-so-new wedding band back from the
engraver's shop in Brisbane Arcade, Kath. He did

a brilliant job spacing my three requested words across the inside of the band, my cheeseball line taken from the three words I nervously whispered to Fiona when I so desperately wanted to hold her hand at that Sting concert in late 2000. We were sitting side by side up in the cheap seats because I was only earning $26,000 a year in my first journalism job. My wallet was empty, but you better believe my heart was full, Kath. I was giddy in my seat. I was the fifth Beatle that night and I wanted to hold her hand. And her perfect hand was just waiting there for me to hold, Kath. I swear there was a moment when she rested her arm gently on the arm rest between us and she turned her palm up to the ceiling. If ever a hand needed to be held it was that hand on that arm rest on that night. Maybe we get three, four, five of these moments, tops, in a lifetime. Maybe we get a moment like that only once and then it's gone forever.

Then Sting played a love song and suddenly I knew I only had a verse, a bridge and a final chorus to make my move. I rubbed the sweat from my right palm across my tight black jeans and I leaned over to a girl with green eyes and open ears and I whispered the first three words that shot from my heart to my head, a soft and fragile plea, a hope, a wish, a dream: 'Sway with me?'

Of course, Kath, I could have asked Duncan
Vickers in that Brisbane Arcade workshop to
engrave just one lone, perfect three-letter word
on the wedding band, the word the girl with green
eyes said back to me as she gripped my hand
before I even had a chance to grip hers. 'Yes,'
she said.

Greg wrote me a letter about you, too, Kath. 'Mum
and her Olivetti,' he wrote. 'Her weapon that she
used to fire at injustice and hypocrisy wherever she
saw it. That Olivetti fired off shots all over the
globe.

'She was not aligned to any particular political,
religious or social movement; that would have
blocked her aim. She never wished to be bound
by a party line. She was the sole member of the
Kath Kelly Party — one headstrong woman and her
trusty sidekick, the Olivetti. She didn't suffer the
deceitful or the self-righteous one bit. It didn't
matter who you were. I saw her stick up for people
under attack many times when others would have run
for cover. I saw her defending a young cashier once
from an abusive customer. She marched him from the
store then returned to comfort the young girl. The
lesson — don't be an arrogant pig next to Mum in a
shopping queue.'

He directed his last paragraph at me, Kath. He
made me cry with his last paragraph, Kath.

'Mum immediately spotted a raw honesty and
genuineness in you, Trent,' he wrote. 'She saw it
a mile off. I think, in a way, she saw you as from
the same street as her, so to speak. I couldn't
agree with her more. She was your friend over
the past decades and remains your friend, even
in death. Life can kill love, but, it would seem,
death can't.'

And I know what love is. Love is a sky-blue
Olivetti and a blank piece of paper for a story
that has not yet been written. Anything is possible
in that story. That story can go wherever it needs
to go and that story does not have to end.

I got your gift, Kath. It now sits on an antique
sewing desk we have at the entry to our house.
There's a sheet of blank A4 paper tucked in it that
waits in permanent readiness. The ink ribbon is
wet, the 'o' hammer is as clean as a whistle. The
idea is that anyone who comes to our house – kids,
adults, anything else with the ability to write –
is welcome to tap a few words on Kath Kelly's
mighty sidekick. But there's a catch. Only stories
about love are allowed. Stories of the ones we
love and the ones we've lost, stories about what we

think love is, stories of love gone wrong and love
that's about to be found. Love stories.

I got your gift, Kath. Thank you. Might be the
most beautiful gift I ever got.

Trent

Dear Eric,

Hello from Australia. My name is Trent and I am
delighted to be your new sponsor. I am forty-two
years old and live with my wife, Fiona, and our two
daughters, Beth and Sylvie.

The people at ChildFund Australia tell me your
favourite colour is yellow. Yellow is my third
favourite colour, behind blue and green. I live
in a city called Brisbane, which is in a state
called Queensland, a place I think you would love
because it is filled with many lovely yellow things:
bananas, beaches, pineapples and sunshine.

I spend my days writing stories. Lately, I have
been writing stories about love, at a desk on a
busy corner of Brisbane, the very same desk at
which I'm typing this letter to you now. It's almost
time for afternoon tea here in Brisbane, which
means it's probably breakfast time in Uganda. It's
winter here, but it's warm and the sky above me is
bright blue and covered in thin rippled clouds that
make it look as though someone has thrown a bag of
flour across the top of the world. A friend recently

gave me a cloud classification guide, so I can safely tell you those kinds of clouds are called cirrocumulus clouds. I wonder what your sky looks like right now? I have enclosed my friend's cloud classification guide with this letter, so maybe you can tell me what clouds you sometimes see above you?

I also hope you enjoy the enclosed Wolverine comic. It's the genuine article from way back in 1988, when I was your age. In case you're unfamiliar with Wolverine, he's a superhero mutant who wears a yellow costume, is as tough as nails, as sharp as a tack and never gives up on anything he sets his mind to, which reminds me a lot of what I've read about you. If I ever had a tough day when I was your age, Wolverine and his friends, the X-Men, always made me smile again, so I hope they do the same for you.

ChildFund Australia asked me to enclose a photograph of our family. That's us down at the basketball court of our local park. That's me in the Pearl Jam shirt. I've got my arm around Fiona. I read about how your favourite thing to do, Eric, is to pick yellow flowers on the way to school and church. Well, if I had to describe Fiona, I'd say she's something like a big bunch of freshly picked yellow flowers. The girl with the brown hair is

Beth. She's fourteen and loves puppies, hip-hop dancing and buying the red properties in Monopoly. Last week, she wrote her first original song on acoustic guitar and made her dad cry. The girl with the blonde hair is Sylvie. She's twelve and loves Star Wars, mid-1990s Leonardo DiCaprio and fried eggs on toast for dinner. Sometimes before she turns her light out at night, Sylvie turns her head on her pillow and calls across the hallway of our house to her sister, whose bedroom doorway faces Sylvie's. 'Hey, Beth,' Sylvie whispers. And Beth turns her head on her pillow to see what Sylvie wants. Then Sylvie puts her hands together and forms a love-heart symbol with her fingers and thumbs. Then Beth smiles and forms her own love-heart with her fingers and thumbs, and that's when Sylvie smiles and turns her bedside light out.

This probably sounds silly to you, but the other night I asked Sylvie if she could remember, just every now and then, to form one of those love-hearts with her fingers and thumbs for you, Eric, and maybe raise it up to the sky, by way of her bedroom ceiling. I want you to know she's been sending those love-hearts up to you, Eric. Of course, you're thirteen thousand kilometres away on the other side of the world, so you'll never know when she's sending those love-hearts up to you.

You'll have no proof of the love she's giving you.
But I assure you it exists, so you can go right
ahead and believe in it anyway.

Love to you and all of your family, Eric, from me
and all of mine.

I'll write again soon.

Trent

SENTIMENTAL

WRITER

COLLECTING

LOVE

STORIES

ACKNOWLEDGEMENTS

I believe in love and I believe in stories. I believe a story is the greatest gift we can give each other. Fiona was right. I was sitting on that corner because I was reaching out for the glimmers of the good stuff to balance out the bad stuff. Deepest and sincerest thanks to every last person who stopped by that desk on the corner of Adelaide and Albert and shared some love through a story or a photograph. You gave me your glimmers. You gave me your good stuff. Thanks to every last random person in the streets of Brisbane who did not run for their life when I asked them to stop and confess their deepest thoughts on love. There were so many stories in the end that I ran out of room to tell them all, but I guess that means it's time I asked the grown-ups to let me do the sequel. Love always deserves a second chance.

Thank you, Danielle Smith, for taking that beautiful shot of Paul proposing to Victor that day. Thank you, Bruce and Denise Morcombe. Thank you for the tea, and the inspiration, Sister Angela Mary Doyle. Thank you, Tracey Gregg. Thank you, Sunny Avenue. Thank you, dear Viv and Ned and the extended Overton family. Thank you, Reg Coyne and Johnny White.

Thank you, Catherine Milne, Scott Forbes, Pam Dunne, Graeme Jones, Belinda Yuille, Sarah Haines, Darren Holt, Elizabeth O'Donnell, Erin Dunk, Jim Demetriou, Brigitta Doyle and the entire HarperCollins Australia love bus that drove this book into being. Thank you, Alice Wood, and welcome to this glorious universe, Matilda. You'll like it here. Turns out the place is filled with love and Cherry Ripes.

And, finally, thanks to Judy Clark and Greg Kelly and your beautiful families. This book exists because of you. You gave me the same good stuff your mum gave this world. A whole lotta kindness. A whole lotta strength. And a whole lotta love.

BOY SWALLOWS UNIVERSE

TRENT DALTON

The bestselling, critically acclaimed and award-wining novel that has taken Australia, and the world, by storm

Brisbane, 1985: A lost father, a mute brother, a junkie mum, a heroin dealer for a stepfather and a notorious crim for a babysitter. It's not as if Eli Bell's life isn't complicated enough already. He's just trying to follow his heart and understand what it means to be a good man, but fate keeps throwing obstacles in his way – not the least of which is Tytus Broz, legendary Brisbane drug dealer.

But now Eli's life is going to get a whole lot more serious: he's about to meet the father he doesn't remember, break into Boggo Road Gaol on Christmas Day to rescue his mum, come face to face with the criminals who tore his world apart, and fall in love with the girl of his dreams.

A story of brotherhood, true love and the most unlikely of friendships, *Boy Swallows Universe* will be the most heartbreaking, joyous and exhilarating novel you will read all year.

'Without exaggeration, the best Australian novel I have read in more than a decade' *Sydney Morning Herald*

www.harpercollins.com.au/trentdalton

ALL OUR SHIMMERING SKIES

**Darwin, 1942, and as Japanese bombs
rain down, motherless Molly Hook, the
gravedigger's daughter, is preparing to run ...**

From best-selling author Trent Dalton,
All Our Shimmering Skies is a story about gifts
that fall from the sky, curses we dig from the earth and the
secrets we bury inside ourselves. It is an odyssey of true
love and mortal danger; of the darkness and the light; of
bones and blue skies. A buoyant, beautiful and magical
novel abrim with warmth, wit and wonder;
a love letter to Australia and the art of looking up.

'A work of shimmering originality and energy,
with extraordinary characters and a clever, thrilling
plot ... unputdownable' Toni Jordan,
Sydney Morning Herald/The Age

www.harpercollins.com.au/trentdalton

Trent Dalton is the author of **Boy Swallows Universe** (HarperCollins, 2018), a critically acclaimed national bestseller and winner of the 2019 Indie Book of the Year Award, the MUD Literary Prize, and the UTS Glenda Adams Award for New Writing and the People's Choice Award at the 2019 NSW Premier's Literary Awards. At the 2019 Australian Book Industry Awards, the book won a record four awards, including the prestigious Book of the Year Award. **Boy Swallows Universe** has been published across thirty-four English language and translation territories. His second novel, **All Our Shimmering Skies**, was published by HarperCollins in October 2020 and has also become a national bestseller. He's also a two-time winner of a Walkley Award for Excellence in Journalism, a four-time winner of a Kennedy Award for Excellence in NSW Journalism and a four-time winner of the national News Awards Features Journalist of the Year.